D0984800

WITH LIBERTY AND
JUSTICE FOR ALL

WITH LIBERTY AND JUSTICE FOR ALL

THE MEANING OF THE BILL OF RIGHTS TODAY

by

HAROLD V. KNIGHT

Introduction

by

ROGER BALDWIN

Revised Edition

1 9 6 8

OCEANA PUBLICATIONS, INC.

Dobbs Ferry, New York

The author gratefully acknowledges permission from the respective publishers to reprint excerpts of copyright material from:

LOYALTY OF FREE MEN by Alan Barth, © 1951 by Alan Barth, The Viking Press, Inc.

ALMANAC OF LIBERTY by William O. Douglas, © 1954 by W. O. Douglas, Doubleday & Co., Inc.

DIVIDENDS AND DEMOCRACY by Lewis D. Gilbert, © 1956 by L. D. Gilbert, American Research Council.

POLITICAL FREEDOM by Alexander Meiklejohn, © 1960, Harper & Row.

CHURCH, STATE, & FREEDOM by Leo Pfeffer, © 1966, Beacon Press.

GRAND INQUEST by Telford Taylor, © 1955, Simon and Schuster, Inc.

LABOR IN A FREE SOCIETY, Michael Harrington ed., © 1958, University of California Press.

To my wife, Ruth

—*my "Goddess of Liberty"*

Acknowledgements

My special thanks are due:

Dr. Richard A. Perchlik, chairman of the Department of Political Science, Colorado State College, for reading my manuscript and making suggestions—many of which I accepted;

Mrs. Harriet Hixenbaugh who did much of the typing and retyping;

My wife, Ruth Gallup Knight, who not only learned to type so she could help me but also proved a school teacher is a better proof-reader than this writer;

My many friends—attorneys, educators, and other civil libertarians—who encouraged me to undertake this project and who may or may not recognize ideas which I have gleaned from them.

HAROLD V. KNIGHT

Table of Contents

Introduction

by

ROGER N. BALDWIN

This book, written in popular language about the law of the Bill of Rights by a layman with practical experience in applying it, deals with the amazing revolution of recent years in the liberties of all Americans. The central element of this revolution is the fact that issues which before were the exclusive concerns of the States now are the concern of the federal government. Practically all constitutional rights have been nationalized; from the Pacific to the Atlantic, the Lakes to the Gulf, every American is guaranteed precisely the same rights by decisions of the ultimate umpire, the U. S. Supreme Court.

This remarkable shift in powers to the federal government has accompanied the growth of the welfare state and the consequent responsibility of the national government not only for equal civil rights, but for those economic and social rights which mark the modern State. Not only the Supreme Court but Congress, the states and effective public opinion have reflected the demands for racial equality, freedom of conscience, belief, association and communication, justice in the courts, the protection of minority rights, and higher standards of living and work.

Mr. Knight brings to his exposition of these dramatic developments in law and practice, his experience as the former executive director for a decade of the Colorado Civil Liberties Union. As my colleague in the persistent defense of the Bill of Rights by the national ACLU, I may be a prejudiced judge of what he has accomplished in clarifying so readably the complex problems of civil liberties which have sharply split the U. S. Supreme Court. Many books have appeared on the new concepts of law and their striking effects on the practice of rights, but I know of none other than this that I would commend as highly to the general reader for accuracy, fairness and lucidity. Though it is not in any sense officially endorsed by the American Civil Liberties Union, it parallels closely its policies and philosophy. Old hand that I am in this field, even I picked up a number of fresh insights from Mr. Knight's observations.

Despite the great progress achieved over the years, I would not be regarded, nor should Mr. Knight, as entirely happy with the civil liberties record. The Supreme Court majority in key cases has failed to protect freedom of speech and association for Communists. It has failed to agree on any intelligible yardstick to measure obscenity—perhaps an impossible task. Congress has failed to implement effectively the guarantees of a racial equality still to be wholly accepted by public opinion. But the exceptions do not detract much from the gratifying forward thrust of expanding liberties.

So pronounced has that been that efforts to resist have failed, as Mr. Knight records. The South has been coerced by federal military power into obedience to court orders for racial equality in education. The movement to upset by constitutional amendments the courts' decisions on school prayers and one-man one-vote representation in state legislatures failed. Supreme Court decisions are enforced, however tardily, and effective public opinion accepts them. This book's major value is to contribute to that opinion which on the whole is so little aware of the dramatic advance of so recent a revolution in law.

The pace of advance does not lessen. The Civil Liberties Union has more cases on appeal involving new problems of civil liberties than it has ever had at one time, and the prospects are for no fewer in the complexities of a changing democracy. Mr. Knight speculates on them in a final chapter devoted to the effects of the phenomenal growth of cities, the huge welfare agencies, the vast automated industries. As the powers of government grow so does the need to challenge their abuses. Whether that need is met depends on the courage of citizens determined to assert them. This study shows that the revolution in rights depended in large part on the pressures citizens exerted on courts and legislatures. The result has been to extend liberty and to restrict power. Government itself has even given birth to many agencies to protect the liberties won.

I like to recollect an observation of Justice Brandeis long ago that the basic liberty of all is "the right to be let alone." Even if it is not entirely practical in a complex society, it breathes the spirit of what most people feel should be their private freedoms beyond the reach of officials or neighbors. The Bill of Rights was conceived in that intent; this study of its meaning today faithfully voices it.

Part I

THE PRIMACY OF THE INDIVIDUAL

1

Everybody Talks About Freedom

"Give me liberty, or give me death."
—Patrick Henry

"We hold . . . that all men are endowed by their Creator with certain unalienable rights, that among these are life, liberty, and the pursuit of happiness. That to secure these rights, governments are instituted among men."
—Declaration of Independence

"Our democracy can be kept strong only by the dedication of every new generation to the discipline of liberty. In knowledge of the Bill of Rights, and in loyalty to its propositions rests our faith in the future."
—from policy statement by
California State Board of Education

Americans have a great heritage of stirring words and noble ideals—words and ideals which reverberate throughout the whole world.

1

Do we take our heritage for granted? Are we prone to make lip service a substitute for applying these ideals and words to our life today? Indeed, what do words like "liberty", "freedom", "justice", "equality", and "constitutional rights" really mean as they relate to concrete situations and current problems?

Recently, a curious statement appeared in the "letters-to-Editor" column of a metropolitan daily. The writer said: "The Pledge of Allegiance is to be recited, not discussed."

Such candor may express an attitude more prevalent than most of us would like to think. Discussion means controversy and many Americans shy away from becoming involved in controversial issues and decisions.

Aristotle pointed out long ago that the struggle for equality was one of the greatest of revolutionary forces. Certainly this force is being demonstrated in the aspiration of the peoples of developing nations throughout the whole world. It is being demonstrated in America by those who until now have been disadvantaged by race or color, by ethnic culture, or economic poverty.

The drive for liberty and the drive for justice are other powerful forces in a democratic society which prizes the dignity and worth of each individual.

In the final phrase of the Pledge of Allegiance, "with liberty and justice for all," is summed up our American heritage expressed in the Bill of Rights and related constitutional guarantees. This book proposes to discuss the meaning of that phrase and nothing more. He who believes the phrase is but for reciting might as well close this volume right now, for his mind has already been closed.

Average American Dubious

As a Fourth of July feature a few years ago, a reporter for the *Madison* (Wisconsin) *Capital Times* asked 113 persons to sign a petition to Congress which contained the text of a bill he wanted passed. All but one refused. Twenty Madisonites wanted to know if he was a Communist or something.

What did the text of the petition contain? Nothing except quotations from the Declaration of Independence and the Bill of Rights! This happened in the city named for James Madison, the principal drafter of the Bill of Rights!

In an unnamed American city, another story goes, the postal employees wouldn't allow a copy of this same Bill of Rights to be posted on the post office bulletin board because, they thought, as they read it, that it was controversial! Only after the governor of the state in which this happened gave them a signed statement that it was not a subversive document was our American Bill of Rights permitted to hang in this American post office!

The Madison experiment has occasionally been copied since, sometimes with slightly better results. For example, two junior high school boys secured signatures of nearly half the 101 persons they contacted in their Washington, D.C. neighborhood on a typewritten "petition" which contained nothing but the Bill of Rights—the first ten amendments to the Constitution of the United States. The boys told a reporter that only 22 persons recognized the document for what it was!

Other surveys indicate that these amendments would have a hard time being adopted today, particularly when citizens were questioned on specific rights.

The Paradox of Freedom

Everybody professes to want freedom. In the abstract, liberty and justice are vast concepts to which all subscribe. Why then is it when these philosophical ideas are applied to concrete situations they become controversial—and to some, even dangerous?

Several reasons for this seeming paradox may be cited— words have different meanings, words are misused, within the philosophical concepts are contradictions, and priorities among conflicting rights must sometimes be chosen, both as between individuals and as between the rights themselves.

Can any person enjoy complete freedom? Is "liberty and justice for all" a realizable absolute or is it a goal toward which America strives but never reaches? What do the words really mean?

Advocates of abolishing the graduated income tax call their proposal the "liberty amendment." Organizations interested in upholding Bill of Rights guarantees talk about constitutional liberties. "Freedom now" is a favored slogan of the civil rights movement. "Freedom School" is a name taken by both extreme rightists and extreme leftists to designate their respective indoctrination centers. Obviously they attach differing meanings to the term.

The English language is full of semantic tricks. More significant than the semantics of general terms are the questions raised when they are applied to specific situations. Most Americans favor religious freedom and separation of church and state, but do they favor excluding religion from the schools? Most believe in equal justice, but do they favor freeing a poor man because he was convicted without having adequate legal counsel? These are but two illustrations of many controversial questions to be considered.

Basic Rights

The phrase "with liberty and justice for all" suggests a division of the basic rights in the American democratic, free society. These rights may be summarized in very general terms as:

Liberty—recognizing freedom to think, believe, express, and act;

Justice—giving every man his just due through fair procedure;

Equality—according all men equal protection and equal opportunity under the law.

These rights are referred to as "civil" rights or "civil" liberties. Somewhat arbitrarily the term "freedom" may also be used to encompass the three divisions, since they are all essential in a free society.

These categories are not mutually exclusive. Sometimes they overlap. Occasionally they conflict. Our heritage is of one fabric—basically that each individual is important and has rights which government does not give and cannot take away. One corollary is that government itself is restrained in relation to the individual. A second is that government restrains other individuals from interfering with those rights. Another is that both government and individual action can encourage the exercise of such rights.

The practice of enumerating specific guarantees of individuals and restraints on governments in writing goes back hundreds of years. It goes back, indeed, to the Magna Charta which King John was forced to sign in 1215. In English usage such documents became known as "bills of rights." All of the original colonies put such "bills of rights" into their constitutions as they became independent states. The American Bill of Rights was added to the United States Constitution as the First Ten Amendments.

A few other paragraphs of the Constitution, some of the subsequent amendments, and similar provisions in state constitutions, likewise place restrictions on government in relation to citizens. Although the Declaration of Independence does not have the legal force of law, its philosophy permeates the interpretation of basic rights.

Significantly, neither the Declaration of Independence nor the Bill of Rights enumerate all the rights and freedoms that American citizens have.

In fact, both documents specifically say the opposite.

In the Declaration of Independence, we find:

> "We hold these truths to be self-evident, that all men are created equal, that they are endowed by their Creator with certain inalienable rights, that *among these* are Life, Liberty, and the pursuit of Happiness . . ."

The Ninth Amendment reads:

> "The enumeration in the Constitution of certain rights, shall not be construed to deny or disparage *others* retained by the people."

Likewise, the Tenth Amendment declares:

"The powers not delegated to the United States
by the Constitution, nor prohibited by it to the
States, are reserved to the States respectively, or
to the people."

The Contemporary Approach

The historical development of every idea embodied in
the Bill of Rights—in the centuries of English and Colonial
history preceding its adoption, in the adoption itself, and in
its interpertation since—is a fascinating study. Many scholarly
books have been written from the historical view.*

Almost every day a newscast, a newspaper report, or a
magazine article demonstrates that some part of the Bill of
Rights affects some of us or all of us, right here and now.
It is from the viewpoint of a journalist that this author proposes to survey the whole range of modern issues encompassed
in the Bill of Rights. This volume is designed not for the
lawyer nor the law student but for the average American
who wants to understand the meaning of it all. The danger
of oversimplifying complex issues is always present, but an
even greater danger is ignorance of the rationale and inter-
relatedness of the Bill of Rights as the bulwark of freedom.

References to court decisions must be made, for it is these
which apply the basic rights to concrete, contemporary situations. But this is not a casebook in law. Perhaps it will stimulate some readers to pursue the study of legal opinions in the
civil liberties area further, for indeed this is an intriguing
field.

Critics of the United States Supreme Court, the fountain-
head of the interpretation of the Bill of Rights, maintain that
in recent years it has gone far beyond the concepts envisioned
by the Founding Fathers.

In a certain sense this is true. It is no accident that during

---

* Chapter 20 provides a brief sketch of historical highlights of
the struggle for freedom. The bibliography lists books which provide
a much more thorough historical perspective.

the past 25 or 30 years the Supreme Court has rendered more decisions concerning the Bill of Rights than during the 150 years previous.

The Founding Fathers could not have conceived of the complexities of modern life—instant communication, rapid transportation, congested urbanization, knowledge growth, pluralistic religious and ethical beliefs, ethnic diversity—all of which demand new applications of the concept of liberty and justice for all.

Worldwide Aspiration

Throughout the world, moreover, emerging peoples are aspiring to achieve equality, freedom and justice, the promise they find in the American Revolution. Our revolution has a competitor in the world today, the Communist revolution. One of its basic tenets is that if an individual is free from economic exploitation—meaning capitalism—he has no interest in other liberties. Indeed, a Russian law professor told a UNESCO conference on human rights ". . . in a socialist society the individual has no desire for liberation from the state."

Such an idea is completely alien to our American premise of the primacy of the individual. The world about us is watching to see if the application of our professed ideals can really operate in an era of profound technological change. Our American tradition holds that economic and social freedoms can be attained without sacrificing political and individual freedoms.

Our tradition also holds that individual freedom implies individual responsibility. You make your choice and you take the consequence. One who dresses and acts like a beatnik can scarcely be expected to be a junior executive at the same time.

Our tradition, as well, implies some freedoms government can neither give nor take away, the inner spirit which is free in spite of slavery, imprisonment, voluntary self discipline, or even martyrdom. The philosophical and spiritual aspects of freedom go beyond a survey of the relation between government and individual rights. Yet our commitment to a free society rejects the idea that persecution and martyrdom are essential to demonstrate man's capacity for inner freedom.

Freedom and Law

Governments are instituted, says the Declaration of Independence, to secure rights of all men. This implies a paradox for, in a real sense, all law places restraints on individual action.

The law interferes with one's "pursuit of happiness"—if that is what it is—to drag-race down a city street disregarding speed limits, red lights, and traffic signs. Obviously, restraints are necessary to protect the rights of others to life and liberty. Indeed, the law, in this case, protects the offender against himself.

"Give me liberty or give me death," cries a school boy in a stage whisper after the teacher tells him to stay after school for disobeying the rules. "Give me liberty or give me death," writes an irate businessman in protest against having to fill out forms required by a government regulatory agency.

Both misapply Patrick Henry's classic statement. Rules and regulations there must be. Questions might be raised, however, as to whether they are fair and whether they are fairly applied.

A person is free, or has liberty, as he has, and to the extent he has, a wide range of effective choices as to what he thinks, feels, says, and does. A free society seeks to make the range of real choices open to an individual as wide as possible without denying a similar range to others. As the old saying goes, your freedom ends at my nose.

2

"All Men Are"... Are They?

"We hold these truths to be self-evident, that all men are created equal. . ."
— DECLARATION OF INDEPENDENCE

"No person shall be . . . deprived of life, liberty, or property, without due process of law. . . ."
— FIFTH AMENDMENT

". . . A new nation conceived in liberty, and dedicated to the proposition that all men are created equal."
— ABRAHAM LINCOLN
IN THE GETTYSBURG ADDRESS

What do these ideas mean? What did they mean to the men who wrote them? Where did they come from? What does equality mean today?

Does "all men" include women? Persons of different races, creeds, national origin? American citizens only, or also aliens? Does it apply to people all over the world?

Obviously, all men are not created equal in physical and

9

mental capacities, nor in the circumstances of our environment.

The Declaration of Independence and the Gettysburg Address stated a philosophical ideal. It is a moral and ethical goal, derived from belief in the worth and dignity of every human being. The Constitution translated this ideal into the principle that every person should enjoy equal protection of the law and equal opportunity under law.

Government, the all-inclusive organization of society to which all must belong and to whose rules all must be subject, can affect only some of the choices open to the individual. It cannot change many factors limiting the range of choice open to a particular person.

Yet, as the dynamic, living Bill of Rights story will demonstrate, government can and does enlarge the range of choices available to each and to all.

Certainly the actions which make meaningful the guarantees of equality before the law to disadvantaged minorities multiply their effective opportunities immensely.

Likewise, guarantees of the freedom to express, to hear and see, to learn, to believe, to associate, and to act make more, and more meaningful, choices possible.

The guarantees of justice and fair procedures in dealing with crime and, perhaps even more important, with the relationships between each individual and organized society, make less restrictive the rules and regulations of modern life.

Civil Rights—An Enlarging Circle

Much of our national history is written in the struggles to apply that principle to enlarge the circle of equal citizenship. In practice various groups have not always been included in the phrase "all men"—slaves, immigrants, racial and religious minorities, women, and the poor.

At present, obviously, the struggle of Negroes to be accepted in the circle of full citizenship is an overriding issue of American life. "Civil rights" has come to refer almost exclusively to this movement, although by dictionary meaning the terms "civil rights" and "civil liberties" are almost interchangeable.

The progress the nation has made in the civil rights struggle can be highlighted by the stories of three men and a woman. All were travelers. All were Negroes. They lived over a span of more than a hundred years. Each was involved in a landmark decision of the United States Supreme Court.

The four included Dred Scott, a slave who was held to be property rather than a citizen; Josephine DeCuir, who sat in a Mississippi riverboat cabin reserved for whites because the state law said she could; Homer A. Plesy, seven-eighths Caucasian and one-eighth African, who would not sit in a railroad car with "separate but equal accommodations"; and Marlon D. Green, a veteran aircraft pilot who didn't put his color on an employment application.

Civil Rights and Interstate Commerce

Dred Scott was a Negro slave whose owner brought him to Wisconsin, a free state, from Missouri, a slave territory. Scott sued for his freedom on the ground that he had been freed when his master had brought him to a free state. In its famous decision in *Scott v. Sanford,* the Supreme Court held he was not a citizen and therefore he had no right to sue. He was the property of his owner whose rights to property were protected by the Fifth Amendment! Congress had no power, therefore, to free Scott, to forbid his owner from taking him into "free territory"—or, indeed, to exclude slavery from any territory. Because it overturned the "Missouri Compromise" this 1857 decision, highly unpopular in the North, foreclosed a political solution to the slavery issue and thus contributed to the coming of the Civil War.

It is a long distance, in time and in concepts of human rights, between the Dred Scott decision and the case involving Marlon Green a century later. Green, a U. S. Air Force pilot, sought employment as a pilot on various commercial airlines. He was asked to come to Denver and take the flight test by a well known airline. It did not know he was a Negro. He had more flying experience than five other applicants tested at the same time. He was admitted to be a qualified pilot by the employment manager. In spite of such qualifications, he alone of the six taking the test in June, 1957, was not hired. Colorado is one of many states having a Fair Employment Practices Act, which like the United States Civil Rights Act of 1964, forbids discrimination in employment.

It was nearly eight years after he took the test that Mr. Green became a regularly scheduled pilot on the run between Denver and Dallas, with the pay and seniority rights of those hired in 1957. It took six years and six hearings before Colorado courts and the Colorado Anti-Discrimination Commission until the U. S. Supreme Court decided the case. It took over a year more before Continental Airlines, Inc. accepted the ruling of the CADC (now the Colorado Civil Rights Commission) that Mr. Green was entitled to a 195. seniority rating.

The Colorado Supreme Court as well as the lower district court upheld the contention of Continental Air Lines, Inc. that Colorado's FEP law did not apply to employees engaged in interstate commerce. This contention the nine justices of the U. S. Supreme Court rejected.

In reaching this unanimous conclusion the justices went back to what previous Supreme Courts had said in cases involving Miss DeCuir. They went back a long way, back to the period following the Civil War. Congress and several Southern states had passed laws very similar to recent civil rights legislation—prohibiting discrimination based on race. Legislatures of Southern states, during this "Reconstruction Era" were composed of Negroes and Northerners, known as "carpetbaggers," who had come to help them. The Thirteenth Amendment had been adopted forbidding anybody engaged in the rebellion from sitting in the state legislature.

Miss DeCuir's story figured in Mr. Green's case because Louisiana passed a law forbidding discrimination in accommodations for passengers on public conveyances during the Reconstruction Era. Miss DeCuir sued the owner of a riverboat going up and down the Mississippi because she was not permitted to sit in the first class cabin while it passed through

Louisiana. The Supreme Court ruled to the effect that the state law caused a burden on interstate commerce. A steamship could not change its seating rules every time it went from one state to another. So the Louisiana law was declared unconstitutional.

That was in 1878. In 1946 another group of justices used this ruling to invalidate state laws requiring segregation of passengers according to race! In the case of Pilot Green the Supreme Court held the Colorado law aided, rather than hindered, Federal policy. It cited the Civil Aeronautics Act and other laws and regulations which forbid racial discrimination.

"Equal But Separate"

Nearly twenty years after Josephine DeCuir had sat in the first class cabin of a Mississippi riverboat, Homer Plesy, one of whose great-grandparents was Negro, sat down in a railway coach going through Louisiana. By that time white citizens had regained control of the Louisiana legislature and, like those in numerous other states, had passed "Jim Crow" laws. One required railways to provide "equal but separate accommodations for the white and colored races" and to assign passengers according to race.

Mr. Plesy sat in the white section and refused to move. His arrest and ultimate appeal to the United States Supreme Court set the pattern for race relations in the United States for over fifty years.

All of the justices, except one, decided that the equal protection guarantee of the Fourteenth Amendment was not violated by separation of the races.

Opponents of recent civil rights decisions say the Supreme Court decided on the basis of sociological factors it had no business considering. In the Plesy case, in 1896, the Supreme Court majority certainly expressed sociological views. It declared that "in the nature of things" the Fourteenth Amendment could not have been intended to enforce "a comingling of the two races upon terms unsatisfactory to either." Enforced separation did not "necessarily imply the inferiority of either race to the other." If the colored race assumes the law stamps it as being inferior this is only because it chooses to do so. "The argument also assumes that social prejudices may be overcome by legislation."

That last statement is still heard today. Those favoring laws banning discrimination counter it by pointing out that a person may think or feel as he pleases about anybody. Only when he acts on the basis of his prejudice does the law step in to protect the rights of others. One can contemplate robbing a bank, but until he acts he has committed no crime.

Lest one think the question of separation of the races was confined to a section of our nation, the majority decision in the Plesy case quoted at length from an early Massachusetts court opinion justifying separate schools for whites and Negroes. Just as children and women do not have the same civil and political powers as men, this early day opinion held, so the state may establish separate schools for different ages, sexes, and colors.

"Our Constitution Is Color Blind"

In a prophetic dissent Justice John M. Harlan, grand-father of the present Justice John M. Harlan, declared in the Plesy case: "In my opinion, the judgment this day rendered will, in time, prove to be quite as pernicious as the decision made by this tribunal in the Dred Scott case."

That time came a half century later. In 1954 the Supreme Court finally overturned the "separate but equal doctrine". In its famous school desegregation decisions it declared unanimously "that in the field of public education the doctrine of 'separate but equal' has no place. Separate educational facilities are inherently unequal."

In this decision, as in others which in the Fifties preceded and followed it, the high court accepted the first Justice Harlan's belief: ". . . in the eye of the law, there is no superior, dominant, ruling class of citizens. There is no caste here. Our Constitution is color blind. . ."

This is the basic meaning of the civil rights movement. Through laws adopted by various states, through court action and administrative rulings, the color blindness of the law has removed legal barriers to equal opportunity in employment, education, public accommodations, housing, and voting. The Civil Rights Act of 1964 culminated a trend which has been gathering momentum for a long time.

Discrimination, and the effects of discrimination, are not eradicated by a "stroke of a pen" be it judical, legislative, or executive. Law, and interpretation of law, can and do make possible opportunities to assert rights.

Conflicting Rights and Public Policy

Do not these rights conflict with the rights of others to exercise their freedom of choice? How are arguments like the following to be answered?

"I have a right to hire whom I please. If I want to hire only redheads with blue eyes in my plant, that is my business."

"A man has the right to choose his customers—those whom he will serve in his restaurant, admit to his theatre, allow in his hotel. Where will our freedom be if the government can force us to rent or sell our hard-earned property to anyone who wants it without freedom of choice on our part?"

Here, indeed, competing rights conflict. Freedom of choice, the essence of liberty, of the owner collides with the right of the prospective employee or customer to equal opportunity to be employed or to be served.

The resolution of conflicting rights provides a broad battle-ground where many unsolved issues remain to be met. That is one reason why the study of the Bill of Rights is so dynamic. The final word on many questions is yet to be uttered.

On the specific issue of discrimination versus free choice, some might pose the question in the terms of human rights as opposed to property rights. Such explanation is too simple. Human beings with sensibilities and feelings are on both sides. The right to work or to obtain lodging has economic value just as much as tangible property. Others might state the conflict in terms of "liberty" versus "equality." A division of rights under such terms is valuable in order to make meanings more understandable, but in reality liberty and equality are aspects of the same ideal.

In the area of equal treatment irrespective of race, color, creed, or national origin—as in many other areas—choices as to permissible conduct have to be made. That is what law-making, indeed, government itself, is all about.

Take traffic laws as an illustration.

Those who consider themselves middle-of-the-road, figuratively speaking, don't actually straddle the yellow line down the center of the highway. If they did they would soon be run over—or else arrested. There was a time, however, when the safest way to drive a Model T down a high-crowned dirt road was to keep in the two ruts in the middle, carefully moving over to negotiate passing the infrequent on-coming car.

Government has power to regulate the conduct of the individual in many areas for the common good. States have police power for "preservation of the public peace, health, and safety"—as the "safety clause" added to every bill passed by one state legislature puts it. The "police power" and considerations of "public policy" have been well established as legislative perogatives of state governments. As for Federal legislation, the courts have relied heavily on the Constitutional provision giving Congress the power "to provide . . . for the general welfare of the United States" in upholding much social legislation enacted.

Those opposing civil rights legislation, to be consistent, must be prepared to also eliminate all regulations regarding pure food and drugs, sanitation, minimum wage and maximum hour legislation, utility rates, etc., etc. Many laws enacted during the past century would not survive if the test invariably placed rights of a single individual above the welfare and rights of others. Carried to its ultimate conclusion this test is a path which leads to anarchy.

Public Accommodation, Housing, Employment

Laws on discrimination are far from new. Since the Middle Ages English common law required inn-keepers to accommodate any well-behaved traveler—and his horses. Laws requiring segregation, whether a proprietor wanted to separate his customers or not, were enforced in many states until recently. If an owner's freedom of choice was limited by such laws, logic would dictate that his freedom to discriminate could also be limited for the public good.

For many years, some states have had laws forbidding discrimination by anybody offering services to the public. Ohio's public accommodation law, for example, dates back nearly a century, although a U. S. senator from that state was surprised to learn of its existence!

Laws and regulations against discrimination in housing are more recent in origin. "Restrictive covenants" were clauses in deeds for property by which successive purchasers agreed never to resell to certain groups, such as Negroes, Orientals, and Jews. Since 1948 such clauses have been unenforceable under a Supreme Court ruling.

Several states have adopted laws banning discrimination in rental and sale of real estate. In upholding such laws, state courts have generally held that public policy takes precedence over the rights of private contract. President Kennedy's executive order barring discrimination in any housing assisted or insured by federal agencies has not resulted in any drop in home construction as some had feared.

Even though California voters adopted "Proposition 14" —by a large majority—to nullify that state's fair housing law, its supreme court held the initiated proposition could not be enforced because racial bias in housing clearly violated the Fourteenth Amendment's equal protection clause for those discriminated against.

Fair employment legislation, in principle, is no different than many other legal restrictions placed on employers as to sanitation, safety, maximum hours, minimum pay, etc. Employees give up many freedoms to choose when, where, how, and with whom they will work as they follow the policies of a particular employer. Modern industry and commerce would be impossible under absolutely free choice of either employer or employee.

In explaining the equal employment opportunity section of the 1964 Civil Rights Act to seminars of employers, an official of the National Association of Manufacturers, Charles A. Kothe, declared: "The law declares no new rights. The rights that it asserts are rights that adhere in the Constitution. The law has to do only with redressing wrongs."

This section prohibits employers, labor unions, and employment agencies (except those with fewer than 25 employees or members) from discriminating in hiring, firing, promotion, pay or membership on account of race, religion, national origin, or sex.

Some predict the ban on discrimination in employment because of sex may produce more litigation than racial discrimination. Women may be expected to demand positions in echelons heretofore reserved almost exclusively for men.

Women are not a numerical minority, but the story of their efforts to attain equal rights contains the account of many battles—in America and in other countries. Once a Canadian court ruled that women were not legally persons and therefore ineligible to sit in Parliament! That ruling was quickly overturned!

Indians constitute one minority group who have long occupied a no man's land in regard to their rights as Americans because those on reservations are usually subject to tribal law, rather than to that of the state. It has been commonly held that they do not enjoy the protection of constitutional rights. Recently a U. S. Court of Appeals held that this is not so.

Mrs. Madeline Colliflower, a Blackfoot Indian on Montana's Ft. Belknap Reservation, was charged with pasturing her cattle on someone else's field. She was convicted by a tribal court without any witnesses or cross examination. The U. S. Court of Appeals held that while tribal courts are. in some respects, autonomous, they must observe fundamental constitutional guarantees of fairness.

Rights of Individuals

Almost every minority group in America has at one time or another felt that they were the object of discriminatory practices. "Minority rights" is a phrase sometimes used. In reality, however, minorities have no rights. Majorities have no rights. Only individuals have rights. And, under the American concept of law, one individual has the same rights as any other.

Individuals differ immensely in capacities and capabilities, in circumstances and in inclinations. Where membership in a particular group causes certain individuals to be advantaged or disadvantaged, cultural, social, and economic factors are involved. No group is inherently superior to another, no group inferior. Modern science confirms that in this sense, "all men are created equal" and ". . . in the eye of the law, there is no superior, dominant, ruling class of citizens."

America has moved steadily, and in recent years, speedily, toward recognizing that all men have equal civil rights. The problems which remain—and they are great—to make equality of opportunity meaningful are to be resolved in the realm of public policy. The foundation of constitutional rights on which solutions can be erected has been firmly laid.

3

One Man's Vote

"No state shall . . . deny to any person within its jurisdiction the equal protection of the laws."

—FOURTEENTH AMENDMENT

"Equal representation is so fundamental a principle in a true republic that no prejudice can justify its violation. . ."

—THOMAS JEFFERSON

"The right to vote freely for the candidate of one's choice is the essence of a democratic society, and any restrictions on that right strike at the heart of representative government."

—CHIEF JUSTICE EARL WARREN

"The concept of political equality from the Declaration of Independence to Lincoln's Gettysburg Address, to the Fifteenth, Seventeenth, and Nineteenth amendment can mean only one thing—one person, one vote."

—ASSOCIATE JUSTICE WM. O. DOUGLAS

These quotations go to the heart of our democratic system—participation in decision-making in government "of the people, by the people, for the people."

All Americans undoubtedly would agree that the right to vote is important—even the third who do not exercise that right in any given election! Most would assume that any person over 21, except mental incompetents and convicted criminals, should have the right to vote.

This assumption, of course, has not been true regarding Negroes in spite of the Fifteenth Amendment which declares the right to vote shall not be denied "on account of race, color or previous condition of servitude." Although about one million Negroes became registered voters during the years between 1958 and 1964, not until the Voting Rights Act of 1965 was the door opened to full franchise of this minority group. Backed by provision for federal intervention where the right to vote is denied, it is expected that two million more Negroes will eventually achieve the most precious of American rights, the right to vote.

Equality in Voting

Another ancient dispute has been recently renewed. Even if a person has the right to vote, is his vote worth as much as another person's vote? Should a district with a population of a couple of hundred thousand and one with a million each be represented by one Congressman? Should members of the state legislatures each represent approximately the same number of voters? In recent apportionment decisions, the United States Supreme Court held the Fourteenth Amendment's equal protection clause required that one person's vote be worth as much as any other's in selecting legislative representation. These decisions are making drastic changes in many state legislatures and in Congressional districting. The arguments they raise go back to the founding of our nation.

Jefferson advocated the "one man, one vote" principle. He urged that the constitution Virginia adopted in 1776 be changed to provide that both houses of the state legislature would be apportioned according to population. The upper house was based on geographical areas. Jefferson did not succeed.

He was opposed by George Washington, who expressed dread of "tumultuous populaces of large cities". Another fellow Virginian, James Madison, held property owners alone were the safe custodians of liberty. Alexander Hamilton feared selfish passions of the masses misled by demagogues.

Justices Warren and Douglas and the majority of the present justices whose views they represent can also find historical precedents for Jefferson's position.

His view prevailed in many states. The original constitutions of thirty-six states provided both houses would be based completely, or predominantly, on population. The Northwest Ordinance of 1787 declared "The inhabitants of said territory shall always be entitled to the benefits . . . of a proportional representation of the people in the legislature."

In the "great compromise" between the large states and the small states in the Constitutional Convention, each state was given two senators while the House of Representatives was apportioned according to population.

This solution was necessary to unite thirteen independent states into a single nation. It has often been used as a precedent for basing membership in one house of state legislatures on territorial subdivisions. For example, Los Angeles county, with four million population has had one member in the California Senate, the same as sparsely settled counties with as few as 14,000 inhabitants.

The analogy between Federal-state relationships and state political subdivisions breaks down. The original states not only gave up some of their sovereignty in forming the United States, but they also retained all the powers not delegated to the Federal government. Every state admitted to the Union since enjoys all such powers not delegated.

Subdivisions within a state—counties, municipalities, etc. —by contrast, exercise only powers granted them by state law. They are administrative creations of the state.

In recent decisions on state legislative apportionment, the Supreme Court called the analogy "factually as well as constitutionally without merit."

Apportionment—Pros and Cons

Advocates of a constitutional amendment permitting apportionment of one legislative branch on factors other than population advance additional, and perhaps more effective arguments. Many states have a great diversity of geographical, social, and economic interests. Again taking an example from California, if the metropolitan areas of Los Angeles dominate both legislative branches, those in the rest of the vast state fear that water resources will be channeled to fill Southern California's pressing needs, to the ruin of the rest of the state's economic growth.

This argument is a two-edged sword. Metropolitan areas which have burgeoned in population in recent decades argue that rural dominance of state legislatures has prevented adequate solutions of urban problems. Indeed, growth of federal government in the form of grants and aid is attributed to the inability of local and state governments to meet needs.

Fifty years ago most Americans lived in small towns or rural areas. Today four-fifths of them reside in urban centers. Changes in the composition of legislative bodies have not kept pace with this revolutionary development.

Legislators generally failed to reapportion not because of any theories about a "federal plan" or "balance of interest". Theorizing came after the malapportionment became so marked as to require justification. While state constitutions differ greatly as to the composition of their legislatures, most of them provide for periodic adjustments to reflect population changes.

Such requirements have been honored more often by ignoring than by fulfilling. Redrawing of district lines is a painful process, particularly to legislators who are going to lose their seats. Reapportionment becomes a political football. Some states redistricted just enough to claim constitutional requirements had been met. Some did nothing. A few, notably, Massachusetts, Oregon, and Washington kept both houses fairly districted on a population basis.

A Full Strength Vote

In the years following World War II, a group of citizens in fast-growing Atlanta sought to enhance their vote through the courts. In Georgia a peculiar "county unit" rule gave a rural voter 99 times the voice of an Atlantan in selecting state officials and U. S. Senators. Under this system, each county, large or small, cast one vote for each office, according to the majority in that county.

The Atlantans failed the first time their case reached the United States Supreme Court. In 1946 the high court had held in a landmark case challenging Illinois malapportionment, *Colegrove v. Green,* that voting was a political issue with which it would not interfere. This view holds that the U. S. Constitution does not impose upon the courts the duty or the right to correct all political wrongs, and some of them— including malapportionment—were left to an informed, civically militant electorate and an aroused popular conscience. When in 1950 the high court dismissed the first Atlanta case on these grounds, Justice Douglas disagreed. In a dissent he said:

> "There is more to the right to vote than the right to mark a piece of paper and drop it in a box or the right to pull a lever in a voting booth. The right to vote includes the right to have it counted. . . It also includes the right to have it counted at full value without diminution or discount. That Federally-protected right suffers substantial dilution . , . (where a) favored group has full voting strength . . . (and) groups not in favor have their votes discounted."

Thirteen years later eight of the nine justices agreed with Justice Douglas that voting involved the equal protection clause of the Fourteenth Amendment. Georgia's "county unit" rule was outlawed.

Meantime, in Tennessee some urbanites found no matter how informed and civically militant they may be they could not arouse the popular conscience—or rather the conscience of legislators enough—to reapportion the Tennessee legislature. Every reapportionment bill introduced since 1901 had failed. Meantime the population had almost doubled. Most of the increase was in the cities. Tennessee voters didn't have a chance. They could not initiate a constitutional amendment or a measure.

Under such circumstances the Supreme Court decided lower federal courts could determine if the equal protection guarantee had been violated by malapportionment. If so, they could offer relief.

Less than a year after this 1962 historic landmark decision, in *Baker v. Carr,* suits on malapportionment had been filed in at least 34 states. Obviously some citizens in each of these states felt that their rights to vote had been discounted.

In deciding one of these cases from Colorado, the Court went further. Even where voters can initiate and vote on reapportionment, "a citizen's constitutional rights can hardly be infringed simply because a majority of the people choose to do so."

"Simply" is a mild word, indeed. This matter-of-fact statement of the court sets forth one of the great principles of American democracy. But, as expressed by an earlier Court, "One's right to life, liberty, and property . . . and other fundamental rights may not be submitted to vote; they depend on the outcome of no elections."

Colorado voters had, by an overwhelming majority, adopted a constitutional amendment "freezing" the composition of the state senate while requiring districts for state representatives to be "as equal as may be" in population. Why did voters approve a proposal whereby two-thirds of the population would elect only one-fifth of the Colorado Senate? One reason might be tradition. Another might be that the proposal was some improvement over the existing malapportionment of both houses. Chief Justice Warren pointed to another factor that probably influenced many urban voters, particularly in Denver. Instead of voting for 17 representatives and eight senators, as in the past, each Denver voter would cast his ballot for one representative and one senator. That simplified ballot has voter appeal.

Effect of "One Person—One Vote"

Significant changes in government may develop as the result of such reapportionment. Some predict the trend toward centralization may be reversed. State legislatures representative of new metropolitan growth may be able to deal more realistically with such problems as housing, transportation, sewage disposal, air pollution, etc., to name only a few. Increasingly, metropolitan areas have gone to the federal government for help, by-passing state legislatures which were rural-dominated. Likewise, rural counties and smaller cities which have looked to legislators from their particular locality to protect specific interests may seek greater home-rule authority to make decisions on the municipal and county levels. Some express belief that the influence of special business interests in the legislature will be reduced because such interests have been able to make alliances on non-rural issues with rural legislators in the past.

The "one person, one vote" principle cannot be applied too literally. Court decisions allow for some variations in numerical strength in voting districts as a practical necessity. Furthermore, population, as determined by the census, is the measure—not the number of eligible voters or of actual voters. A suburban area where young families live will have fewer residents of voting age per thousand population than an apartment house district where few children live. A military base in a county may account for a large percentage of the population—people who may not stay long enough to meet the residence requirements for voting. Mental incompetents and persons convicted of felonies are ineligible to vote, but inmates of mental and penal institutions are counted in the census.

Population remains, however, the only practical method applying the "one person, one vote" principle.

The Expanding Franchise

This controversy over giving votes equal weight is but the latest chapter in a long historical trend. Since Colonial

times in America—as in other democratic countries—the
circle of those eligible to vote has been successively expanded.
Today universal, adult suffrage has been nearly achieved—
in theory, if not always in practice.

In Colonial America, as in England at the same time,
only those owning a certain amount of property could vote.
The value of property required varied from colony to colony.
By the time of the Revolution these requirements had been
lowered so most tradesmen and artisans—men of modest
means—could vote.

The U. S. Constitution recognized the different voting
requirements in the various states. Voters for members of
the House of Representatives, says Article I, Section 2, "shall
have the qualifications required for the most numerous
branch of the state legislature." As originally contemplated
in the Constitution, representatives, of course, were the only
federal officials which were to be elected by popular vote.
Senators were appointed by the state legislatures. Presidential
electors could be chosen in any manner each state legislature
chose. Soon, of course, voting for presidential and vice presidential candidates by the electorate became the universal
custom.

By the 1820's requirement of ownership of property as a
condition of voting had been dropped in all states, although
in a few only men who paid taxes could vote.

After the Civil War the Fifteenth Amendment forbade
denial of voting rights because of "race, color, or previous
condition of servitude." In response to this amendment, other
restrictions were imposed on voting in some states to discourage Negroes from voting. You could vote if your grand-
father could. You could vote if you paid a poll tax, or if
you could read and interpret the Constitution. You could
vote in party primaries only if you were white. One by one
most of these restrictions have been removed by judicial
decisions or by legislation. An important assault on the denial
of the franchise to Negroes comes in the Civil Rights Act
of 1964, with its provision that a sixth-grade education shall
be deemed sufficient evidence of literacy. This act also pro-

vides machinery for Federal action to prevent denial of voting rights in Federal elections. (Even the sixth grade literacy presumption bars a large number of citizens from voting in certain Southern states.)

The Seventeenth Amendment, adopted in 1913, provided for the direct election of U. S. Senators by the voters of each state—another extension of the "one person, one vote" principle.

Note that Justice Douglas did not speak of "one man, one vote." While the statements of the Declaration of Independence and Lincoln about all men being created equal used the word "men" in its generic sense, when it came to voting "men" meant only males. It seems strange in this age of women's rights that it took nearly a century and a half of our national existence before women were guaranteed the right to vote. This guarantee is contained in the Nineteenth Amendment, adopted in 1920, which forbids any state from denying or abridging the right to vote because of sex.

Preceding the enactment of this amendment, of course, was the long struggle for women's suffrage. In its methods of demonstrations, picketing, and petitioning, as well as the resistance of its opposition, the women's suffrage movement can be compared to the civil rights revolution of the Sixties.

The frontier territory of Wyoming—where more women were wanted—was the first to give women a vote. This was in 1869. The following 50 years a majority of the states gave women the franchise.

The two most recent Constitutional amendments also relate to voting. The Twenty-Third, adopted in 1961, enables residents of the District of Columbia to vote for president and vice president. The Twenty-Fourth, adopted in 1964, prohibits the denial of voting for Federal office by a state because of failure to pay a poll tax.

Back of the final adoption of this amendment was a long battle over the abolition of poll taxes as a prerequisite for voting. Most of the states which had such a poll tax had abandoned it before adoption of the Constitutional amendment. In 1966 the Supreme Court gave the death blow to the poll tax in the other states by declaring it could not be required as a condition to vote in any election.

Two states, Georgia and Kentucky, have lowered the voting age from the customary 21 to 18 while Alaska sets it at 19 and Hawaii at 20. This issue is being debated in other states.

Protecting Minority Interests

If state legislatures are to be apportioned strictly on population, how are minority interests to be protected? Some say if both houses represent only population, states might as well abolish one branch, adopting a unicameral system like Nebraska's.

This is not necessarily so. Members of the upper house may be elected for longer terms and from larger areas. Voters may choose members of one house from single election districts, while they may elect more than one from multi-legislator districts in the other.

State legislatures vary greatly in size. Some are already unwieldy. Others could be enlarged without diminishing their effectiveness. Such enlargement might help protect diverse economic and geographical interests in a state. One spokesman from an area dependent on protecting irrigation rights, for example, may convince his colleagues that his position is right. The art of politics is not wholly dependent on appeal to self interest. Elected representatives legislate for all the people as well as their particular constituencies. The legislative process, to a considerable degree, consists in a few persuading a majority to accept a point of view or in achieving a coalition based on compromise.

Each legislator, as indeed each voter, is a member of diverse interest groups, each a minority in itself. To illustrate, a doctor in a small town sent to the state senate may join with fellow physicians from the city to support a health bill. As a school board member he works with educators over the whole state to secure adequate appropriations for the schools. As a legislator from a rural area he seeks to have

highway construction funds distributed in a manner to assure good roads in less populated areas.

State legislatures may be criticized on various grounds.
One criticism, however, falls flat. They cannot be accused
of being inaccessible. As long as Americans are free to speak
and write to their legislators, to lobby and to make suggestions, to join organizations and pressure groups—that long
will legislatures be open to diverse and conflicting points of
view. If citizens fail to express their opinions—or fail to have
opinions—they, not the legislators, are open to censure.

Should legislators from populous areas be elected from
single districts or at large from the city or county? This
issue was raised, as noted above, in the extreme case from
Colorado where Denverites voted for 25 different legislators.

Chief Justice Warren, while holding no constitutional
issue was involved, pointed out three objections. Ballots are
long and cumbersome. Intelligent choice among candidates is
difficult. Voters have no legislator specifically chosen to represent them.

Strong arguments are advanced on the other side. Voting
according to party rather than for specific individuals increases party responsibility. Single districting encourages
political bossism because ward leaders have undue power in
selecting legislators. It increases likelihood of gerrymander-
ing—setting boundary lines to protect the party in power.
Able candidates with city-wide support cannot win in the
district where they live because in that particular area their
party is in the minority.

Perhaps a compromise would be districts large enough
to elect two, three, or four members to each house, but no
more, or single districts for one branch, multi-legislator districts for the other.

The right to meaningful franchise includes not only the
right to vote and to have one's ballot counted at face value.
It also implies the right to effective choice and the right to
get on the registration rolls.

Residence Requirements

Twenty million Americans move every year. Many of these lose their right to vote because they do not meet the residency requirements of either their new home or their old. This mobility factor was recognized by the President's Commission on Registration and Voting Participation, appointed by the late President Kennedy.

This commission recommended that residence requirements not exceed six months in a state and not more than 30 days in a local subdivision. It also made a score of other recommendations, all designed to facilitate registration and voting. Only the individual states, of course, can act on such issues.

Civil liberties attorneys have challenged the residency voting requirement as applied to presidential elections. They claim such requirement discriminates between long-term and short-term residents, in violation of the Fourteenth Amendment. Here, indeed, is a "frontier issue" in applying constitutional guarantees. Its proponents estimate at least 3,700,000 more American adults, otherwise eligible to vote, would be able to cast ballots for president and vice president. In a brief order without opinion, however, the U. S. Supreme Court upheld Maryland's one year residency requirement.

The right to vote implies a responsibility to vote. American voting records show only about two out of three potential voters actually go to the polls. In European democracies, such as the Scandinavian countries, well over ninety percent of the eligible voters cast ballots. Even taking into consideration some mitigating reasons for non-voting—mobility, obstacles to easy registration, one-party system in some states— the American voting record could be improved.

If Americans really believe in the primacy of the individual and equality under law they can demonstrate their faith by participating in government through voting.

Part II

LIBERTY FOR ALL

4

First Amendment First

"Congress shall make no law respecting an establishment of religion, or prohibiting the free exercise thereof; or abridging the freedom of speech, or of the press; or the right of the people peaceably to assemble, and to petition, the government for a redress of grievances."

—THE FIRST AMENDMENT

"This then is the appropriate region of human liberty. It comprises, first, the inward domain of consciousness; demanding liberty of conscience in the most comprehensive sense; liberty of thoughts and feelings, absolute freedom of opinion and sentiment in all subjects, practical or speculative, scientific, moral or theological . . . liberty of tastes and pursuits; and . . . freedom to unite for any purpose not involving harm to others."

—JOHN STUART MILL

"If there is any fixed star in our constitutional constellation, it is that no official, high or petty, can prescribe what shall be orthodox in politics, nationalism, religion, or other matters of opinion or force citizens to confess by word or act their faith therein."

—JUSTICE ROBERT H. JACKSON

"It is time enough for the rightful purposes of civil government for its officers to interfere when principles break out into overt acts against peace and good order."
—THOMAS JEFFERSON

"It is beyond debate that freedom to engage in association for the advancement of beliefs and ideas is an inseparable aspect of the 'liberty' assured by the Due Process of the Fourteenth Amendment, which embraces freedom of speech."
—JUSTICE JOHN M. HARLAN

"Freedom of press, freedom of speech, freedom of religion are in a preferred position."
—JUSTICE WM. O. DOUGLAS

It is no coincidence that the Founding Fathers placed the freedoms enumerated in the First Amendment foremost in the Bill of Rights.

Freedom to choose what one says, publishes, reads, hears, believes, feels, joins, and does within a wide range of effective alternatives—this constitutes the essence of liberty. For the individual, freedom of choices makes self-fulfillment. For the community, for the nation, for society, liberty offers avenues to progress and development.

Choices involve risks. Freedom may be dangerous to an individual and to the state. Many speak without thinking, write without knowing, believe without seeking, join without reasoning. Some talk when it would be better to listen.

Freedom opens the way for oddballs and neurotics, for subversives and fabricators. It also promotes creativity and the joy of self expression.

The First Amendment, to those who wrote it, meant much more than granting the privileges of free expression for such worthy or unworthy ends. They shared a tradition of many struggles over hundreds of years against the power of the English crown to suppress dissent and criticism of whatever the rulers ordained as orthodox. Whether religious or political, they mistrusted interferences by government in the realm of ideas. They accepted the risk where truth is discovered and people distill wisdom from the noisy market place of ideas and competing policies.

Those who adopted the First Amendment in the first session of the Congress of the new United States went beyond the traditions of England.

A New Idea—Separation of Church and State

Separation of church and state, in particular, was a most revolutionary step. Union of church and state was the accepted rule in England, as it was in Europe—as it had been throughout history. In the Middle Ages, as in Rome, in Greece, and in ancient Palestine, the rulers of the state were either subject to the religious authority or were themselves the religious authority.

Rhode Island, alone among the original thirteen colonies, had from its founding complete religious freedom and absence of any official recognition and tax support for churches. Virginia adopted Thomas Jefferson's bill completely separating church and state only two years before the Federal Constitution was drafted.

Thus the "no establishment, free exercise" clause of the First Amendment followed a long time trend exclusively American. It was debated and worked over more than almost any clause in the Bill of Rights. In fact the Senate and House could not agree, so the final wording as it appears in the First Amendment was written by a conference committee.

First, the Senate rejected three versions which merely forbade laws preferring one sect or denomination over another. Then it passed a version forbidding any law "establishing articles of faith or mode of worship." This the House rejected as too narrow a prohibition. So a compromise was worked out: "Congress shall make no law respecting an establishment of religion, or prohibiting the free exercise thereof."

Interpretation of this two-sided restraint has been and continues to be the subject of sharp controversy. Indeed, the application of each of the clauses of the First Amendment to specific situations has probably produced more differences of opinion and more court tests than the other nine amendments in the Bill of Rights put together.

Differing Intent Indicated

What are the limits on free expression? Do the limitations apply to Congress or to all branches of the federal govern ment? Have they been extended to the state governments? What did the first Congress intend when it framed the First Amendment? If this amendment had not been adopted would Congress be free to legislate on religious matters or limit freedom of speech and press? Does the First Amendment's "no establishment" clause really add to the powers of Congress one to support religion as long as there is no discrimination? Has the development of our nation expanded our concepts of freedom far beyond anything the Founding Fathers envisaged? Has the United States Supreme Court gone too far in recent interpretation of First Amendment rights?

These are questions which have been asked and are being asked. Judges disagree among themselves, so it is no wonder that ordinary citizens wonder about the answers.

The intent of the Congress which adopted the First Amendment cannot give the answers to all the questions asked today. History, however, throws significant light. Those who drafted the Constitution were of the opinion that no Bill of Rights was necessary because the power of Congress did not extend to the press, to speech, or to matters of religion. Only those powers specifically enumerated in the Constitution were granted the Federal government.

Others in the states, however, were fearful the federal government might usurp powers not specifically prohibited to it. These, it should be noted, knew only too well the experience of English and colonial history.

The Constitution was ratified with the understanding that the first Congress would submit amendments for ratification comprising a Bill of Rights.

In submitting his draft for consideration, James Madison

told the House of Representatives the "great object" of the Bill of Rights was to "limit and qualify the powers of government." Furthermore, he declared it was not written "to imply powers not meant to be included in the enumeration."

This view is followed by those who give the broadest possible interpretation to the rights to freedom of speech, freedom of press, and freedom of religion. The quotations which start this chapter are from men who, in general, share this broad view. Others would define these freedoms much more narrowly. Exponents of each position can cite historical precedents for their particular stands.

A Preferred Position

One generalization may be made. Freedom of expression is and has been a growing concept, evolving and changing as the nation—and the world—grows and changes to meet new situations. Factors which have made change inevitable include at least these: the widening circle of full citizenship discussed in the last section, the growth of universal, popular education, the technological revolutions in the means and the speed of communication, the expansion of government services on every level, the tolerant acceptance of differing religious and philosophical ideas, and the emergence of radically different economic and political systems in the world—communism and fascism—which are threats to political democracy and economic free choice.

First Amendment freedoms can be dangerous, but democracy itself is dangerous. It puts its trust in the people. In interpreting most of the United States Constitution courts assume a law to be constitutional unless proven otherwise. But laws relating to suppression of ideas—freedom of the press, freedom of speech, freedom of religion—such suppression must be assumed to be unconstitutional unless it is unmistakably proven—beyond a shadow of a doubt—that such expression would constitute a real, present, and terrible danger to the fabric of society itself. This is what Justice Douglas meant when he declared that these freedoms are in a preferred position. Even Thomas Jefferson, one of the greatest civil libertarians who ever lived—saw the necessity for government "to interfere when principles break out into overt acts against peace and good order."

When does that occur? The chapters which follow in this section deal mainly with answers to that question.

5

Free to Express

"Congress shall make no law . . . abridging the freedom of speech, or of the press. . ."

— FIRST AMENDMENT

"One of the objects of the Revolution was to get rid of the English Common law on liberty of speech and press."

— JUSTICE HUGO BLACK

"The fact that speech is likely to result in some violence or in destruction of property is not enough to justify its supression. Among free men, the deterrents ordinarily to be applied to prevent crime are education and punishment for violations of law, not abridgements of the right of free speech and assembly."

— JUSTICE LOUIS D. BRANDEIS

"The most stringent protection of free speech would not protect a man in falsely shouting, 'Fire!' in a theatre, and causing a panic."

— JUSTICE OLIVER WENDELL HOLMES

."Speech concerning public affairs is more than self-expression. It is the essence of self-government."

— JUSTICE WM. J. BRENNAN

40

All of these brief quotations on free speech are from court decisions made since World War I.

This fact is significant. It indicates that in our own time controversy has raged over what the limits on freedom of speech and of the press are or ought to be.

Free speech, someone says, is as American as apple pie. A person is free to speak or print anything he pleases. Why talk of limits when there are no limits?

But there are limits, as such words as "treason", "incitement to crime", "libel", "slander", "pornographic" intimate.

A Necessity of Self Government

The late Dr. Alexander Meiklejohn, noted educator and philosopher, expressed a position more absolute than any the United States Supreme Court has taken in permitting unbridled expression. Yet in his famous book, *Political Freedom*, he acknowledges limitations within the First Amendment. A brief sampling of the ideas expressed in that book may help clarify what the First Amendment meant to the founding fathers and what it means today.

Meiklejohn points out one of the good dictionary meanings of "abridge" is "to decrease." Thus Congress could make no laws decreasing the free speech permitted by existing laws but it could legislate to enlarge and increase it. It is "freedom of speech" and not "speech" itself which may not be abridged. One may not speak anything, anywhere, anytime. The legislature may and must prohibit certain forms of speech—libel, slander, speech that incites to crime, or which results in treason.

Another meaning of "abridge", used by Blackstone in his commentaries on English law is, "restrict." The purpose of the first amendment's absolute, unqualified prohibition against any law abridging freedom of speech or the press, according to Meiklejohn, "is not that everyone shall speak, but that everything worth saying shall be heard. . ."

"And this means though citizens may, on other grounds, be barred from speaking, they may not be barred because their views are thought to be false or dangerous. No plan of action shall be outlawed because someone in control thinks it unwise, unfair, unAmerican. No speaker may be declared 'out of order' because we disagree with what he intends to say."

Here Dr. Meiklejohn was using a town meeting as an illustration where rules such as recognition of the chair, time limit, speaking to the "question before the house", etc. must prevail if the chaotic anarchy of babel is to be avoided.

But he declares absolute the prohibition against barring speech because of the ideas expressed:

"That prohibition holds good in war as in peace, in danger as in security. The men who adopted the Bill of Rights were not ignorant of the necessities of war or of national danger. In fact it would be nearer the truth to say that it was exactly those necessities which they had in mind as they planned to defend freedom of discussion against them. Out of their own bitter experience they knew how terror and hatred, how war and strife, can drive men into acts of unreasoning suppression. They planned, therefore, both for the peace which they desired and for the wars which they feared. And in both cases they established an absolute unqualified prohibition of the abridgement of freedom of speech. The same requirement, for the same reasons, under the constitution holds good today."

Dr. Meiklejohn says:

"The reason for this equality of status in the field of ideas lies deep in the very foundations of the self governing process. When men govern themselves it is they—and no one else—who must pass judgment upon unwisdom and unfairness and danger . . . The principle of freedom of speech springs from the neces-

sities of the program of self-government. It is not a
law of Nature or of Reason in the abstract. It is a
deduction from the basic American agreement that
public issues shall be decided by universal suffrage."

Historical Development "Concerning Public Affairs"

Justice Brennan refers to the same aspect of free speech
in the quotation cited. "Speech concerning public affairs"
does not embrace the total concept of freedom of speech,
but this aspect is highly significant in its historical development. The differentiation between speech concerning public
affairs and other speech helps find the way through the maze
of convolutions that mark interpretations of the First Amendment. ("Freedom of speech" as a general term, of course,
includes freedom of the press. The written word is but an
extension of the spoken.)

Those who insisted that freedom of speech and the press
be guaranteed by amendment to the Constitution were well
aware of the attempts of the English crown to suppress criticism of the government—in England and in the Colonies.
Only a few years before had John Peter Zenger been acquitted by a jury although he had dared to publish a newspaper criticizing the activities of the royal governor. The
framers of the Constitution had, indeed, provided that no
member of Congress can be questioned on any statement
made in either House except in that House. Madison and
other drafters of the Bill of Rights insisted that all citizens—
not just those elected to office—were free to express opinions
on public affairs. This is the basic intent of the freedom of
speech and press clause of the First Amendment.

Whether, as Justice Black declared, one of the purposes
of the Revolution was to get rid of the English common law
on liberty of speech and press has been argued pro and con
in the courts. As developed over centuries, English common
law holds that no one can be restrained from publishing or
saying something, but one can be punished—or held accountable—after publication or utterance. This is the doctrine of no prior restraint.

The Issue Raised During World War I

As applied to comment on public affairs the issue did not really arise until about the time of the first World War. In the very early days of the Republic the notorious Alien and Sedition Acts were passed under which critics of the "political powers that were" found themselves fined and imprisoned. These laws were set to expire at the end of John Adams' administration so its opponents, who elected Thomas Jefferson president, could not use them. Thus a court determination of the Acts' constitutionality was never made.

During World War I America was engaged in a struggle which prevailing opinion thought threatened her existence. Americans of German descent were harrassed. German language papers were banned. Eugene Debs and many others who expressed any opposition to the war were jailed. Religious pacifists who opposed the draft were prosecuted.

It was in a case involving such a pacifist, *Schenk v. U. S.,* that Justice Holmes made his famous analogy to a man falsely shouting fire in a theatre and causing a panic. He went on to say:

"... the question in each case is whether the words are used in such circumstances and are of such a nature as to create a clear and present danger that they will bring about substantive evils that Congress has a right to prevent."

What is a "clear and present danger"? That is always the hard question. If a person thinks he smells smoke is he falsely shouting fire? Like most analogies and figures of speech, this one should not be stretched too far. Granted that a government has the right and duty to resist its overthrow by unconstitutional means, those in government, being human, may be prone to consider sharp criticism a threat to government itself.

Pacifist Schenck circulated a pamphlet urging resistance to the draft during World War I. The Supreme Court decided that such a pamphlet did indeed constitute "a clear and present danger."

In view of the much more liberal treatment afforded conscientious objectors during World War II, to say nothing of opposition to Selective Service during the Viet Nam War, this decision sounds a bit naive.

Attempts to Draw a Line

In the past four decades, successive Supreme Courts have grappled to find the line separating permissible speech from revolutionary incitement to overthrow the government. The "clear and present danger" theory has been embroidered and embellished. Court decisions on free speech and press issues are full of such phrases as "bad tendency" which would ultimately harm the state, "clear and probable danger," "substantive evil to society," "balancing theory," "the gravity of the evil discounted by its improbability" as justifying invasion of free speech necessary to avoid the danger.

As might be expected sharp differences of opinion have prevailed among justices on almost all of the decisions involving freedom of speech and press.

Justice Black, one of the most vigorous exponents of interpreting strictly the First Amendment once said that the balancing theory—weighing individual rights against public good—could be used "to justify almost any action the Government may wish to take to suppress First Amendment freedoms."

He offered an objective standard which comes very close to Jefferson's statement that there is time enough for government officers "to interfere when principles break out into overt acts against peace and good order."

Justice Black declared: "Freedom of expression can be suppressed if, and to the extent that, it is so closely brigaded with illegal action as to be an inseparable part of it."

That standard, it may be said, does not reflect—yet— the thinking of a majority of the U. S. Supreme Court. Certainly Congress and the executive branch since World War II have shown preference for the sliding scale of the balancing theory, which takes account of the international political climate and the tensions and dangers of the Cold War.

In adopting the Smith Act, the McCarran-Walter Internal Security Act, the Subversive Activities Control-Act, and other measures directed against the Communist conspiracy, Congress obviously acted on the premise that it would be too late, under modern circumstances, to wait until the subversive forces started overt action against the state. Even the advocacy of the use of force and violence to overthrow the government was sought to be banned by the Smith Act.

This law was declared constitutional, under the balancing theory, in 1951. Since then, however, subsequent decisions on this and other internal security laws have placed so many restrictions on the nature and amount of evidence needed for convictions that the whole attempt to suppress the American Communist Party by law has proven ineffectual. On narrower grounds than the basic free speech issue, courts have required proof of knowledge that the Party advocates use of force and violence. More is required than an abstract theory that some day in the indeterminate future the government ought to be overthrown. A relationship between advocacy and incitement to some kind of action must be shown.

The problem of drawing the line between permissible expression and illegal revolution against which the government may protect itself may go on for a long time. At the moment, however, it does not seem as important as it did in the Fifties.

Attempts to Control the Press

During our history various attempts have been made to restrict or control the expression of the press on public affairs. Some efforts have been most subtle, others quite blatant.

In the latter category was a tax imposed by the Louisiana legislature during the Huey Long regime in the Thirties. This tax applied to the gross receipts of advertising revenues of newspapers—but only to papers with large circulation. It just so happened that these were the papers which opposed the Huey Long machine. The courts held such a tax interfered with freedom of the press. Likewise declared unconstitutional was a Minnesota law of the same depression period permitting any state court to enjoin publication of any "malicious, scandalous, and defamatory newspaper, magazine or other periodical."

More recently—in 1964—the U. S. Supreme Court has moved to protect critics of public officials against criminal and civil libel suits brought by the officials attacked.

A jury in Alabama had awarded the city commissioners of Montgomery a $3,000,000 judgment against the New York Times for running a full page ad in defense of Rev. Martin Luther King. Although not mentioned by name, the commissioners complained that the description of events in their city constituted personal libel. The ad contained some minor errors of fact.

The high court—unanimously—overturned the judgment, declaring that a "good faith critic" is entitled to protection from libel suits by public officials criticized. An official can recover damages even for a defamatory falsehood relating to his official conduct only if he proves that the statement was made with " 'actual malice', that is with the knowledge that it was false or with reckless disregard of whether it was false or not."

The Court pointed to the "profound national commitment that debate on public issues should be uninhibited, robust and wide open, and that may well include vehement, caustic, and sometimes unpleasantly sharp attacks on government and public officials."

The Times attorney had declared the Alabama court judgment "poses hazards for freedom of the press not encountered since the early days of the Republic."

Regardless of whether any newspaper could survive a series of such damage suits, the Court pointed out, "the pall of fear and timidity created an atmosphere where First Amendment freedoms cannot survive."

During hot political campaigns one hears it said that some scurrilous accusation against a candidate must be true. Otherwise the candidate would sue for libel. This is not necessarily so. Aside from protecting the right to uninhibited sharp political debate, it is most difficult to prove libel. He who sues for libel opens his whole past to searching interrogation by hostile cross-examiners.

To label an individual—or organization—"Communist" has been held libelous per se, that is in itself, if made with knowledge that the accusation is false or with reckless disregard whether it is false or not.

Yet a New York district court dismissed the libel suit brought by Dr. Linus Pauling against William Buckley, editor of the *National Review,* for accusing him of being a Communist sympathizer. The court held that Dr. Pauling, scientist and Nobel prize winner, was a public figure who had expressed himself freely on various issues and therefore was subject to criticisms. If this position stands up on appeal, it will substantially extend the doctrine in the New York Times case to almost any person in the public eye as well as to public officials and candidates for public office.

Freedom of Information

If expression of ideas regarding public issues is to be really free, if debate is to be "uninhibited, robust, and wide open" then it follows that information regarding public affairs must be available.

This aspect of free speech and free press raises a number of questions. Herein lies the basis of the not infrequent conflicts between agencies of government and representatives of the press. Here "the press," of course, include all mediums of mass communication—radio and television as well as newspapers and magazines.

In one sense reporters have no special right of access to information not available to others. Although newspapermen have claimed the right to refuse to divulge sources of information—and a few have gone to jail rather than disclose such sources—the weight of judicial decisions is that where necessary to serve the ends of justice in court proceedings they are required to tell how they obtained their information. Newsmen have not been accorded the professional status of attorneys, physicians, and clergymen who cannot be questioned on what is told them in private.

Newsmen, however, have a particular responsibility to inform. Therefore, as a matter of practical necessity, they are accorded special privileges in reporting news of public concern—such as the right to attend news conferences or be in particular places where the general public is barred.

Sometimes these privileges are abused, as vividly pointed out by the Warren Commission Report on the tragic assassination of President Kennedy and the events which followed. This report criticized the Dallas Police Department for not adequately controlling "the great crowd of newsmen that inundated . . . the department building" and laxity in screening press credentials. This permitted Jack Ruby to slip unnoticed into the crowd that November Sunday morning and shoot Lee Harvey Oswald. The Warren Commission also criticized the newsmen themselves for a "regrettable lack of self-discipline" and failure to respond properly to the demands of the police.

The time factor as a limit on the right to information was cited:

> "The commission recognizes that the people of the United States, and indeed the whole world, had a deep-felt interest in learning of the events surrounding the death of President Kennedy . . . However, neither the press nor the public had the right to be contemporaneously informed by the police or prosecuting authorities of the details of the evidence being accumulated . . . The courtroom, not the newspaper or television screen, is the appropriate forum . . . for the trial of a man accused of a crime."

Public Officials and the Right to Know

The reporting of less sensational matters—the day-to-day activities of policy-making and administration by governmental officials—poses less dramatic problems.

Every holder of political office, from the village councilman to the President of the United States, desires that his actions appear in the most favorable light. It may be natural, therefore, that an official would prefer that the press be informed after an action has been taken—probably by a press release, a "hand-out"—rather than permit it to observe the process of decision-making where the arguments pro and con and the compromises reached are in full view.

When government agencies or officials attempt to withhold or edit information newsmen accuse them of "managing the news." Officials complain, on the other hand, that the press selects, distorts, or even fabricates the news so as to present a false picture. Examples can be cited on both sides of the argument.

Nevertheless, it is the citizens' right to know—not the political desires of an officeholder nor a newspaper's desire to profit from sensational exposés—which is the real concern.

Largely as the result of efforts of newspapermen's associations, twenty-nine states have passed "open meeting laws" requiring all governmental bodies to conduct business in public—although sometimes discussion prior to final vote is permitted to occur behind closed doors. Thirty-seven states have open record laws, requiring public records to be open to inspection.

In 1966 Congress enacted into law a similar freedom of information bill, making accessible all records of all Federal agencies except personnel files, trade secrets, private business data, and classified-security information. It further clarifies an old statute relating to disposition of records which has been used in modern times to bar reporters from access to public documents.

Why such a law is desirable is illustrated by an instance in 1962 when the National Science Foundation said it would not be "in the public interest" to disclose cost estimates of the unsuccessful bidders for the "Mohole Project". This project involves drilling through the earth's crust on the ocean floor. When White House intervention reversed this secrecy rule, reporters found that the firm winning the contract was not the lowest bidder.

Such laws are no cure-all. In one state the exceptions written into the law enable school and municipal boards to hold more closed sessions than before the "open meetings" law was passed! In another instance a reporter attempted to use the "open records" law to get the details of a juicy divorce case!

Just what are public records and what is private information? Although secret court trials—"star chamber proceedings"—are barred in the American system of justice—there are exceptions. Hearings in juvenile cases are almost always private and the records sealed.

One of the arguments used in support of executive sessions is the example of a school board examining a morals charge made against a teacher. Isn't it better, whatever decision is reached, that the matter be kept quiet? One instance is cited where a teacher was fired on a morals charge by a school board and hired by a board in a neighboring district—both in secret sessions. In another case, a superintendent fired a principal on morals charges and his reasons for doing so were made public. The principal sued the superintendent for slander and won a heavy judgment which bankrupted the unfortunate official. Had the proceedings been kept secret, there would have been no slander suit—but the principal would have been discharged on the basis of faulty information—possibly malicious.

In its 1963 report, the Freedom of Information Committee of Delta Sigma Chi, journalistic fraternity, charged that freedom of the press "is at its lowest ebb today in the history of our federal government." It particularly charged the Defense Department with controlling the release of all news emanating from its far-flung operations, and other branches of the Federal government with shrouding their activities in a "blanket of secrecy" even less justified for security reasons. "On the other hand," the report continued, "the American people are being deluged today with more governmental propaganda than at any time in the history of our country."

Responsibility for a Responsible Press

In this and other demands for freedom of information from government sources the assumption is implied that the press is responsible—that it will report fairly and accurately, within the limits of good taste, and with an awareness of the existence of libel laws.

Is this assumption always justified? Norman Cousins, himself the editor of the magazine *Saturday Review,* has cited several instances where the press has been less than responsible and has even jeopardized delicate international negotiations.

One related to the agreement reached between President John F. Kennedy and Premier Nikita Khrushchev over the removal of Soviet troops in Cuba. The announcement was to be made simultaneously in Moscow and Washington in order to avoid the charge that either side had succumbed to pressure. But a press "leak" in Washington before the scheduled time almost wrecked the agreement.

Cousins also told how he acted as intermediary between Khrushchev and the Vatican over the release of several Catholic bishops and archbishops held for years in Communist jails. The Soviet leader feared the press would print lurid interviews about "Red tortures" when the churchmen were released. So it was agreed that the first bishop to be freed would be whisked out of Vienna and taken to a seminary without meeting the press. Nonetheless the day the prisoner was released, Cousins said he received a call from the Russian ambassador in Washington, reading him "in a cold voice" the headline "Bishop Tells of Red Torture." Cousins reported a check with the Vatican showed the bishop had seen no one "and the story was a complete fabrication. It was four months before we could arrange release of the second bishop."

A third example of press irresponsibility cited by the *Saturday Review* editor illustrates, perhaps "slanting by selection" which is at the same time less portentous and more frequent. When a commencement speaker listed a score or so of great authors which students should read, from Plato to George Bernard Shaw, the headline came out: "Students Urged to Read Marx"!

Obviously, news stories—and headlines particularly—necessarily select and emphasize certain aspects of the total body of facts. That selection may be a fair and representative presentation of the truth, or it may truthfully reveal its bias.

Responsibility of Readers

Readers of the press, as well as publishers and editors, have a responsibility for freedom of the press. They exercise that responsibility by questioning what they read and hear, and by reading and listening to more than one viewpoint. Where a city has only one newspaper, this may present a problem, but there are weeklies and monthlies, not to mention pamphlets and books, radio and television programs which provide a variety of views. Small periodicals expressing non-conformist viewpoints often exert an influence far greater than their tiny circulation indicates.

While some daily newspapers which enjoy a monopoly situation restrict their news and editorial columns to a single point of view, more, even in cities where they have no competition, find it good busines to present a variety of columnists with sharp differences and to carry special Washington and foreign news, syndicated by such papers as the New York Times, Los Angeles Times, Washington Post, and others with large and specialized staffs of reporters.

It has been charged that newspapers are influenced by their advertisers as to what they print. More nearly the ultimate truth, however, is the fact that both publishers and advertisers need readers.

The better informed more readers are the more information they will demand—and get—from the press. Whatever the shortcomings of the press and the broadcasting industry may be at the moment, in the end the only guardians of freedom of communication—freedom to express—are the people themselves.

6

Free to Hear and See

"All ideas having even the slightest redeeming social importance—unorthodox ideas, controversial ideas, even ideas hateful of the prevailing climate of opinion —have the full protection of the guaranties, unless excludable because they encroach upon the limited area of more important interests."
—JUSTICE WM. J. BRENNAN

". . . 'liberty' assured by the Due Process clause of the Fourteenth Amendment . . . embraces freedom of speech."
—JUSTICE JOHN M. HARLAN

"When you display more interest in defending your freedom to suffocate the public with commercials than in your freedom to provide provocative variety—when you cry, "Censorship", and call for faith in the founding fathers' wisdom only to protect your balance sheet —when you remain silent in the face of a threat which shakes the First Amendment's proud oak to its very roots—you tarnish the ideals enshrined in the Constitution and invite an attitude of suspicion."
—E. WILLIAM HENRY
FEDERAL COMMUNICATIONS COMMISSION

Freedom of speech and press on public issues is the essence of self government. That was the theme of the last chapter. What about freedom of expression on matters regardless of whether they concern public policy? That is a question attempted to be answered in this chapter.

Public Speech in a Public Place

Some of the ramifications of the answer may be posed by considering a very simple situation—a man speaking on a street corner or in a public park. Under what circumstances, if any, may the police arrest him?

Do they have such a right:

— If he does not stop talking if they ask him to?

— If he has not secured a permit?

— If he is presenting a position so obnoxious to his listeners that they threaten a riot?

— If he gathers a crowd of enthusiastic supporters who become noisy?

— If he is blocking the sidewalk?

— If he is selling patent medicine?

— If he uses offensive language?

— If he vilifies a group or specified individual?

— If he attacks the government?

— If he incites to violence?

— If he uses a loud speaker which disturbs the peace for blocks around?

Such questions as these have been answered in numerous court decisions over the years. Some of the answers conflict with each other. Many of the cases which reached the U. S. Supreme Court were decided by a five-to-four or six-to-three vote of the justices.

Out of these decisions, however, has evolved a general consensus. Justice Felix Frankfurter once reviewed the cases involving free speech and free press. His summary may be paraphrased as follows:

Ordinances prohibiting or requiring a permit for distribution of handbills or pamphlets are invalid although antilittering ordinances are permissible. Laws requiring licensing for soliciting have been held invalid when applied to religious spokesmen or labor organizers. Discriminatory taxes on itinerant peddlers are improper. Requirement of licenses purporting to regulate use of streets and parks are not permitted if used to arbitrarily suppress free expression. A permit and license fee for a parade are permissible if the only grounds for refusal are "considerations of time, place and manner so as to conserve public convenience." A city may subject the use of its streets and parks to reasonable regulations but officials cannot be given power arbitrarily to suppress free expression, no matter under what cover of law they purported to act. The use of sound equipment may be regulated to prevent disturbance of the peace, but not to suppress free speech. One decision overthrew a conviction for common-law breach of peace, but another upheld a statute forbidding use of "fighting words"—offensive, derisive, or annoying words—in a public place directly tending to cause a breach of peace by the persons to whom the remark was addressed.

In general the time, place, and manner of speech may sometimes be regulated if done in good faith to maintain public peace, assure availability of streets for their primary purpose of traffic, or "for equally indispensable ends of modern community life"—to quote Justice Frankfurter. But the "net of control must not be cast too broadly" and the particular circumstance of a situation must be considered.

Limitations on the "soap-boxer" or others exercising rights of speech and press may be classified as those involving preservation of public order, libel or slander, censorship of the obscene and pornographic, and purely commercial enterprise. As usual, such classification may be somewhat arbitrary and overlapping.

The statement, quoted above, that freedom of speech is embraced in the term "liberty," provides a new angle to an examination of these areas. The states, under the Fourteenth Amendment, and the Federal government under the Fifth, cannot deprive any person of liberty "except by due process of law." As applied to freedom of expression, "due process" means at least that all must be treated alike. From the "preferred position" doctrine of the First Amendment it would appear that the reasons for any restrictions on expression must be overwhelming. Freedom to express ideas not only about public issues but about any subject is the essence of personal and social development.

Preserving Public Order

Father Terminello was a Chicago Catholic priest who had been suspended by his bishop because of his attacks on others. He had his enthusiastic following. In a private hall packed with both friendly and unfriendly listeners, and hundreds more milling about outside, he stirred his listeners to a frenzy. He pilloried Negroes, Jews, and Catholics. He cast aspersions on the widow of a U. S. President.

Seventy policemen could not prevent disturbances. Stench bombs were thrown. Windows were broken. Clothing was torn. Father Terminello was convicted under an ordinance making any "misbehavior which violates the public peace and order" a breach of the peace. He appealed to the United States Supreme Court.

Feiner also appealed his conviction in a free speech case. He had spoken on the sidewalks of Rochester, N. Y. in favor of the Progressive party during the 1948 election campaign. He collected a crowd of 75 or 80 persons on the sidewalk. He engaged in name-calling, telling Negroes they should rise up in arms. Passers-by had to walk in the street. A member of the audience had protested. The two officers present twice asked Feiner to stop talking. He refused. After about twenty minutes they arrested him.

How did the Supreme Court decide these cases in 1949 and 1951 respectively? It would appear the major difference between the two was that Terminello had "hired a hall" while Feiner spoke in a public place. Whether that factor entered into consideration or not, the Court reversed the conviction of Terminello and upheld that of Feiner. In both instances the justices were split. These cases indicate the difficulty of finding the thin dividing line between giving free speech a preferred position and maintaining public peace and good order. An earlier decision drew the line at the point of a "clear and present danger of riot, disorder, interference with traffic upon the public streets, or other immediate threat to public safety or order." In other cases courts have held that police have a duty to keep peace by protecting the speaker from violence.

The majority in the Feiner case upheld his conviction, not for making a speech or for its contents, but for the reaction it invoked.

In the Terminello case, five justices held the suspended priest was protected by the First Amendment. Four held that he had lost that protection by using "derisive, fighting words" which incited disturbance.

Speaking for this minority, Justice Robert H. Jackson compared the incident to the tactics used by Hitler's Nazis before they took power. Like other extremists, they organized mass demonstrations in confident expectation that their opponents would organize a counter demonstration. They knew their cause thrived on the resultant publicity, turmoil, and claim to martyrdom at the hands of police.

Regardless of the legal issues, to deprive rabble rousers of their opposition is just about the hardest blow that can be struck against them. Perhaps that is asking more than human nature can endure. Many civil libertarians, however, believe that ignoring the fulminations of those seeking to provoke disorder is a better tactic than bringing them into court.

Libel and Slander

This same question arises in considering libel and slander. These forms of publication and speech are not, by legal interpretation, protected by the First Amendment. Yet "winning" libel and slander suits often turn out to be empty victories.

Libel is defined as any defamatory writing that falsely suggests that a person has committed a crime, or that tends to injure him in his business or profession, or that exposes him to ridicule, hatred or contempt. Slander pertains to similar defamation by speech.

The remedy lies not in suppressing publication of libel or utterance of slander, but in a civil suit for damages. If malicious intent can be proven, libel and slander may also be criminally punished.

As indicated in the last chapter, statements made on public issues are not libelous unless malicious intent is proven—knowledge that an accusation is false or reckless disregard of whether it is false or not.

Defamation by libel or slander on private matters is also hard to prove. Oftimes the publicity of the suit in which the plaintiff may find his whole past opened up by the defense in an attempt to prove "fair comment," will prove more damaging than the original statement. A "nominal award," a damage judgment of a few cents or a few dollars, may give the person suing a "moral victory" which is of dubious satisfaction. Yet the right to protect one's character and reputation from defamation has developed as a freedom basic to an individual's integrity in our Anglo-Saxon concept of justice.

Successful libel suits—and there have been some—may provide high drama. Indeed, the Broadway hit, "A Case for Libel" consisted almost wholly of excerpts from court transcripts of the successful case brought by Quentin Reynolds, noted war correspondent, against Westbrook Pegler, another famous newspaper columnist. Here, as developed in court by the brilliant attorney, Louis Nizer, the libel that Reynolds was unpatriotic, faking, profiteering, was repeated persistently. Here the intent to injure, the jury decided, was deliberate and actual.

Another problem arises when the theory of libel is applied, not to a specific individual or specific organization of individuals, but to a class of individuals. As far back as World War I, Illinois adopted what is known as a "group libel" law. This law makes it a criminal libel to falsely and maliciously expose religious or racial groups to contempt, derision, or obloquy. After World War II, a person was convicted under this law for distributing leaflets portraying Negroes as de-praved, criminal, unchaste and lacking in virtue. The U. S. Supreme Court upheld the group libel law on the grounds it was designed to prevent violence and disorder.

The Court, as one might expect, divided on the consti-tutional issue. Justice Felix Frankfurter, while upholding the right of the legislature to pass such a law, expressed doubt that it would meet the evil as intended. It "might itself raise new problems. . .."

Neither Congress nor legislatures of other states have favored proposals for group libel laws.

Education and enlightenment, through positive promo-tion of good human relations, appear to be better answers to the hate-mongers than legal suppression.

Obscenity and Pornography

Like libel, obscenity does not come under the protection of the First Amendment. Yet a publisher or purveyor of the allegedly obscene or pornographic has the right to judicial determination. In other words, the liberty of free speech and press cannot be denied except by due process of law.

It is not enough for a policeman to riffle through a juicy-covered paperback, looking for a purple passage, and then confiscate all of the stock of that title. It is not enough to tell the proprietor not to sell any books or magazines on a proscribed list, official or compiled by some private organiza-tion. It is not enough to create a board of censorship to issue or deny a permit to show a movie before it can be exhibited.

As in other free speech-free press areas, prior restraint is not permissible. After a book or periodical is published or a movie shown, action may be brought against the publisher or distributor on the ground that the work is obscene. The court—the judge or the judge and jury—decide the issue.

Laws against obscenity are very old—and very universal. This was noted by the United States Supreme Court when, in 1957, it finally sought to establish a definition of what is obscene. Such a definition has been attempted many times—by courts, by moral crusaders, by creative artists and writers, by literary critics, by almost anybody. Agreement has been, and is, almost totally lacking. Moreover standards vary from age to age, and from culture to culture.

On the list of banned books have appeared, at one time or another, many of the classics—the Greek tragedies, Shakespeare, even parts of the Bible, to name but a few. Truly, censorship on the grounds of a work being detrimental to morals has encompassed much more than what is considered obscene or pornographic. Realistic portrayal of sex in art and in literature has marked the greatest creative productions of many past ages.

"But implicit in the history of the First Amendment is the rejection of obscenity as utterly without redeeming social importance," wrote Justice Brennan, continuing his quotation at the head of this chapter. "This rejection for that reason is mirrored in the universal judgment that obscenity should be restrained, reflected in the international agreement of over 50 nations, in the obscenity laws of all the 48 states and in the 20 obscenity laws enacted by the Congress. . ."

Today's Test of Obscenity

Matter is obscene, as defined in the landmark Roth case in 1957, if, "considered as a whole, its predominant appeal is to prurient interest, i.e., a shameful or morbid interest in nudity, sex, or excretion, and if it goes substantially beyond customary limits of candor in description or representation of such matters."

To be proscribed as obscene, however, such matter must be "patently offensive because it affronts contemporary community standards relating to the description or representation of sexual matters" and it must be "utterly without redeeming social value."

This threefold test the high court applied in 1966 to *Fanny Hill,* first published in England in 1750. A majority found it not "utterly without redeeming value" and therefore not subject to banning.

At the same time, however, the court upheld convictions in two other pornography cases involving publishers who blatantly advertised their material with "an exploitation of interest in titillation by pornography". In one case the appeal was frankly to sex deviants; in the other it was frankly a sensual leer.

The Court seems to be saying that if a seller portrays material as meeting the threefold test of obscenity, it will accept that judgment without looking at the material itself. This adds a fourth test of obscenity, "pandering", which may possibly vitiate the other three.

The fact that fourteen differing opinions were written in the three 1966 obscenity cases indicates how far from being clarified are the limits of expression in this area.

Yet certain things are clear.

It is not sufficient that an isolated excerpt be objectionable. It is not enough that the publication as a whole might have a deleterious influence upon youth or any group of particular susceptibility. Sex and obscenity are not synonymous. The portrayal of sex per se is not sufficient to deny the constitutional protection of freedom of speech.

Justice Black objected to the Roth test—although more liberal than any before—because it is very subjective. What are "contemporary community standards"? (A later decision appears to make them national in scope.) How do you define "dominant theme" or "prurient interest"? Or, for that matter, "average person"?

He would apply the same test to obscenity as to other expression, to be "suppressed if, and to the extent that, it is so closely brigaded with illegal action to be an inseparable part of it."

It is axiomatic in law that thought does not constitute a crime. It may be morally wrong to think about robbing a bank or killing someone, but until one begins to put thought into action, he has committed no crime. "Immoral" and "illegal" are not synonyms.

In the realm of pornography, however, it is the stimulation to lustful thought that is sought to be made illegal as socially harmful. Many psychiatrists would dispute that it is really harmful, holding that the vicarious imagining may actually deter overt conduct. Such a view, however, is probably not acceptable to prevailing community standards.

If one suggests to another that he commit murder, that suggestion becomes an "inseparable part" of any illegal acts which follow. By analogy, if that which is obscene impels to illegal acts, it ought be suppressed. The difficulty in applying this test is that some neurotic or sociopathic persons can be stimulated to anti-social acts by the most innocent of suggestions.

Censorship of expression of ideas which in past generations have been deemed seditious, sacreligious, or generally offensive, has dissappeared in American life. In spite of the greater candor and freedom in expressing ideas relating to sex, the problem of "hard core" pornography remains a difficult one.

Obviously, individuals and organized groups of individuals have the right, under *their* First Amendment freedoms, to protest against any book, magazine, or movie as being objectionable and to make their objections known to others, including the sellers or exhibitors. But when they seek to extend their boycott of the material they consider objectionable to force the vendor to accept their standards, they are interfering with the freedoms of others.

Attempts have been made to protect youth from material which might not be considered objectionable to mature persons. The Supreme Court in 1962 found the Rhode Island Commission to Encourage Morality in Youth exceeded constitutional boundaries by forcing a wholesale distributor to stop handling books and magazines which it believed should not be available to persons under 18.

Not the law but the home, the school, and other segments of the community have the responsibility of setting the standards of good taste for the young to emulate.

Freedom to hear and see is not absolute but it is too important to be restricted by what any one person or group thinks ought to be heard or seen.

Airwaves — Control or Censorship

Advent of radio and television, of course, brought a new dimension to freedom of expression. Because the number of broadcast channels were limited in any area, a government agency had to be given authority to determine who should be granted the lucrative franchises and under what circumstances they should operate. The Federal Communications Commission is that agency which decides who among applicants for a specific channel is to receive a license to serve "the public convenience, interest, or necessity." Furthermore the FCC passes periodically on renewals of radio and TV licenses, with or without hearings. It reviews the program content to assure balance and diversity which it believes will meet the taste, needs, and desires of all substantial groups of the listening public.

Regulation of public utilities which are natural monopolies has long been a function of governmental bodies. Here the product distributed, however, is not electric power, or gas, or water but *ideas*. How can the FCC examine the content of radio and television without impinging on the First Amendment right of expression? This is the dilemma. Thus far the FCC has sought to solve it by quantitative measurement of time allotted to various categories—entertainment, news, education, religion, and numerous others. The FCC has not gone into the content of the various categories except for the equal time provision for political candidates and the "fairness doctrine." The latter requires a license to make his facilities available to opposing views when one side of a specific "controversial issues of public importance" has been presented.

When atheists asked for time to reply to religious broadcasts, the FCC held, that their request did not involve "a controversial issue of public importance."

It was because the Pacifica Foundation, which operates several non-profit FM radio stations, permits any group, including atheists and communists, to broadcast their view—no matter how unpopular—that the FCC took four years to renew its licenses. The FCC finally rejected the charge that Pacifica Foundation was Communistically inclined.

E. William Henry, one-time FCC chairman, excoriated the broadcast industry for ignoring this free speech struggle while besieging Congress for the law forbidding FCC to regulate the length and frequency of commercials. The quotation at the beginning of this chapter is from that address.

To anyone who listens to the radio or views television it is obvious that the goal of "balance and diversity" in programming has been far from achieved. Can it be without censorship? That, however, is a frontier issue of freedom to be considered again in the final chapter, "A Look Ahead."

7

Free to Teach

"Socrates met death not in defense of any creed, but the right to think things through with the full freedom of an unbiased mind."

—James T. Shotwell

"Teachers and students must always remain free to inquire, to study and evaluate, to gain new maturity and understanding; otherwise our civilization will stagnate and die."

—Justice Earl Warren

"Where suspicion fills the air and holds scholars in line for fear of their jobs, there can be no exercise of free intellect. . . A problem can no longer be pursued with impunity to its edges. Fear stalks the classroom. The teacher is no longer a stimulant to adventurous thinking; she becomes instead a pipe line for safe and sound information. A deadening dogma takes the place of free inquiry. Instruction tends to become sterile; pursuit of knowledge is discouraged; discussion often leaves off where it should begin."

—Justice William O. Douglas

What is academic freedom? Do teachers, by the very nature of their profession, have rights peculiar to that profession? Or does their situation require a particular application of the First Amendment guarantee of freedom of expression, applicable to all?

While differing answers to these questions may be given, the role of education in a free society poses a number of issues of great import. These will be explored in this and the next chapter.

The Nature of Teaching

Academic freedom asserts teachers must be free to teach, and students to learn.

A good teacher presents material related to the subject matter at hand so his students learn as much as they can. This involves presentation of facts, but much more than that.

Facts are facts, one hears it said, so let's stick to facts. They may be incontrovertible or may seem incontrovertible but oftimes their interpretation becomes most controversial.

This is true even in the realm of physical science and mathematics. How many of our scientific and technological advances would have been made if scientists in the laboratory had not questioned "incontrovertible" facts, explored daring hypotheses with the full freedom of an unbiased mind, experimented until they proved or disproved each hypothesis? This is the essence of the scientific method.

One need not be an Einstein to successfully challenge such a "fact" as "one plus one always makes two." R. Buckminister Fuller, noted architect and designer, demonstrates how one plus one may make four in a popular lecture. He holds up a triangle in each hand. Then he breaks apart the sides of one triangle and inserts each side in the angle of the other triangle to form a three-dimension pyramid. Then he has four triangles!

How much more subject to diverse and controversial interpretations are matters dealing with human aspirations, values, and relations! Does a good teacher stimulate a student to "think things through with the full freedom of an unbiased mind"? Should he? What is the difference between education and indoctrination?

Some questions which might be asked concerning the treatment of a specific issue might be these:

Does the teacher—or text—strive to present all sides of an issue objectively? Does he keep his own opinion to himself or does he tell the class of his own strong viewpoint? Does he present materials which are slanted toward a special interest, be it organized labor, the manufacturers' association, or a coalition of patriotic societies? If these materials are propaganda—and they are if they substitute appeal to emotions for reason or if they ignore significant facts—are they labeled with their source? Are students furnished with information from other sources or challenged to find them?

The late Zechariah Chafee, Jr., distinguished constitutional law professor, tells how the classroom of Professor Thomas Nixon Carver of Yale "a conservative of the toughest fiber" was "the most fertile nursery of Socialists." Chafee writes:

"He was determined to be more than fair to economic theories with which he disagreed, but his lectures made socialism so unattractive that undergraduates, in and out of his courses, started the Harvard Socialist Club to combat his influence."

This was around 1910 and one of its members was Walter Lippman, now sometimes called the dean of American political columnists and certainly no socialist.

Chafee makes the point; "Boys and girls do not really think always like their teachers, nor do they necessarily go on thinking like themselves when in college. Life wears us all down."

It will be noted that Professor Carver did not hide his own strong convictions, but he tried to lean over backwards in presenting other viewpoints. That, indeed, is a mark of a teacher with professional integrity. Furthermore, he was dealing with a field in which he had competency—in this case, economics.

Teaching Controversial Material

A quite different situation occurred recently in a small city in one of the Mountain States. A teacher of high school mathematics kept giving his students right-wing literature— leaflets and pamphlets and posters urging affiliation with organizations deemed extremist. The school board came up with a resolution which said:

> "While both sides of controversial issues may be presented in classes where the same are relevant to the subject matter of said classes, the principles of such issues or organizations shall be neither advocated nor condemned."

Is this an adequate statement? Are there ever only two sides to a controversial issue? Are there some issues on which a teacher should be free to advocate or condemn principles? Attitudes toward the Bill of Rights, for example? Should there be a difference between the methods of teaching in college, where students are presumed to be mature enough to challenge what they read and are told, and teaching in high school, where they may accept everything uncritically? Or do they?

In this complicated world it is doubtful that any issue can be presented with complete objectivity or, indeed, with completeness. Scholars spend entire lifetimes investigating controversies within a tiny segment of knowledge. Perhaps on most issues the goal should be a "balanced presentation"— an opening of doors to show a variety of viewpoints—rather than an exhaustive treatment of all viewpoints.

This view of academic freedom is, needless to say, not universally shared. In discussing a suggestion that a large university might well have one or two avowed Communists, as well as advocates of other unorthodox views, on its campus, William F. Buckley, Jr., editor of the *National Review*, had this to say in one of his syndicated columns:

> "There are, of course, two views of academic freedom, and the distinction is important.

"The one supposes that no questions are closed. By this definition it is not a closed question whether the Communists are more nearly right about our bones of contention, or we are. Hence we should have 'one or two' (a bourgeois concession by Dr. Sibley) Communists on campus to ply their point of view.

"The other view of academic freedom says something like this: We do not by all means know all that there is to know about things, but some things we do know, among them that Communists and communism are barbarous recrudescences that aim at overthrowing everything we have painfully learned over the millenia about the meaning of man and man's freedom.

"Subject to that general acquiescence, it is important to allow professors to advance their ideas on how to advance civilization."

At least two questions occur concerning this view:

What about past eras when one issue or another was "known" beyond doubt and therefore beyond discussion? In different ages could you not substitute "papist," "protestant," "Gallileo," "evolutionist," "Jacobin," for Communist and come out with an argument equally valid for the times for suppression of discussion?

If communism is the "barbarous recrudescence," why not let its advocates expose it and themselves?

Finally, what is the fundamental difference between the idea that the evils of communism are so apparent they need not be discussed, and the idea of the Soviets that a member of socialist society "has no desire for liberation from the state"?

This phrase is quoted from a consultant to the United Nations Commission on Human Rights, Boris Tchechko.

Marks of a Good Teacher

More will be said later concerning the advisability, or rather the inadvisability, of employing teachers subject to the discipline of the Communist Party. Much, but by no means all, of the controversy over academic freedom results from the fears and pressures engendered by the Cold War, the threat of real or fancied infiltration of Communist thinking into the educational system. Perhaps the next most prevalent source of controversy is literature which portrays conduct, particularly sex conduct, not acceptable to prevailing moral standards.

These issues must be placed in context, however, of the purpose of education. Is it to put students in gray flannel suits, to borrow a phrase denoting the conformity supposedly required in the advertising and public relations world? Or is it to develop gray matter, to teach students to think for themselves, to study the facts and draw their own conclusions?

Good teachers may express views they do not hold to stimulate thought and discussion. (So do good students, sometimes.) During an attack on a state university by conservatives who alleged a proponderence of professors were expounding ultra-liberal doctrines in the classrooms, a newspaper proposed to send its reporters to cover class lectures.

Does freedom of the press extend to reporting what is said in classrooms? Is there a difference between a campus lecture open to the public and regular classes? Would teacher and student be inhibited in their search for truth if what they said in the classroom might find its way into public print?

On a somewhat related issue, should school administrators —or others—listen in on what goes on in a classroom over the inter-room system? At least in some states, any citizen is entitled to visit a classroom in a public school at any time.

Academic freedom to educators means, above all else, that the professional conduct and competency of teachers is to be judged by other educators. Just as doctors and attorneys determine the standards of their respective professions, so teachers should determine theirs. That aspect of academic freedom is not acceptable in some quarters, for reasons to be examined.

In discussing the nature of teaching in relation to academic freedom, one factor is assumed. That is the maturity of the students governs how material is taught, particularly controversial material.

A teacher, at any level, who uses his position to exclusively propagandize a particular ideology—be it political, religious, or food faddist—is not the best teacher.

Nonetheless where students are mature enough to challenge such teachers and draw their own conclusions, such slanted teaching may stimulate thinking. Where younger pupils accept, rather than challenge, the attitudes of the teacher, professional competency—including objectivity—is even more necessary.

Grade and high school teachers, no less than college professors, however, have rights to academic freedom in particular as well as the rights guaranteed to all Americans.

In a western state a young man was hired to teach a fifth grade of slow learners. On the first day of his teaching a newspaper revealed he had refused to answer questions of the House UnAmerican Activities Committee on First Amendment grounds. The superintendent told the papers the teacher would be forced to resign. The teacher asked help from a civil liberties lawyer who pointed out that the use of a constitutional right was no reason for canceling a contract. The school board lawyer agreed. The teacher stayed for years and was liked by his pupils, their parents, and even by the superintendent who had sought to get rid of him.

Teachers as Employees

Teachers in public schools, state-supported colleges and universities are public employees. Those in private schools and colleges are usually under some kind of governing board of trustees.

In tax-supported institutions what is the role of the tax-paying citizen, the voters, the school patrons, the board of education, and the legislature in determining educational policy? Who influences educational policy in private institutions?

These questions complicate issues of academic freedom.

Teachers in public-supported schools are employed by boards elected by the voters or, in some state institutions of higher learning, by boards appointed by elected officials. True, the teachers are usually picked by the school administration, but in theory the governing board is ultimately responsible. Back of the school board is the state legislature which controls the purse strings, directly or indirectly, by limiting the taxes the local board can raise. The lawmakers also legislate on standards and methods of teacher certification, tenure, required oaths, etc. Where does the responsibility of the teacher lie? To encourage scholarly research? To teach what their employers, the taxpayers, want them to teach? In case of doubt, to play it safe?

Teachers in private schools and colleges have a different situation. They do not necessarily enjoy full academic freedom. If they teach in sectarian or denominational schools they may be expected to adhere to the tenets of the particular faith. Some church-related colleges and universities, however, as a policy employ professors of a differing faith as a means of challenging their students.

Even though a school may approach life from particular viewpoints, if it is to be educationally sound, it must permit consideration of viewpoints other than its own. Some of the independent, privately-endowed institutions of learning provide the maximum academic freedom because they are free from public pressures as well as from private interests.

Sometimes this independence requires courage to say "no." Some years ago an extremely wealthy Southerner offered a fabulous endowment to a university on one condition—that it teach the doctrine of white supremacy. Be it said to the credit of Southern universities and colleges, he could not find a single institution which would accept his money on this condition.

The Teacher as Citizen

What about the role of a teacher outside the classroom? Does he have the same rights as other citizens to speak, write, or join in activities dealing with any subject and any viewpoint he pleases? Or does he have particular responsibilities and obligations?

One answer was given by the president of the Portland State College of Oregon. He circulated a memorandum to the faculty assuring teachers of their right to "speak as clearly as they wish" on subjects of their choosing, outside the college, as long as they do not appear to be official spokesmen of the school.

On the other hand, Wayne State Teachers College in Nebraska cancelled the contract of an English teacher it had hired when the Nebraska State Board of Education learned he had allowed a speaker to talk in opposition to the House UnAmerican Activities Committee in his own backyard in Columbus, Ohio. He had offered his home as a forum after the speaker had been denied permission to speak on the campus of Ohio State University. Fortunately for this teacher, his old contract was renewed at Ohio State.

A California district court of appeals reinstated a Lassen Junior College teacher who had been accused of "unprofessional conduct" by school officials because he wrote letters to the local newspaper criticising the educational level of the county public school system. The court agreed teachers had the same First Amendment rights of free speech as other citizens. In this instance the teacher in a public school system was protected by a state law on teacher tenure. A teacher in a private, denominational college in western Pennsylvania, Grove City College, had no such legal redress when he was fired on the grounds he was an "incompetent teacher." Although known to be a Quaker pacifist when hired, he was dismissed after becoming actively engaged in a debate which broke out on the campus over pacifism. Six of his colleagues resigned from the faculty in protest.

The American Association of University Professors is an organization which investigates instances of alleged violation of academic freedom in institutions of higher learning, whether private or public. In the case of private institutions— and public ones in many instances—the only weapon the AAUP possesses is the professional disapproval of the academic community. The number of cases which it has been called upon to probe has increased significantly in recent years. Many of these, though by no means all, involved allegations of past or present association with Communist or Communist front groups or opposition to loyalty oaths..

Tenure

Teacher tenure is highly important to academic freedom because without tenure no teacher would feel secure in exercising his academic freedom so essential to good teaching.

Tenure means, simply, that after a probationary period which determines a teacher's fitness in a particular system, he can be removed only for adequate cause. Such cause includes such offenses as criminal conduct, gross immorality, treason, neglect of duty, and incompetence. More important than the grounds for dismissal, however, are the methods.

Alan Barth in *Loyalty of Free Men* describes these methods as including the right "to be judged by a group of the teacher's professional colleagues as well as by the institution's governing body, under procedures in conformity with Anglo-Saxon traditions of justice—written charges, confrontation of accuser, and a chance to be heard in his own defense."

In other words, teachers should have a fair hearing before being dismissed—if they have taught long enough to acquire tenure. The probationary period varies, but two or three years is average. Tenure policy and method of hearing is sometimes determined by state law, other times by the institution's governing body. Occasionally even probationary teachers are given the opportunity of a hearing if charges reflecting on their moral character or loyalty are involved. Whether the hearing is open or closed should depend on the circumstances. It would seem that the teacher involved should have some say on whether he wants the charges against him— and his defense—made public.

Does this mean that teachers are entitled to privileges beyond other public employees or other public citizens? Not necessarily! In almost all instances where public employees—

federal, state, or local—are covered by civil service regulations provisions are made for hearings, often with appeal, before dismissal. Yet academic freedom does present a special case. The reason is not that teachers are entitled to special privilege but that without explicit protection the learning process would be corrupted by forcing teachers to teach only what is acceptable to the community. Many would say that most instruction is bland enough already—that teachers naturally hesitate to become embroiled in controversy anyway. So any protection which gives teachers encouragement to induce students to think things through with an unbiased mind ought to be jealously guarded.

Teachers and Loyalty

This brings us to the crux of the controversy which has ranged since World War II. What about teachers—or would-be teachers—who are Communist Party members, have been members in the past, or who have supported causes which are said to be subversive or Communist-infiltrated, or who know others in such positions?

One attempt to answer this multiple question—at least to try to assure the loyalty of teachers in educational institutions—has been the requirement that they take "loyalty oaths." Such oaths affect many groups of citizens, not just teachers, and have a long and interesting history. Yet teachers, particularly, have been singled out.

Most states require teachers to take oaths of office. Over half require a positive oath (or affirmation) of support to the state and federal constitutions and laws and faithful performance of duty. Such oaths are generally required of all public officials, from the President on down. Who could object to such an oath or affirmation? Could any subversive honestly take such an oath? Or what subversive would hesitate to falsely swear to any kind of oath?

The kind of oath many find objectionable is the negative oath requiring one to swear that he is not a member of the Communist Party or a supporter of its principles, or a member of other "subversive groups."

The form of test oaths—required in more than a dozen states—differs considerably, but the purport is the same— a teacher is suspect until he clears himself. He is not, from the standpoint of oath advocates, innocent of subversive tendencies until proven guilty.

Why, they say, should anybody object to taking such oaths unless he has something to hide?

Protection against self incrimination is for the innocent as well as for the guilty. One might have belonged to an organization to support worthy purposes back in the days when it was thought liberals could work with Communists on specific issues—peace, better race relations, or a large number of ends. One might have joined even the Communist Party with idealistic motives and become disillusioned. Who of us would want to swear to all our past mistakes when we apply for a new job?

A more basic objection to test oaths for teachers is that they should be judged on their performance in the school— not on what they have done or believed in the past, or even what they do and believe outside the classroom in the present.

In one of the first U. S. Supreme Court decisions in this area, the justices in 1962 unanimously declared unconstitutional a Florida law requiring every government employee to swear that he had never lent his "aid, support, advice, counsel, or influence to the Communist Party." Cramp, a schoolteacher in Orange county for nine years, refused to sign such an oath. In the complaint which he filed he declared he was not a Communist and that "he has not, does not and will not lend aid, support, advice, or counsel, or influence to the Communist Party."

In spite of the fact that Cramp had made all of the required declarations, the high court held that somebody might interpret the oath differently, and therefore might bring perjury charges against the teacher. It held the words "aid" etc. were unconstitutionally vague and indefinite.

Justice Potter Stewart took occasion to say, "It would be blinking at reality not to acknowledge that there are some among us always ready to affix a Communist label upon those whose ideas they violently oppose."

The high court has struck down similar loyalty oaths for teachers in Arkansas, Washington and Arizona. The Washington state decision, in 1964, voided a 1931 law requiring teachers only to teach "reverence for law and order and undivided allegiance to the government of the United States" as too vague. It also voided a 1955 act requiring all state employees to swear they are not members of the Communist party or "knowingly of any other subversive organization" on the same grounds.

The Arizona case in 1966 involved a law similar to the 1955 Washington law. Here the court declared the oath unconstitutional because it "threatens the cherished freedom of association protected by the First Amendment."

The Arkansas law, the first to be declared unconstitutional—in 1960, required teachers to report all organizations they had belonged to or contributed to for five years previous.

State courts in New Jersey and New York have made various rulings that teachers could not be compelled to disclose the names of former Communist colleagues, were entitled to invoke the Fifth Amendment protection against self incrimination before investigating committees, and could not be dismissed for Communist Party membership which ended several years in the past.

Barth points out that there are good reasons why a faculty should be unwilling to admit a Communist into its fellowship. "In the light of what we have learned during the last twenty years, anyone so emotionally unstable and lacking in judgment as to be willing to submit to the party's discipline would seem to lack the qualifications for university tenure."

He makes a distinction, however, between a university "like any other employer" exercising care to avoid granting tenure to a Communist, and discovering that a faculty member "whose performance as a teacher has won him permanent status" was or has been a Party member.

8

Free to Learn

"The spirit of liberty is a spirit which is not too sure it is right."
— JUSTICE LEARNED HAND

"Education's job is to balance exuberance with rational suspicion. It's job is to balance dogma with quiet doubt."
— ATTORNEY GENERAL NICHOLAS KATZENBACH

"I do not believe for a minute that you are losing faith in democracy, in the Constitution, in American liberties, and in the concept of law and order. I find you making your elders uncomfortable precisely because you have the bad taste to take these concepts literally."
— U.S. REPRESENTATIVE EDITH GREEN
TO A 1965 GRADUATING CLASS

Students have made their elders uncomfortable from time immemorial. Demonstrations and hi-jinks on the campus are nothing new, although the forms of protest and rebellion have varied from generation to generation and from university to university.

Visible, voluble forms of protest, of course, are an extreme manifestation of academic freedom. Are there limits to the academic freedom of students? What are they?

Teachers must have freedom to teach if they are to be more than "a pipeline for safe and sound information" (recalling the quotation from Justice Douglas). The end of teaching, however, is the student. Several questions arise concerning the freedom of students to search and seek for truth, to express themselves, to associate with others, to participate as citizens in activities outside the classroom.

School as Community

Does a student have the same freedoms as others? Does the limit of his freedom vary with his age, grade, and maturity? Should any material on any subject be "off limits" to a student? Does a school constitute a special kind of community within which principles inherent in a democratic society should be operative? How independent of school administration should students be in running student government and publishing student papers and magazines? In forming and running clubs and organizations? To bring speakers to the campus, to petition, to distribute literature, to demonstrate, to engage in political activity, on or off the campus? Should the school have disciplinary power over students for behavior outside of school?

Obviously, the range of problems of freedom of expression for students parallel the First Amendment problems for all Americans. At least two factors, however, set students apart. First, the responsibility that goes with freedom is relative to the degree of maturity. In high school, and even more in lower grades, more guidance of the teacher is expected by the students as well as by the school administration and parents. In college, however, students are expected to show greater independence and initiative, both as to how and what they study and as to their extra-curricular activities.

Secondly, the learning process means students are exploring, testing, expressing ideas in a search for truth. Conclusions reached and expressed may oftimes be tentative—subject to revision on the basis of additional facts or more mature judgment.

While learning facts, students are also learning participation within a community. While no school or university is completely divorced from the world around it, in a real sense, it is a community unto itself.

To what extent is a student accountable to the school community? To what extent to the general community outside? Answers to these questions may depend on a variety of circumstances in which they arise.

The Right to Read

One such circumstance arises in the selection of materials —textbooks, required readings, approved reading lists, etc. Are students to be barred from reading any particular book? If so, who is to determine what books are to be banned? Perhaps more important, since no student can read everything and no school can afford to buy every publication, who is to select recommended reading? The individual teacher? The faculty as a whole? The librarian? The school administration? Some outside group or organization?

Pressures from outside the schools and universities to determine what shall be and what shall not be read have been noticeably felt in recent years. Such pressures have ranged from efforts to restore the McGuffey readers, used 100 years ago, as the grade school textbooks in a small community (Twin Lakes, Wis.) to the extensive operations of *America's Future, Inc.* This organization, headquartered in New Rochelle, N.Y., has "evaluated" more than 400 social science textbooks in general use. It is critical of many of them for giving too much space to the role of government in economic affairs and more to freedom of religion, press, and speech than to free enterprise and the right to work. "Evaluation" is one thing. Use of these findings to pressure legislatures, school boards, and teachers to discontinue certain texts is something else.

It is assumed of the academic world that teachers and textbook writers are qualified to select educationally competent books and that competition insures a wide variety. If this is not true, then American education is indeed in a bad way.

In selecting titles for reading lists, a teacher's aim might be to encourage students to choose from books of merit in any particular category which will make an educational contribution and which, in style and content, are readable by the particular group of students.

The National Council of Teachers of English has probed the problem of selecting reading material in depth in a pamphlet, "The Students' Right to Read." This study defends the right to judge the value and impact of any literary work as a whole even though it may contain words, phrases, or incidents to which some may object or which do not conform to conventional morality.

Then the pamphlet has this caution:

> "The teacher must exercise care to select works for class reading and group discussion which do not place students in a position of embarrassment in open discussion with their peers, but he must be free to recommend for individual reading any work he feels has educational significance for the individual student. In addition the teacher needs the freedom to discuss with the student any work that the student reads whether the teacher has recommended it or the student has discovered it for himself."

This statement relates primarily to English literature at the high school level. More often than not the criticism leveled at particular books are based on their use of profanity and "dirty" words, or of realistic portrayal of sex. Yet pressures are also felt to censor literature for other ideas advanced. Some would eliminate from the high school reading list Shakespeare's *Merchant of Venice* because of its portrayal of Shylock, an individual Jew. Mark Twain's *Huckleberry Finn* has been banned or rewritten to omit reference to "Nigger Jim," a name which did not have the derogatory connotation when used by Twain that it has today. Is the cause of human relations advanced if minorities keep from the students any unfavorable reference from the historical past?

Student Organizations

"Student activities" covers a wide range. Even in grade school, election of class officers and the conduct of "meetings" by them is useful in teaching democratic procedures by action. Throughout junior and senior high school and in college, student self government becomes increasingly important in dealing with real issues within the school community.

Questions arise as to the degree of autonomy to be exercised by the students and the control to be maintained by the school authorities.

High school principals, traditionally, have legal veto power over student activities. A study of the American Civil Liberties Union by its academic freedom committee suggests, however: "The wise principal in an enlightened community uses this veto seldom and with great reluctance, and explains his reasons carefully."

It proposed high school students ought to have certain rights, such as a democratically organized student government "with a clear budget of power."

College students (a term which includes university students) are obviously more "on their own" than high school students. Even here, however, a legal theory says that the college is "in loco parentis" meaning that the school authorities stand in place of the parents and have the same rights of control and discipline.

While persons under 21 are, in some instances, still minors in the eyes of the law, parents nowadays who treat young men and women in their late teens as children are not very wise. Likewise, knowledgeable college authorities recognize that allowing maximum freedom to students contributes significantly to educational goals. Sometimes such recognition requires these authorities to resist the demands of parents, alumni, legislatures, or other governmental or private groups to interfere with student activities.

Student government is the vehicle by which students may regulate student-sponsored activities, organizations, publications and other matters subject to their jurisdiction.

Should the academic authorities interfere with the by-laws or elections of such student governments? Should the academic authorities set scholastic eligibility requirements for major student offices? Should they require non-discrimination and inclusion of all members of the student body in the electorate of the student government? Should faculty members, administrators, or members of the college's governing body have any voice or vote in policy matters beyond this?

Rights and Limits of Association

As in any other community, students as citizens of the academic community should be able to form and join associations of their choice—for educational, political, social, religious, or cultural purposes. To what degree, if any, should such voluntary associations be subject to regulation?

The ACLU study, *Academic Freedom and Civil Liberties of Students in Colleges and Universities,* suggests that procedures for official recognition and registration should be set up by the student organization. Another suggestion is that meeting rooms, bulletin boards, and other campus facilities should be made available, as their primary purpose for educational use on a non-discriminatory basis. Organizations should not be required to file a list of their members. Discrimination by social clubs and fraternities on the basis of race, religion, color or national origin ought not be permitted. The faculty advisor should be chosen by the student organization. He should advise but should have no authority or responsibility to regulate or control its activities.

These suggestions grow out of many situations on many campuses. Colleges and universities differ considerably in their relations with voluntary student organizations. Variously, official recognition of organizations is made by the administration, an administration-faculty committee, a faculty-student committee, or the student government. Perhaps as important as who makes the rules, is that they be clearly stated and uniformly administered.

Why is it necessary for official recognition? Obviously if the group is to use campus facilities, publicize its activities through bulletin boards, distribution of leaflets, etc. such recognition is desirable. Clandestine organizations among students lend themselves to rumor and suspicion, founded or unfounded.

Organizational activity is complicated if it comes, wholly or largely, from non-students. That is amply demonstrated in the student riots in 1964-5 on the Berkeley campus of the University of California. The leaders of the "Free Speech Movement" were largely students. Yet they were protesting against administration restrictions on non-student political activities on the campus, including distribution of literature and speech-making.

Courts have been extremely reluctant to interfere with campus regulations of such activities. But there are a few decisions holding that streets through campuses are public thoroughfares where the rights of speech, assembly, and press exist the same as in other public places.

Campus Publications

Student publications constitute another activity where questions of control and freedom of expression arise.

On most campuses the student newspaper is the organ of the student governing body which all students support through compulsory student fees. Directly or indirectly, it may be subsidized by the college by being given office space, circulation facilities, etc.

How is the editor and staff selected? To whom is he responsible—the administration, a faculty committee, a student council, or a publication board composed of representatives of each?

Whose opinion does he represent? The editor's and staff's, the student body, the school's administration, faculty, alumni? Or should the paper be open to expression of opinion by any student or faculty member?

Should material be reviewed before publication by the faculty advisor or publication board? Or if something offends the administration or faculty, should the editorial staff be subject to discipline, or even removal?

In answering these questions, one should keep in mind the dual nature of campus journalism—a means of disseminating information and opinion and a training ground for democratic participation, including freedom of expression. The ethics and responsibility of journalism may well be pointed out to fledgling journalists, but only in instances of extremely poor judgment and after proper hearing, should they be denied opportunity to learn from their prior mistakes.

What has been said about campus newspapers generally also applies to literary and humor magazines—where the taste, or lack thereof, and youthful humor may sometimes offend the sensibilities of adults. Publications dependent on voluntary student support, however, generally fail if they lack real merit.

Political Activity

Do student organizations have the right to bring and hear outside speakers on the campus? This question arises most often in relation to controversial political figures. One of the most fruitful methods of inquiry is to listen to speakers presenting views radically different from those generally accepted. Sponsoring a speaker does not imply, necessarily, agreement with his views.

After a period of years when speakers from certain groups, notably Communists, have been banned from various campuses, it appears that the trend is now toward permitting college students to hear any and all viewpoints. This trend was augumented by a decision of the highest New York state court in 1964 reversing the ban on a Communist speaker who had been scheduled for one of the state colleges. The Michigan Coordinating Council on Higher Education, in November 1963, called for a policy on all state universities and colleges permitting liberty for all speakers to speak on any campus on any subject, with the exception of advocacy of illegal acts, or acts designed to overthrow the government. Subsequently Communists spoke on two campuses, and Governor George Romney refused to intervene to cancel the appearances. Likewise a proposed state constitutional amendment making it illegal for Communists to appear on Michigan campuses suffered crushing defeat in the state legislature.

Prior to this policy statement, not only Communists but also representatives from some civil rights organizations had been denied the right to speak on some Michigan campuses.

The Regents of the University of California lifted a ban on Communist speakers, with the proviso that university officials may require any or all of three conditions;

(1) that the meeting be chaired by a tenure professor,
(2) that the speaker be subject to questions from the audience,
(3) that speakers be appropriately balanced as to views in debate.

In Seattle, counter-pressures resulted in the reinstatement of a speech to high school students by a member of the Socialist Workers party after the original date had been cancelled because of pressure from members of the John Birch society.

One problem faced by a student group in selecting speakers, in a university where freedom to present any speaker is recognized, was outlined by a student forum chairman at Colorado State University. He invited two segregationist leaders to speak after a Negro civil rights leader had spoken, hoping one would accept. Both did, so the university was accused of being biased!

Significant support for freedom of students to hear came from a rather unexpected quarter when the Colorado Department of the American Legion, at its convention, upheld its commander who had refused to protest the appearance of a Communist speaker on a Colorado campus. A member of the Legion's Americanism committee had sought to ban the appearance because, he said, that was in accord with the Legion's anti-communist stand. But the commander upheld freedom of speech as part of the essence of Americanism.

Students as Citizens

On and off the campus students exercise their privileges as citizens to engage in political activity, to demonstrate, to protest.

Occasionally such activities may bring them in confrontation with the law. Whether the alleged infraction of the law is deliberate civil disobedience to dramatize its injustice or whether it is ordinary lawlessness, certain questions arise.

What is the responsibility of the college administration? To ask that any disciplining be handled by the institution rather than by the civil authorities? To insure the rights of students to due process—right to counsel, etc.? To impose campus discipline—ranging from withdrawing certain privileges to suspension—in addition to any fines or other penalties imposed by the courts?

Such questions might arise from incidents ranging from speeding to the international complications caused by a group of students arrested and jailed for disorderly conduct while on a spring holiday at a Mexican beach town. When they returned they were reprimanded—but not expelled—by the university administration.

Traditionally, colleges have been considered to have jurisdiction over their students except in cases of serious crime. Yet this tradition is subject to abuse if not safeguarded by the same kind of fair procedures required of the courts.

How far should a student's activities and attitudes in school follow him after he leaves school? How much should teachers tell prospective employers? On this point the ACLU academic freedom committee says:

"The teacher-student relation is essentially a privileged one. The student does not normally expect that either his utterance in the classroom, or his discussions with teachers outside classrooms, or his written views, will be reported.

"Since the best education calls for probing, sharing, hypothesizing, and for uninhibited expression and thinking out loud by the student, disclosure by the teacher to a source outside the college community of a student's expressed opinion, or making a statement based on such an opinion, becomes a threat to the educational process."

Do you agree? Granted information regarding a student's ability to write in a certain way, to solve problems of a certain kind, to reason consistently, work with other people, is important in helping a student get a proper job. But how about questions relating to his loyalty and patriotism, political, religious, moral and social beliefs? Can a teacher answer these without violating the privileged student-teacher relations.

After the school records were used in court testimony by a school principal against a former pupil, the Maryland ACLU declared "no expression of belief or non-belief, nor any expression of belief on morals, politics, association or other matters of private concern should be made part of the permanent record of any student."

Do you agree?

9

Free to Believe

"Congress shall make no law respecting an establishment of religion, or prohibiting the free exercise thereof; . . .

FIRST AMENDMENT

"If there is any fixed star in our constitutional constellation, it is that no official, high or petty, can prescribe what shall be orthodox in politics, nationalism, religion, or other matters of opinion or force citizens to confess by word or act their faith therein."

JUSTICE ROBERT H. JACKSON

"The content of the term 'religion' is incapable of compression into a few words. . . . It is a belief finding expression in a conscience which categorically requires the believer to disregard elementary self-interest and to accept martyrdom in preference to transgressing its tenets."

JUDGE AUGUSTUS N. HAND

"Religion is a concern between God and the soul with which no human authority can intermeddle."

ISAAC BACKUS IN 1774
(A NEW ENGLAND BAPTIST)

Today some 115 million Americans, nearly two-thirds of the population, are members of some church or synagogue. This percentage is at least two or three times greater than when the United States became a nation. Active membership in religious organizations in America is far greater than in European countries with state churches.

Separation of church and state, the one original idea in the First Amendment, has worked amazingly well. Yet the concept has produced, and still produces, difficult problems and sharp controversies as this and the following chapter will indicate.

Right to Mix Religion and Politics

Thomas Jefferson's metaphor "wall of separation" has been used so frequently in the discussion of church-state relations that one would almost be led to think it appeared in the Constitution.

As with any figure of speech, however, it is not to be taken too literally.

The "wall of separation" has been used as an argument against churches or clergymen taking a stand on social and political issues of the day. Yet where is it more important to express moral judgments and values than in the realm of social legislation? The free exercise of religion certainly means that an individual—either alone or in association with others—has the right to express his religious insights by seeking to influence government action. From the abolition of slavery and of child labor to the promotion of international justice and civil rights, the voice of religious people, organized and individually, has been loud and effective.

You might have a strong conviction that capital punishment was morally wrong, that it did not accord with the religious teachings that judgment belongs to God and that life was sacred. Others, from equally religious convictions, might disagree, but you and others like you certainly have the right to lobby for repeal of the death penalty in your state.

Contrast this example with a conviction, equally strong

on religious grounds, that a movie which makes light of the doctrine of the Virgin Birth should be banned. Obviously, those who share this conviction have the right to persuade all they can, particularly those within their own church, that this film should not be seen. But do they have a right to have a law, forbidding the showing of the film to anybody on the grounds it is sacreligious, enforced? The Supreme Court, in the case of *The Miracle* said "No." It held that "sacreligious" as defined in the law was "vague" and that motion pictures were entitled to the same protection of freedom of expression as the press.

Separation of church and state means that government cannot interfere with the religious convictions of individuals. It also means that religious groups cannot use government to obtain special favors or interfere with the liberties of others. It does not mean that religious groups cannot express opinions on issues. To invoke ecclesiastical authority, however, to pressure an adherent to vote a certain way is considered a breach of the wall.

Free to Spread Ideas

In interpreting the "free exercise" part of the religious liberty clause, the courts have firmly, and quite jealously, guarded the rights of individuals and religious organizations to spread their ideas. When it comes to acts which conflict with laws designed for protecting public health, welfare, and order, the issues are not quite so clear. Probably in no area of interpreting what the Constitution means have U. S. Supreme Court justices disagreed so strongly among themselves as in decisions involving application of the "free exercise" and "establishment" clauses of the First Amendment. (Yet the unanimity of several cases dealing with religion in the early Sixties may indicate that judicial consensus is being reached.)

The courts have declared unconstitutional ordinances and laws as follows:

> Requiring a license for distribution of religious pamphlets or prohibiting distribution of religious leaflets.

Prohibiting solicitation of funds for religious purposes in public places.

Prohibiting of licensing door to door religious
solicitation.

Forbidding religious solicitation by mail except in
case of fraud.

It may appear simple to distinguish between "religion"
and "fraud" but the Supreme Court said, "—one man's fraud
may be another man's religion." Statements are fraudulent
only if the maker does not believe them to be true.

Close questions have been reversed. In 1942 the Supreme
Court upheld a municipal ordinance which imposed a license
tax on book selling as applied to Jehovah's Witnesses. The
very next year the Court reversed itself, declaring:

"A license tax certainly does not acquire constitutional validity because it classifies the privileges protected by the First Amendment with the wares and
merchandise of hucksters and peddlers and treats them
all alike. Such equality in treatment does not save the
ordinance. Freedom of press, freedom of speech, freedom of religion are in a preferred position."

The fact that a religious circular offers books for sale
does not make it commercial advertising, distribution of
which may be legally regulated.

Legislation has been upheld, however, requiring even religious groups to conform to parade regulations designed to
prevent serious interference with the normal use of the
streets. These regulations required securing a license and
paying a fee bearing a reasonable relation to the cost of
policing the parade.

A child labor law prohibiting boys under 12 and girls
under 18 from selling magazines and newspapers was held
to apply to children selling religious tracts, even though they
were under direct supervision of their parents. The Supreme
Court held that the family is not beyond regulation in the
public interest—here the welfare of children—even against
the claim of religious liberty.

This, and most of the other decisions mentioned, concerned the Jehovah's Witnesses, a sect whose methods of spreading its ideas and whose vehement attacks on other religions made it subject to many attempts to legally restrict its activities.

Free Not to Believe

Free exercise of religion means freedom not to believe as well as freedom to disseminate one's beliefs. In 1961 the Supreme Court unanimously held unconstitutional a provision in the Maryland constitution requiring all public officials to swear or declare that they believe in the existence of God. The plaintiff, Roy R. Torcaso, had been denied a notary public license because he refused to take this oath. In its decision the Maryland Supreme Court expressed a rather shocking opinion holding disbelief in a Supreme Being equivalent to "the denial of any moral accountability for conduct" which renders a person incompetent to give testimony or serve as a juror, as well as to hold public office.

The Maryland court claimed, "The historical record makes it clear that religious toleration . . . was never thought to encompass the ungodly."

While the early history of some colonies and some states might give credence to such an interpretation, the ideas of Jefferson and Madison on separation have long prevailed. The Jesuit dean of the Boston College Law School, the Rev. Robert F. Drinan, S.J., in a letter to the New York Times said the *Torcaso* decision conformed to Catholic theology, in that it was unfair to require an office holder to have a gift of faith which "he cannot in any way merit or obtain since it comes freely and unmerited from God."

Limits In Action

Free exercise of religion may, however, be curbed when it goes beyond belief and opinion to result in action "inimical to the peace, good order, and morals of society." So said the Supreme Court in upholding laws against the practice of polygamy, which was an essential ingredient of the Mormon religion until banned by Federal laws in the 1870's.

The government can also require action which may be contrary to religious belief if necessary to public health and welfare. As early as 1905 the Supreme Court upheld statutes requiring vaccination for smallpox of even those, such as Christian Scientists, who do not believe in medical treatment. Here the law's purpose is not to protect the health of an individual willing to take a risk, but to prevent him from passing the disease to others.

Although not a matter of life or death, fluoridation of drinking water has proven a feasible way of reducing tooth decay of large numbers of people. Although never before the U. S. Supreme Court, a state court held fluoridation of the public water supply was within the state's power to protect the health of its residents in spite of religious objections of some. Likewise the state has temporarily taken a child from custody of his parents when they refused to permit a life-saving blood transfusion, because they, as Jehovah's Witnesses, believed it was contrary to the words of the Bible. Another state passed a law forbidding the handling of poisonous reptiles if it endangers public health and safety, curbing the practice of snake handling by one sect.

The same reasoning has been applied in California in the use of peyote, the button of one type of cactus, in the religious ceremonies of the Native American Church, composed mostly of Navajo Indians. This plant, not considered a narcotic by the U. S. Food and Drug Administration, produces mild, pleasant hallucinations when chewed but is said to produce no after effect. Its use has also been banned by the Navajo tribal council. A. U. S. Circuit Court of Appeals rejected a suit by the Native American Church to have the ban lifted on the grounds that it infringed on free exercise of religion. The circuit court held the Bill of Rights did not apply to tribal regulations. The U.S. Supreme Court has never passed on this question.

Can the religious conviction that certain conduct is morally wrong be used to prohibit that conduct on the part of those who do not share this conviction? After a Connecticut law had been on the books nearly a century forbidding prescription and use of birth control devices, the Supreme Court declared it an unconstitutional invasion of privacy. Earlier it had refused to rule because, it said, the law had never been enforced. Richard Cardinal Cushing, Catholic prelate of Boston, pointed out that while he might not, in good conscience, approve repeal of an anti-birth control law he would make no effort to impose his will on others.

Conscientious Objection

Some knowingly disobey certain laws which transgress the dictates of their consciences, willing to suffer the civil penalties. They witness in the spirit of Peter, who refused the demand of the authorities that the apostles stop teaching, saying: ". . . We must obey God rather than man."

Judge Augustus N. Hand, in the quotation at the beginning of this chapter, was considering such an instance in the case of a conscientious objector to war. Progressively the law has become more lenient in exempting such from military service.

During the Civil War conscripts could pay for substitutes. In the First World War the draft exempted from military service ministers of religion and members of certain sects, the "historic peace churches" like the Quakers with a tradition of opposition to war. Laymen of other churches or nonchurchmen who took the conscientious objector position very often found themselves with prison terms of from 10 to 50 years, but amnesty was granted to all CO's some time after the war.

The Selective Service Act of the Second World War provided for alternative service for those who objected to bearing arms whose scruples were grounded in belief in a Supreme Being. Such alternative service ranged from noncombatant ambulance service to forest conservation in Civilian Public Service camps or work in civilian hospitals. Yet a number of CO's went to prison during and after World War II—those who rejected the authority of government to force them to perform any national service, those not members of a religious organization, and those whose conscientious objection was based on ethical and social considerations regardless of belief in a Supreme Being. The average sentence, however, ran about two years, in contrast to the heavy sentences of World War I.

While upholding exemption and broadening the concept of religious motivation, court decisions have held it a matter of legislative decision rather than constitutional right.

In 1965 the Supreme Court skirted the constitutional issue as to whether the draft law's exemption on the basis of religious belief in relation to a Supreme Being created a governmentally-sanctioned form of religion, thus excluding non-theistic or polytheistic religions. Instead it granted CO status to three objectors who had been earlier refused exemption because of non-adherence to orthodox religious beliefs. The test is, the Court held, whether a given belief that is sincere and meaningful occupies a place in the life of its possessor parallel to that filled by the orthodox belief in God which clearly qualifies for the exemption.

This position is a long, long way from that taken by the high court majority in 1929 when it denied citizenship to persons whose religious beliefs prohibited them from bearing arms. The majority held the oath prescribed by the naturalization law to ". . . support and defend the Constitution and laws of the United States against all enemies, foreign and domestic . . ." implied a willingness to bear arms. A quarter century later another Supreme Court decision reversed this finding, holding that since this oath did not mention bearing arms the refusal to do so was no bar to becoming a citizen.

Holmes on Quakers

Justice Oliver Wendell Holmes, in the 1929 dissent which became the majority view in 1945, declared:

"If there is any principle of the Constitution that more imperatively calls for attachment than any other it is the principle of free thought—not free thought for those who agree with us but freedom for the thought that we hate. . . I would suggest that the Quakers have done their share to make the country what it is, that many citizens agree with the applicants belief and that I had not supposed hitherto that we regretted our inabiliy to expel them because they believe more than some of us do in the teachings of the Sermon on the Mount."

The same year, however, a bare majority upheld an Illinois court decision which in effect, according to Justice Hugo Black, would bar any true Quaker from the practice of law in that state. An applicant for the bar refused to take the oath, which included a pledge to bear arms, because of his belief in non-violence. In 1961 the U. S. Supreme Court refused to review a Washington State Supreme Court decision upholding the refusal of the State Bar Association to permit a conscientious objector, convicted in World War II, from taking the bar examination. The state court held that the conviction marked him as a man "not of good moral character."

A dissenting opinion in this case pointed to other men in English and American history who "preferred jail, rather than do what (their) consciences said (they) should not do."

Not all conscientious objection concerns refusal to bear arms. Members of the Jehovah's Witnesses sect believe saluting the flag is a form of idolatry forbidden by the Ten Commandments. In 1940 the Supreme Court upheld a local board of education in expelling two school children of a Jehovah Witness family who refused to pledge allegiance to the flag. Three years later, in a similar case, the court reversed itself, holding that the silence of some pupils to the flag salute did not bring imminent danger to society. But it held to the position stated in the 1940 decision that the requirement of an orderly society, including national unity as a component of national defense, may at times have a claim superior to the religious beliefs of individuals. A schoolroom flag exercise, however, was not one of those times.

10

Free from Establishment

"Congress shall make no law respecting an establishment of religion . . ."

—FIRST AMENDMENT

"When religion is good, I conceive it will support itself; and when . . . its professors are obliged to call for the help of a civil power, it is a sign, I apprehend, of its being a bad one."

—BEN FRANKLIN

"The Amendment's purpose was not to strike merely at the official establishment of a single sect, creed or religion. . . The object was broader than separating church and state in this narrow sense. It was to create a complete and permanent separation of the spheres of religious activity and civil authority by comprehensively forbidding every form of public aid or support of religion."

—JUSTICE WILEY RUTLEDGE (1947)

"Legal Christianity is a solecism, a contradiction of terms. When Christianity asks the aid of government, religion never rises above the merest despotism; and all history shows us that the more widely and completely they are separated the better it is for both."

—OHIO SUPREME COURT (1872)

What does "respecting an establishment of religion" mean? Wouldn't "respecting establishment of a religion" have been a clearer statement of intent? Or why didn't the Congress framing the Bill of Rights say "Congress shall make no law establishing religion" which would be shorter?

Issues of church-state relations involving free exercise of religion are relatively simple compared to the problems rising out of the "no establishment" clause.

Since the mid-Forties, in particular, the U. S. Supreme Court has handed down decision after decision interpreting this clause—in relation to school aid, released time, school prayers, Bible reading, Sunday closing, etc.

Meaning of "Establishment"

These decisions have been controversial, within the Court and without. Various theories of philosophy and law have been advanced to defend or condemn traditions which the court has upset.

When the First Amendment was adopted the words "an establishment of religion" had definite meaning. Six states still gave tax support and official recognition to any church with enough adherents to form a congregation. Three states stipulated "Christianity" as the established religion, and half "Protestantism." Congress was forbidden by the First Amendment to aid religion by tax support or otherwise, but the states were free to continue such support. Massachusetts did until well into the Nineteenth Century. The other states with establishment laws were New Hampshire, Connecticut, Maryland, South Carolina and Georgia.

One theory which has been advanced is that the "no establishment" really adds to the powers of Congress that of supporting religion in general as long as there is no discrimination. James Madison, however, in presenting his draft to the House declared that the "great object" of the Bill of Rights was to "limit and qualify the powers of government." It was not written, he said, "to imply powers not meant to be included in the enumeration."

Another broad interpretation is expressed by the following paragraph from an editorial from *Church and State*, organ of Protestants and Other Americans United for Separation of Church and State:

> "We take 'respecting an establishment' to mean *inclining toward substantial involvement*. The traditional Thanksgiving proclamation by the President is in a sense a spiritual or religious act of an official nature. But it is not unconstitutional for it does not incline toward involvement. It projects no interlocking of government with religious organizations. The same could be said of 'In God We Trust' printed on legal tender of the United States Government; or the phrase 'under God' in the pledge of allegiance. These are acts neither establishing religion nor respecting an establishment of religion."

Some non-believers may not agree, but their "free exercise" may be used to ignore such issues as minimal. It may be significant, however, that the motto on the coins did not come into use until the mid-nineteenth century and the phrase "under God" was added in 1954.

Government Recognition of Religion

Other ceremonial recognition of religion by government, such as the opening of daily sessions of Congress and the legislatures with prayers by chaplains, may be considered an accommodation in a pluralistic society to the majority consensus.

Yet what is the difference between starting a legislative day with prayer and opening a school day with prayer, which has been declared unconstitutional? One answer is that the latter becomes instruction because young minds are taught by every experience. Another is that legislators can absent themselves from the morning prayer, but pupils cannot without being singled out as being "different."

Chaplains in penal institutions and in the armed forces certainly "incline toward substantial involvement." Millions of tax dollars are involved to put chaplains on the government payroll and provide facilities for their work.

Such involvement is justified on the grounds that when men are taken away from normal civilian life where each enjoys free exercise of his religious choice, the government should at least provide an opportunity for spiritual activity in their government-maintained environment.

Some denominational leaders have expressed preference that military chaplains not be commissioned officers in the armed services and not be paid by tax funds. The reasoning is that chaplains should be servants of the church rather than under military discipline which might place restraints on their ministry. Is the chaplain preaching the "official line" or out of his own conviction?

Objections have also been voiced against the practice of requiring certain cadets at service academies to attend official religious services either Catholic, Jewish, or Protestant. The objectors believe cadets should be free to attend the church or synagogue of their particular denominational choice.

Do religious displays on public property or use of public property or use of public facilities for religious services "incline toward substantial involvement"? In some communities such practices have engendered bitter controversy.

In one of the Jehovah's Witnesses cases the court held use of public parks for religious addresses could not be banned unless all addresses were banned. Public buildings—including schools when not being used for school buildings—are often available for rental to various organizations, including religious organizations. A Florida court held in one instance, however, that a religious group could not use the public schools after school hours as a permanent arrangement rather than an occasional use.

How about ristmas displays, particularly Nativity creches, on public grounds? These have been objected to, but no court decision has banned them—yet. Would it make a difference whether these or similar displays were financed from tax funds or from voluntary contributions? Regardless of how a court would rule, is it conducive to good will in a pluralistic society for a majority to insist on public displays and practices offensive to some?

Religion and Education

The heart of the current controversy over the "no establishment" clause centers in education. When the Bill of Rights was adopted 175 years ago the problem of religion in the public schools did not exist—because tax-supported schools did not exist. Schools were conducted by the churches. Jefferson advocated free public elementary schools—without religious instruction—to supplement rather than supplant church schools. Nonetheless when free public schools did become predominant in the first part of the nineteenth century they generally supplanted—and copied the church-supported schools. In fact they were often parochial Protestant schools, a situation which originally prompted the Catholics to set up their own parochial schools.

One of the early decisions departing from the pattern came in 1872 when the Ohio Supreme Court ruled a Cincinnati ordinance valid which prohibited religious exercises, including Bible reading, in public schools. The significant quotaton from that decision heads this chapter.

A recent survey showed ten states prohibited Bible reading as a religious exercise before the 1963 U. S. Supreme Court decision banned religious exercises in public schools everywhere. Actually, six out of ten public schools in the United States did not conduct Bible reading and half did not conduct any homeroom devotional service.

Parents have the right to send their children to private schools, under the "free exercise" clause, said the U. S. Supreme Court in 1925. It nullified an Oregon law requiring attendance at public schools. States, however, have the right to compel attendance at some school and set minimum educational standards and curriculum requirements.

In 1930 the high court decided that a state may furnish non-sectarian textbooks to pupils of public and private schools alike, on the grounds that the books were a benefit to the pupil, not to the school or church which operated it. (Several state courts, however, have barred free textbooks and bus transportation to parochial pupils on the basis of state constitutions.)

It is against this background that Justice Hugo Black, in 1947, defined what "establishment of religion" meant in words which have been repeated three times since by the Supreme Court. They are:

> "The 'establishment of religion' clause of the First Amendment means at least this: Neither a state nor the Federal government can set up a church. Neither can pass laws which aid one religion, aid all religions or prefer one religion over another. Neither can force nor influence a person to go to or to remain away from church against his will or force him to profess a belief or disbelief in any religion. No person can be punished for entertaining or professing religious beliefs or disbeliefs, for church attendance or non-attendance. No tax in any amount, large or small, can be levied to support any religious activities or institutions, whatever they may be called, or whatever form they may adopt to teach or practice religion. Neither a state nor the Federal Government can, openly or secretly, participate in the affairs of any religious organizations or groups and vice versa. In the words of Jefferson, the clause against establishment of religion by law was intended to erect 'a wall of separation between Church and State.' "

Justice Black was speaking for the majority in a decision which held that a New Jersey school district could pay the costs of transporting private pupils to private and parochial schools as well as public. The reasoning followed the textbook decision in holding that bus transportation was not an aid "to support any religious activities or institutions" but its purpose was to enable children, regardless of religion, to get to their schools safely.

The application of the "child benefit," the "welfare," and the "police and fire" protection theories to problems of state aid to pupils in non-public schools is still controversial. Should they have the same benefits as public school pupils of the hot school lunch programs, health and dental check-ups, etc.? If these, why not physical education, or indeed instruction in the physical sciences? Where shall the line be drawn between "pupil benefit" and "school benefit"?

School Aid for All

Questions such as these multiply and become more complex with the entrance of the Federal Government into massive aid to schools under the Elementary and Secondary Education Act of 1965 and similar laws in previous years giving aid to institutions of higher learning.

All funds made available for the various programs under the 1965 Act must provide services and benefits to all children, whether they attend public schools, private schools, or are dropouts. It provides (1) for a wide variety of projects for educationally-handicapped children in poverty areas, (2) funds for improving libraries, buying textbooks and other instructional materials, and (3) special, supplementary services such as counseling, remedial instruction, classes for the handicapped and adults, and numerous others not otherwise being provided.

The 1965 Act meticulously seeks to avoid the repeated high court injunction against any tax, large or small being levied to support religious institutions. All federal aid funds are to be administered by public school authorities, state and/or local. Materials are to be "loaned" not given to private school pupils. Where teachers or other personnel who are paid from public funds serve private school pupils they are to do so on a "dual enrollment" or "shared time" basis. Use of federal funds for any religious or sectarian instruction or worship is expressly forbidden.

The idea that pupils be enrolled in both public and parochial schools—the "shared time" or "dual enrollment" concept—is of comparatively recent origin. Prior to the 1965 Act a few school districts provided that pupils could spend a half day in public school taking technical courses and the other half day in the parochial school, receiving a diploma from the latter upon graduation.

Dual Enrollment

Various interpretations and applications of the "dual enrollment" concept have been made in different states, some of which have very specific constitutional bans on aid to parochial schools. In some states classes provided for in the act are barred from being held in parochial schools. In another the state rents space in parochial schools, so technically the public school teacher teaches on public property. In other instances, private school teachers instruct special classes on public school property after school hours. This is held to be a form of "moonlighting," a second job a teacher takes upon herself in which her own school is not involved. In at least two states the United States Commissioner of Education is distributing books and other educational materials directly to the private schools because state authorities believe the permanent loan provision of the act is a subterfuge which does not get around their constitutional ban against distributing textbooks to parochial schools.

If the 1965 Act had not provided assistance for non-public pupils, it could never have been passed. Court challenges to this and other school-aid measures are difficult, if not impossible, because of a 1923 Supreme Court ruling that individual taxpayers do not have standing to challenge laws authorizing expenditure of funds. A bill before Congress to authorize challenges of specified laws in this area was not acted upon in 1966.

Use of Tax Money

Many members of Congress would agree with the Rev. Robert F. Drinan, Jesuit dean of the Boston College Law School, that all of these laws are constitutional under the key statement of the *Everson* decision. Fr. Drinan writes:

"No tax in any amount, large or small, can be levied to support religious activities or institutions, whatever they may be called, or whatever form they may adopt to teach or practice religion."

"This famous sentence proscribes tax support *only* for 'religious activities or institutions' in 'whatever form they may adopt to teach or practice *religion*'. It does *not* proscribe public funds for instruction in secular subjects even though such instruction may be conducted under the auspices of a religious institution."

He further quotes—with hope—what the counsel for the American Jewish Congress, Leo Pfeffer, wrote with apprehension, to the effect that court decisions

". . . lead logically to the conclusion that the state may, notwithstanding the First Amendment, finance practically every aspect of parochial education, with the exception of such comparatively minor items as the proportionate salaries of teachers while they teach catechism." *

Arguments for Tax Support

Four arguments are advanced for tax support of parochial school activities which allegedly do not "teach or practice religion." They may be summarized briefly as follows:

1. By excluding religion from the public schools, the state "establishes" irreligion or secularism. If only they receive public funds, then the secularist philosophy is being preferred. This is contrary to the establishment clause.

2. Education is compulsory. Parents who send their children to parochial schools because the public school concepts offend their beliefs are ". . . deprived of their right to share in the commitment of the state to provide a free

---

* Church, State, & Freedom, P. 476

education for every future citizen." The price of free exercise of religion thus becomes this deprivation.

3. Regardless of whether denial of aid to parochial schools imposes an unnecessary burden on religious observance of those choosing such schools, incidental aid to religion does not invalidate secular aims of the state—in this instance the raising of the nation's standards of excellence in education.

The concept "incidental aid" is drawn from the Supreme Court decision upholding Sunday-closing laws (so-called Blue Laws). Here the court held that the purpose of these laws was secular—to set aside a common day of rest, relaxation and "family togetherness." Such laws did not violate the First Amendment, said the court, in spite of the fact that such laws gave incidental aid to religious adherents who observed the First Day as Sabbath and imposed an indirect burden on those who close on Saturday for religious reasons.

4. Public welfare legislation may not be granted or denied to citizens because of their religious faith or their lack of it. Thus, argues the Boston College law dean, the welfare purpose of providing education can be served without violating the First Amendment, only if public funds are made available for strictly secular purposes to all schools.

Each of these arguments has been, and will be, strenuously refuted. It is impossible to divorce the secular from the religious content in a school whose basic premise is that religion ought to permeate all learning. Aid is not incidental when it may well mean the survival of the school. The state is not obligated to finance alternatives to public facilities which some prefer to utilize, be they schools, hospitals, parks, etc. Religious neutrality of public schools does not mean they teach irreligion. Parents and the churches of their choice have the responsibility for their childrens' training.

Released Time

Although never involving more than ten per cent of the total school enrollment, most states permit pupils to be released from regular classes for religious instruction of their choice, or usually, their parents' choice. Time allowed is from 30 minutes to two hours. Those not choosing religious instruction continue with their usual school work, or go to the library or study hall.

The released time idea was advanced as a means of providing religious instruction, mainly by Protestants, which could not be given by the public schools. It has been the subject of numerous lawsuits, particularly a pair of famous decisions by the U. S. Supreme Court.

In the 1958 *McCollum* case, the court held that released time religious classes could not be held on school premises during school hours. Public funds were involved. Compulsory school attendance meant pressure to attend the religious classes even though pupils could continue regular school classes.

Then four years later, in the *Zorach* case, the court said released time was permissible if the religious instruction was given off the school premises. No public funds were involved, and the court found no coercion being exercised in New York City, where the case originated.

Yet this decision raises questions. "Coercion" is a subtle matter, particularly for children sensitive to the demand of conformity by their peers.

Is a pupil less likely to resent staying in the study hall or library when his fellow classmates are off to a neighborhood church than if they went to another room in the school building? What about the child of a minor Protestant sect who is the only one in the school? (This question was raised by a Seventh Day Baptist.) Will he want to go with a larger group for religious instruction offensive to his parents? Would not the same purpose of religious instruction be served if all pupils were dismissed in time to go to classes in their churches if they wanted to? If not as many went to such classes as during school hours, is that not proof that the power of the state is being used to aid religion?

Religious Exercise vs. "Teaching About"

A decade later the Court took a much closer look at the issue of coercion. In the *Engle* opinion of 1962, striking down the New York Regents' prayer, and in the *Schempp* and *Murray* cases, decided in 1963, banning Bible reading and reciting of the Lord's Prayer, the Supreme Court found that the fact individual students could be excused did not make the practices legal.

"The establishment clause," unlike the "free exercise clause," the Court said in *Engle*, "does not depend upon any showing of direct governmental compulsion and is violated by the enactment of laws which establish an official religion whether those laws directly coerce non-observing individuals or not."

The Regents' prayer was a 22-word supplication formulated by the New York Board of Regents which, it thought, would be acceptable to any faith. Non-believers and those who felt the prayer "watered-down" their specific beliefs might disagree, but the decision was not based on any such basis. With only Justice Potter Stewart dissenting, the majority said:

> "It is neither sacreligious or anti-religious to say that each separate government in this country should stay out of the business of writing or sanctioning religious prayers and leave the purely religious function to the people themselves and those the people choose to look to for religious guidance."

In the *Schempp* case, involving Pennsylvania's statute requiring daily Bible readings in the schools, and the *Murray* case, involving Maryland's similar law requiring both Bible reading and reciting the Lord's Prayer, the 8 to 1 majority held:

> These are religious exercises;

> It is no defense to argue that these exercises may be relative minor encroachments on the First Amendment;

The fact that pupils may be excused is no defense of constitutionality;

The "free exercise" clause has never meant a majority could use the machinery of the state to practice its beliefs.

Justice Stewart, in his dissent, held that if the exercises were compulsory they would be invalid, but, if not, they would be in accord with the neutrality concept by which the government should accommodate to religious belief without preference.

Do these decisions mean that, as has been charged, "religion of secularism" is established in the schools? The majority opinion in denying this, pointed out that the state cannot affirmatively oppose or show hostility to religion, adding:

> "In addition, it might well be said that one's education is not complete without a study of comparative religion or the history of religion and its relationship to the advancement of civilization. It certainly may be said that the Bible is worthy of study for its literary and historic qualities.
>
> "Nothing we have said here indicates that such study of the Bible or of religion, when presented objectively as part of a secular program of education, may not be effected consistent with the First Amendment."

Here the distinction between teaching *about* religion and indoctrination or worshipping is quite clearly drawn. Ten years earlier Justice Jackson pointed out that it would not be practical to teach the arts if exposure to religious influences were forbidden.

> "Music without sacred music, architecture minus the cathedral, or painting without the scriptural themes would be eccentric and incomplete, even from a secular point of view. Yet the inspirational appeal of religion in these guises is often stronger than in

forthright sermons. Even such a 'science' as biology raises the issue between evolution and creation as an explanation of our presence on this planet.* Certainly a course in English literature that omitted the Bible and other powerful uses of our mother tongue for religious ends would be pretty barren. . ."

Elementary School Observations

Obviously, children in grade school are more susceptible to indoctrination than students at higher levels of education. Thus the type of objective study which the Court mentioned suitable for high school seniors or university students might become indoctrination if given in the lower grades. Likewise ceremonials like the invocation which starts each day's session of Congress are considered the free expression of those who participate, while similar prayers for school children would be indoctrination.

Recognition of holidays in the schools offers an opportunity to teach objectively about religion at all grade levels. But the line between learning about the meaning of Christmas, Easter, and the Passover to adherents of various faiths and indoctrination and devotional observance of them is indeed difficult to draw.

Certainly, a teacher who confines Christmas to the Santa Claus myth and Rudolph, the red-nosed reindeer, or Easter to the Easter bunny is presenting a false picture of these holidays. Yet it is for the home, the church, and the synagogue to inculcate the meaning of religious observances. Perhaps such questions as these might be guidelines in school observances:

"Is the art, music, drama, literature, etc. the expression of the pupil or is it imposed by the school authorities?"

** Many scientists and theologians would dispute that this is an issue. They would deny that "evolution" and "creation" were mutually exclusive terms.

"Does the holiday observance contribute to the learning process and does it refrain from encroaching on the time for regular studies?"

"Is it tolerant and sensitive to the attitudes and beliefs of all faiths and of no faith?"

Good will and good sense are more needed here than legal guidelines..

Tax Support and Religious Agencies

Five and a half billion dollars, it is estimated, of Federal funds were made available in the 1966 fiscal year to private church-related groups to operate various parts of more than sixty programs. State and local governments likewise sometimes reimburse such agencies on a fee-for-service basis.

These are mainly in the areas of education, health, housing, and welfare. Issues raised by public support for social services by religious organizations are among the thorniest in the field of church-state relations. The issues are not new although, as noted above, recent Federal aid legislation has augmented them.

Since World War II, hundreds of private hospitals— under Catholic, Protestant, and Jewish auspices—have been built with Federal funds under the Hill-Burton Act. Such hospitals must be open to patients and physicians regardless of faith. Yet questions arise as to the possibility of proselytizing or the imposition of religiously-motivated rules restricting the action of physicians—in prescribing birth-control materials, for example.

While direct general financial grants have not been made to church-related schools, substantial indirect aid by the Federal government—and by some states—accrued to institutions of higher learning, both private and public. This aid has come in the form of scholarships, loans, and grants to students administered through the institution and contracts for research projects given by the government directly to the institution.

From the depression's National Youth Administration which paid students for work benefitting the college, through the GI Bill of Rights, down to the scholarships under the National Defense Education Act, students have received government financial aid irrespective of the orientation—religious or otherwise—of the institution they attended.

Likewise many private universities, as well as state universities have benefitted from government-financed research projects related to defense, health, science, etc.

Some 35 divinity schools around the country are accepting funds from the National Defense Education Act to train theology students. Harvard Divinity School refused to accept such funds on First Amendment grounds.

Tax Exemption and Religion

Income tax deduction for tuition and other school expenses has been proposed as a means of aiding and encouraging education at both the college and common school levels. It would seem that no objection can be raised on First Amendment grounds, particularly since contributions to religious, educational, and various non-profit charitable causes, within limitations, are tax deductible.

Exemption of churches and various religious organizations from taxes, particularly property taxes, has been the rule from time immemorial. Yet certain questions arise.

If a church or church-related college owns rental property or a commercial enterprise—as actually is the situation in many instances—should such be exempt from taxation—either property taxes or income taxes? Should churches and church-related institutions share the community cost of police and fire protection, street maintenance, etc. as they generally do for special improvements—paving, sewers, sidewalks and the like? Should clergymen receive special income tax allowances from their income, as is presently provided?

These issues have been raised not by those unfriendly to religion—or a particular religion—alone. A major denomination, the United Presbyterian, in its 1964 policy statement supporting absolute separation of church and state, says in regard to such a practical matter as tax exemption: "The church must regard special status or favored position as a hindrance to fulfilling of its mission."

11

Free to Join

"Congress shall make no law . . . abridging . . . the right of the people peaceably to assemble, and to petition the Government for a redress of grievances."

—FIRST AMENDMENT

". . . nor shall any State deprive any person of life, liberty, or property without due process of law; . . ."

—FOURTEENTH AMENDMENT

"It is beyond debate that freedom to engage in association for the advancement of beliefs and ideas is an inseparable aspect of 'liberty' assured by the Due Process clause of the 14th Amendment, which embraces freedom of speech."

—JUSTICE JOHN M. HARLAN

"Americans of all ages, all conditions, and all dispositions, constantly form associations." and *"In no country in the world has the principle of association been more successfully used or unsparingly applied to a multitude of different objects, than in America."*

—ALEXIS DE TOCQUEVILLE (1835)

116

Long before modern sociologists wrote popular books about America being a nation of joiners, the perceptive French visitor was impressed with the role of voluntary associations.

It was not always thus. Not only were religious organizations once tied to government by tax subsidies, but political "factions" were discouraged, organizations of workingmen considered illegal conspiracies, and business corporations formed only by special legislative acts.

Even James Madison, the architect of the Bill of Rights, warned against "factions" of citizens "who are united and actuated by some common impulse of passion, or of interest, adverse to the rights of other citizens or the permanent and aggregate interests of the community."

By the time deTocqueville visited America, however, it was apparent that associations, whether political or special interest, pressing for or against certain legislation were an inherent part of a free, democratic government.

By this time, too, workingmen who formed associations to improve their lot were no longer punished as criminal conspirators, although it could not yet be said they were encouraged to organize. General incorporation laws in most states enabled businessmen to assemble capital and talent in corporations without having to ask legislators for special permits. Societies for the promotion of this and for the prevention of that flourished.

Assemble and Petition

Our forbearers who dumped tea in Boston Harbor and marched in front of more than one colonial governor's residence would be quite at home in today's demonstrations. Pickets with banners and placards, chanting slogans and singing songs are nothing new in America. The abolitionists, the suffragettes, the pacifists, the union organizers, the "farm holiday" advocates, and the civil rights demonstrators— among others—have disturbed the apathetic and altered the status quo.

The phraseology may sound a bit quaint but the "right of the people peaceably to assemble, and to petition for a redress of grievances" is as meaningful today as when it was made part of the First Amendment.

The right to assemble is conditioned on being peaceable, but the courts have held that it may be regulated only to protect substantial rights of others. The right to assemble and express views—by sign or voice—cannot be denied simply to avoid inconvenience.

Neither can the right be denied a group so unpopular that their opponents threaten to stage a riot or peace officers fear breaches of peace will occur if the group assembles.

This interpretation was made in a case involving a religious sect. It has become very significant in the civil rights demonstrations. The courts, meaning the Supreme Court and lesser Federal courts following its opinions, have consistently reversed convictions of demonstrators for "breach of peace", "parading without a permit", and similar offenses.

The Supreme Court has also reversed convictions of those engaged in "sit-ins"; seeking service in business establishments in violation of local segregation laws. Here the state, as well as the owner, was held responsible for discrimination.

A group carrying signs and marching on the state capitol grounds rated police protection from the crowd they attracted, said the high court, in exercising their constitutional rights "in their most pristine and classic form."

Protection of demonstrators from onlookers by officers of the law, perhaps under court order, is a visible testimony of the rule of law. Undoubtedly most Southern white peace officers are more in sympathy with the onlookers who would like to stop the demonstrators than with the civil rights marchers they are protecting. But the right of the people peaceably to assemble is and must be protected. The police also have a duty to stop an imminent riot.

Sometimes the line between what is peaceable and what is not is difficult to draw. Advocates of civil disobedience deliberately break the law. They are disappointed if they are not arrested and jailed, to dramatize what they consider the unjustice of the law.

Such tactics as lying in the street to block traffic, or blocking an entrance, or damaging property are breaches of the peace which go beyond the constitutional rights of protest.

Picketing As Expression

Picketing, the demonstrating by persons parading in front of a business establishment, has played—and continues to play—a significant role in labor-management relations. Usually the pickets are employees of the firm who are on strike. The purposes of their picket signs are to dissuade other workers from entering the plant or store and to persuade customers from patronizing the struck business. The pickets, however, may be union members who are not employed by the picketed firm who are telling the world that it is operating under non-union conditions. This latter type is known as "organizational" or "informational" picketing.

As late as 1921 the U. S. Supreme Court held that a state law protecting the right of picketing violated the employer's equal protection of the law. Twenty years later the court, again by a 5 to 4 decision, reversed itself and held picketing was a form of expression guaranteed under the First Amendment.

Yet "picketing by an organized group is more than free speech" Justice Douglas points out,

"Since it involves patrol of a particular locality and since the very presence of a picket line may induce action of one kind of another, quite irrespective of the nature of the ideas which are being disseminated. Hence those aspects of picketing make it the subject of restrictive regulation.

"But since 'dissemination of information concerning the facts of a labor dispute' is constitutionally protected, a State is not free to define 'labor dispute' so narrowly as to accomplish indirectly what it may not accomplish directly."

Thus regulations designed to prohibit violence in picketing situations have been held valid.

"Organizational" picketing has, in some instances, been banned—if it is an integral part of illegal restraint of trade, if the state has a so-called "right-to-work" law, if the place picketed carries goods produced by firms engaged in labor disputes but which is not involved in the dispute itself.

Other court decisions have upheld the right of persons to inform others that an establishment is non-union—provided the purpose of the picketing is informational and not designed to coerce anybody. The line between the two is sometimes difficult to draw.

Association for Economic Activity

Picketing as an essential part of the strike weapon has long played a significant role in efforts of employees to form labor unions to secure better wages and working conditions from their employers. Long after the theory that it was illegal conspiracy for workers to organize had been abandoned, any rights organized labor obtained were hammered out of raw economic struggle. For over a century, the struggle between management and labor pitted the need of the industrialist for the skills of the craftsmen against their ability to maintain solidarity to stay off the job until their demands were met. If hunger forced them back, or the employer could find new workers or new processes to replace them, they had no bargaining power. If, however, the workers possessed needed skills in great demand, they could force their employers to bargain with them on wages, hours, and other conditions.

Only during the Twentieth Century, particularly after 1930, has there grown up a body of labor law embracing modern concepts of union recognition, collective bargaining elections and agreements, majority rule, mediation, arbitration, unfair labor practices, etc.

Does the freedom to associate for advancement of beliefs and ideas extend to freedom to associate for economic activities? The answer to that question concerns not only labor organizations but many other forms of association as well.

The answer to this question was a long time coming in a decision of the Supreme Court, although some legislation appeared to assume the affirmative. Among the first state laws seeking to minimize the raw conflict of labor-management warfare were those which outlawed the "yellow dog" contract. Under it an employee agreed not to join a union as a condition of employment. In 1932 Congress, in the Norris-La Guardia Act, said employees—and employers— had the right to freely associate to negotiate terms of employment. Shortly thereafter the Wagner Act provided, in the National Labor Relations Board, the machinery to conduct representation elections, certify a union as a bargaining agent if it received a majority of votes, hear complaints of "unfair labor practices" and bar them upon finding the employer was unfairly discouraging union organization.

Some years later, in 1945, the Supreme Court spoke on the impact of the First Amendment on economic activities.

Texas had a law requiring union organizers to register and be licensed before soliciting union memberships. A union leader promptly challenged the law by speaking and asking non-union members to sign up—without, of course, registering. The state argued the law merely regulated a "business practice" since the organizer collected dues as well as talking. Four justices agreed that the case involved regulation of commerce, not free speech. The majority, however, held that freedom of speech, press, assembly, and petition did extend to business and economic activity. These freedoms, further, were bound together in a single amendment, and should be construed in relation to each other.

"Free discussion concerning the conditions in industry and the causes of labor disputes . . ." the Court held, are "indispensable to the effective and intelligent use of the processes of government to shape the destiny of modern industrial society."

Disclosure and Exclusion

Alabama banned the National Association for the Advancement of Colored People on the ground it refused to disclose its membership and failed to comply with procedures required of foreign (out-of-state) corporations. As in the Texas union organizer case, the high court held that First Amendment rights could not be denied under guise of regulation of business.

Its statement, quoted at the beginning of this chapter, is the clearest recognition to date of the right to associate. Freedom to engage in association for advancement of ideas and beliefs is an inseparable part of "liberty."

Can a voluntary association be required to disclose the names of its members? In a case involving this issue, Justices Black and Douglas declared:

"First amendment rights are beyond abridgement either by legislation that directly restrains their exercise or by suppression or impairment through harassment, humiliation, or exposure by government."

This statement came in the case involving Mrs. L. C. Bates, president of the N.A.A.C.P. of Arkansas, who refused to obey an ordinance of the Little Rock city council, requiring her to turn over the membership lists of her organization.

The right to associate in privacy, however, is not absolute. Laws requiring disclosure of membership have been upheld in cases involving the Ku Klux Klan and the Communist Party. Here a "clear and serious purpose which cannot be served in any other way" is held to override the right of anonymous association.

Does an organization have the right to exclude certain classes or individuals? For most voluntary associations the answer is obviously "yes."

Some types of organizations, however, have been imbued with powers or prerogatives which make membership practically necessary, under certain circumstances, for one to work or exercise his franchise. Not only trade unions but also business and professional organizations may come under the first category. Certainly to be excluded from a political party reduces a citizen's opportunity to participate in choosing candidates for office.

Civil rights laws ban discrimination because of race, color, religion, national origin or sex in membership in unions as well as in employment. Labor unions are restricted in other ways as to whom they can exclude, whom they may require to belong, and how they can spend their funds. The next chapter will deal with limitations on association for unions, for trade and professional organizations, and for political groups.

Political Parties, How Private?

Even more than labor organizations, political parties are dual in nature. They are both voluntary associations and instruments of public policy through which voters choose elected officials.

Although the courts, years ago, denied the right of a party to exclude Negroes from its primary election—on the ground it was a private organization, Negroes have been barred in certain states from participating in party affairs. The demonstrations of the Mississippi "Freedom Democratic Party" at the 1964 Democratic National Convention highlighted this fact. The partially successful attempt of this group to be recognized because the regular party had refused to allow Negroes to take part in selecting delegates resulted in a new rule being adopted by the National Democratic Party. At the 1968 convention and thereafter no delegation will be seated where Negroes have been excluded in its selection.

Political parties, as voluntary associations, make their rules. Yet in practically all states their procedures are circumscribed by law. Either the law or party rules, or both, determine how and when party officials and party candidates are chosen. How long must a voter be registered as a party member before he can be a candidate or even take part in a precinct caucus or convention? Does he have to pledge his support to the party's entire slate before he can be a candidate on its ticket? These and other questions may be answered either by party rules or by law. If party rules are too restrictive the trend appears to be that the law will take over.

One large group of people are barred by Federal law, the Hatch Act, from taking "any active part in political management or in political campaigns." These are Federal civil service employees and state employees engaged in activities partly financed with Federal funds. They may, of course, vote in all elections, primary as well as general. As mentioned in Chapter 3 many state laws make it difficult, even impossible, for a new party—or even an established minority party—to get on the ballot. To deny a group of dissenting citizens a place on the ballot may not be a denial of their right to associate but it indeed limits their effectiveness.

Limits on Demonstrations

In 1967 two divided decisions of the U. S. Supreme Court put new restrictions on the right to demonstrate. The five-day conviction of Dr. Martin Luther King and other ministers for contempt in disobeying a court injunction against marching in the famed Birmingham 1963 Easter Day parade was upheld. A bare majority held King's group should have appealed the injiction through the courts—meantime obeying it, even though the parade-permit ordinance upon which the city obtained the injunction was clearly unconstitutional. Justice William J. Brennan, for the dissenters, pointed out this decision gave state courts "the power to punish by 'contempt' what they otherwise could not punish at all."

In another civil rights case, trespass convictions of demonstrators before a county jail were upheld—on the basis that a jailhouse was in a different category from the grounds of a state capitol. (See page 118.)

12

Free to Associate—How Far?

"I do not think that a nation is always at liberty to invest its citizens with an absolute right of association for political purposes; and I doubt whether, in any country or any age, it be wise to set no limits to freedom of association."

—ALEXIS DE TOCQUEVILLE

"The constitutional rights of workers to assemble, to discuss and formulate plans for furthering their own self-interest in jobs cannot be construed as a constitutional guarantee that none shall get and hold jobs except those who will join in the assembly or will agree to abide by the assembly's plans."

—JUSTICE HUGO BLACK

"At the point where the mutual advantage of association demands too much individual disadvantage, a compromise must be reached."

—JUSTICE FELIX FRANKFURTER

What are the limits on freedom of association? Does freedom to join imply a freedom not to join? Under what conditions may association be compelled? Under what conditions may it be forbidden?

Answers to these and similar questions continue to be sought in the areas of labor-management relations, professional and trade associations, political activity, and subversive associations.

Compulsory Association

In spite of the statements of Justices Black and Frankfurter, under certain circumstances individuals must be members of an association as the price of holding a job or practicing a profession.

Attorneys are officers of the court in all of the states. In over half of them lawyers must also be members of the state bar associations to practice. This form of compulsory association, known as the integrated bar, has been repeatedly upheld as constitutional.

Physicians are not quasi-public officials in the sense of attorneys-at-law, although their license to practice is granted by a state agency. Membership in the local and state medical societies is practically mandatory for use of hospital facilities. This compulsory association is not a requirement of law, but in effect the ties between the state licensing board and the professional organization are usually so close that a physician not acceptable to the medical society might well find himself in difficulties with the licensing agency. In other professions, the discretion of the state licensing board or authority to grant or withhold a professional license may coerce one applying to hold membership in the professional organization. Ostensibly, however, the criteria of licensing is professional competency.

"Union Security" or "Compulsory Unionism"

It is in the area of labor-management relations that the issue of compulsory association becomes most complex. Some call it "union security," others "compulsory unionism," depending on whether they favor or oppose the practice of negotiating contracts requiring union membership as a condition of employment.

Historically, unions have sought contracts which in addition to providing wage scales, hours, grievance procedure, etc. also provide all employees are governed by it. Obviously, if an employer were free to pay higher wages or give other preferential treatment to non-union employees he would have a powerful weapon against the union.

Under the National Labor Relations Act, a union winning representation rights through election must represent all employees in the bargaining unit. This provides protection for all the workers as well as assurance to the employer that he is dealing with a responsible agent, the officers and committees of the union.

If the union must represent all of the workers in the plant, the argument for the union shop goes, why should not all of the workers support it by payment of dues? Why should "free-loaders" be allowed? What if an employee doesn't want the union to represent him?

Labor laws now provide for government-supervised elections to determine if a majority of the employees want to be represented by a particular union. Before any such laws were enacted, however, strong unions succeeded in obtaining a clause in a contract specifying that the employer would hire only union members, or at least as long as union members were available.. This is the "closed shop" or "preferential hiring," now outlawed by the Taft-Hartley Act. Instead, "union shop" or "agency shop" provisions are permitted. Under the union shop agreement, employers may hire whom they please but the new employees, within a specified time, must become union members. Under the agency shop provision, employees who do not want to become union members pay a fee to the union in lieu of dues to recompense the union for services in negotiating and administering the contract on working conditions. In any case, union shop and agency shop provisions have been negotiated by the employer and representatives of a majority of the employees.

Such agreements do not violate the constitutional rights or freedom of association of employees. So the Supreme Court held in a test of the Railway Labor Act, which authorized union security provisions in contracts between railroads and their employees.

"Right to Work"

On the other hand, the high court has also upheld state laws forbidding denial of employment because of membership, or lack of membership, in any labor union. These so-called "right-to-work" laws (a term to which labor unions strenuously object) have been attacked on the grounds of infringement of free speech, peaceable assembly and petition, equal protection, due process, and impairment of contract.

In other words, the court says in effect that whether union security agreements are to be permitted is a matter of public policy rather than one of constitutional rights. If Congress repealed Section 14B of the Taft-Hartley Act, which permitted states to enforce laws prohibiting union security provisions in labor contracts, it would be saying that promoting industrial peace and stability throughout interstate commerce overrides state restrictions on union-management contracts. It would say in effect, that the law neither requires nor forbids membership in a union as a condition of employment, but leaves such matters to collective bargaining between employer and employees.

To maintain that each employee individually has freedom to contract with his employer is to return to the era when a worker "didn't have the rights of a yellow dog." That was the way union men referred to an agreement between an employer and worker that the latter would not join a union.

The whole history of labor organizations has been based on the premise that only collective action could tend to equalize the economic strength of the individual worker and that of an employer employing hundreds or thousands of workers. The instrument of that collective action has been collective bargaining, the fruit of which is a labor-management contract. As business and industrial enterprises and labor unions have grown big and increasingly complex in modern America, government has played an ever bigger role in writing the "rules of the game" for collective bargaining.

Public policy demands industrial stability as the price of economic well being. The government-guaranteed "right to organize" carries with it a delegation of quasi-governmental functions to a private association. In return, both unions and employers are forbidden to carry on certain "unfair labor practices" according to findings by the National Labor Relations Board, appealable to the courts. Unions are required to adhere to certain regulations as to disclosing financial data, conducting elections, admitting members, etc.

Labor organizations are not the only associations which, although essentially private, have public functions and are subject to public regulation. Responsibility of associations to provide fair treatment within their organization is the subject of another chapter.

Clearly, however, modern society gives rise to circumstances when an individual's unchecked right to contract—his "right to work" without regard to association with others, for instance—conflicts with the well-being of the group. How is the compromise to be reached which Justice Frankfurter finds necessary "at the point where the mutual advantage of association demands too much individual disadvantage"? Where is that point? Who determines it, the individual, the association—or an administrative agency, a legislative body, or the courts? Does the question of compulsory association arise only when regulation of one's livelihood is involved?

Political Action by Associations

Whether it be a labor union, a corporation, a professional or trade association, or some other non-political organization, expenditure of organization funds to influence elections or legislation raises another question. Does such use of money paid by members who oppose the organization's stand in a specific instance deny their freedom of expression?

The Taft-Hartley act prohibits any corporation or labor organization from contributing or spending funds "in connection with any election" where any federal official is nominated or elected. In spite of the broad language, the law has been construed as not applying to an organization paper advocating a candidate's cause—if it is distributed to its regular readers. Employees may be compensated from organization funds even if they are assigned to political activity. Unions raise "voluntary contributions" to carry on political activity, and corporations encourage their officials to give time and money to political activity.

In 1961 a group of union members protested that a substantial share of the dues they paid under a union shop agreement was being used to support political candidates they did not favor. A majority of the U. S. Supreme Court avoided a ruling on the constitutional issue of freedom of expression. It said the union shop provision of the law did not authorize spending a member's dues for political expenditures over his objection. Either such expenditure should be prohibited or objectors' proportionate share of the total dues used for political activity should be refunded. The state court to which the case was sent back held that if no practical method could be found to separate the money spent for political purposes from other union purposes, the union should be enjoined from spending any money for political ends.

Justice Black, in a dissenting opinion, did not believe the constitutional issue could be dodged. Admitting that ordinarily a voluntary organization could use membership funds for political purposes, he pointed out that the law authorizes the union to carry on activities at the expense of employees who do not choose to be members of the group but must under the union shop agreement. He held that spending for political activities under such conditions violated the dissenting members' freedom of expression and was therefore unconstitutional.

Justices Frankfurter and Harlan agreed that the constitutional issue could not be avoided, but they held that political spending by unions was constitutional. Political action at times becomes as important in improving working conditions as collective bargaining negotiation. "A minority of a legally recognized group may at times see an organization's funds used for promotion of ideas opposed by the minority," wrote Justice Frankfurter comparing the minority union member to a taxpayer who saw his tax money used for purposes he did not approve.

Two Supreme Court justices reputed to be among the most conservative on civil liberties issues upheld the union expenditures for political activity—almost always directed to electing more liberal candidates—while one considered most liberal held such expenditures unconstitutional!

Expenditure by Business

Expenditures by business enterprises, incorporated or not, to influence voters or legislators may be legal, but they may find they cannot claim such expenditures as tax deductions. Two liquor firms contributed money to a campaign to defeat an initiative proposal which would have curbed liquor sales. The Treasury Department disallowed the deduction of this money as a business expense under its regulation refusing deduction of sums spent for lobbying or the promotion or defeat of legislation.

This regulation, the Supreme Court held, did not deny the liquor firm their rights under the First Amendment. They were "simply being required to pay for these activities entirely out of their own pockets." Neither individuals nor corporations can deduct political contributions from taxable income.

Corporations have been barred by law from making direct contributions to political parties. Some civil liberties lawyers contend such a ban violates the spirit, if not the letter, of the First Amendment. Corporations are legally artificial persons, and should have the rights of persons to expression. The issue as applied to corporate political contributions has never been clearly faced in a court case. Perhaps the reason is that the ban has been so readily circumvented by individuals within a corporation making the contributions. If the ban were lifted, the same question faced within unions would arise. What are the rights of minority stockholders who do not agree with the position taken by the corporation, almost inevitably determined by the inner management group?

This question also arises as to lobbying activities of corporations—and other groups. The courts have held that Congress can regulate activities of those seeking to influence congressmen and their committees in developing or defeating legislation. This regulation includes registration of lobbyists, disclosure of finances, and possible investigation by congressional committees. It does not extend to attempts to influence public opinion by publication and distribution of books, pamphlets, advertisements etc.

As for the rights of stockholders, most stockholders accept the probability the positions taken by management are for the good of the company. If they feel strongly enough, they can try to change the company policy or sell their stock in it.

Another method by which corporations exert influence on both political issues and specific legislation is through trade associations. While such associations rarely openly back candidates or parties, they do distribute information on voting records of congressmen and state legislators. They engage in lobbying activities, ranging from testifying at legislative committee hearings to entertaining legislators—individually or collectively. The trade associations sometimes put their views before the public in advertisements.

Non-Profit Associations

Non-profit organizations lose their federal income tax-exempt status if a "substantial part" of their activity seeks to influence legislation. The law and internal revenue regulations on this issue raise various questions. How do you draw the line as to what is "substantial"? If an association whose purpose is to work for peace, or for better race relations, urges its members to write their congressmen asking them to support a certain bill, is that "a substantial part" of its activity? Or if it sends a delegation, or even maintains a spokesman in Washington, to keep in contact, does it thereby lose its exempt status? Should any distinction be made between activities of organizations working for what they believe is for the common good and those who stand to reap financial gain from lobbying activity?

Subversive Associations

One type of association which has been subject to regulation, restriction, or prohibition is that aimed at the subversion of lawful authority or violent overthrow of social institutions.

The term "subversive" is susceptible to several different interpretations. The Alien and Sedition laws, passed when John Adams was president, made it unlawful to conspire to oppose "any measure or measures of the government of the United States." During the Civil War, hostility or outright opposition to the Union was considered subversive. During and after World War I, various states passed laws which were directed against assembling to advocate criminal anarchy or criminal syndicalism. State laws attempted to restrict the activities of the Klu Klux Klan.

In the recent years of the Cold War the term "subversive association" almost inevitably refers to Communism. It should be recalled, however, that prior to and during World War II, organizations such as the German-American Bund and other groups with Nazi or Fascist ties were branded as subversive.

Since the enactment of the Smith Act in 1940, Congress has not been negligent in passing laws aimed at subversive association. Their effectiveness over the long run, however, has been about as weak as the old Alien and Sedition laws, which expired when Jefferson became president.

The Communist Control Act

Such laws generally define as subversive those who advocate the overthrow of government by force and violence or those who are agents of a foreign power. The McCarran Act, also called the Internal Security Act or the Subversive

Activities Control Act, was passed in 1950—over President Truman's veto. It was amended by the Communist Control. Act of 1954.

One general conclusion may be drawn from various decisions on these laws. That is, a person must know the subversive or seditious nature of an association before he can be penalized for joining it. This is more difficult to prove than it might seem.

Among numerous other provisions these acts require the registration with the attorney general of "Communist-action," "Communist-front," and "Communist-infiltrated" organizations. Heavy penalties of $10,000 a day for each day such organizations fail to register are provided.

Yet in 16 years no organization has registered, nor in the light of the 1964 decision of the U. S. Supreme Court is likely to. In 1961 the court said it was not unconstitutional to require the Communist Party to register and disclose its membership. But in 1964 the high court upheld an Appeals Court decision that no member could be required to register the Party, for by doing so he would be incriminating himself. The Fifth Amendment, of course, says that no person can be compelled to be a witness against himself. As long as the law provides penalties for individual members, to confess membership in the Communist Party is self-incrimination! Thus it appears the McCarran Act, as it applies to "Communist-action" organizations is unenforceable. It would seem even more difficult to define and penalize "Communist front" and "Communist infiltrated" organizations under procedures called for.

This does not mean that the government is helpless to deal with subversive associations, particularly if they are agents of a foreign power. But, in general, conspiracy to commit illegal acts, not simply membership in an association, is the basis of penalties.

The courts have long distinguished the Communist Party from an ordinary political party. Its role as a legitimate political organization, entitled to run candidates, etc. has been distinguished from its role as part of a worldwide conspiracy dedicated to the overthrow of government, including the United States government, by force and violence.

Congress, in 1954, turned down the proposal of then Sen. Hubert Humphrey that mere membership in the Communist Party be made a crime, but did say the party was not entitled to "any of the rights, privileges, and immunities attendant upon legal bodies".

A New Jersey court used this clause to bar Communists from the ballot. But the U. S. Supreme Court held this section did not deprive an employee of the Communist Party from drawing unemployment compensation.

The Court has upheld the right of government to dismiss an employee for disloyalty, of which membership in a subversive organization is evidence. The employee must have been aware of the subversive purposes and activities. In general, members of subversive associations must be accorded their rights—due process, privilege against self incrimination, specific standards of definition, etc.—before being penalized, either criminally or by civil disabilities, such as loss of a job. As to the latter, there are conflicting decisions. Some of them will be considered in the chapter, "Punishment Without Crime," dealing with powers and procedures of legislative investigating bodies and administrative agencies.

13

Free to Act

No person shall be...deprived of life, liberty, or property without due process of law; nor shall private property be taken for public use without just compensation.

—FIFTH AMENDMENT

". . . Nor shall any state deprive any person of life, liberty, or property, without due process of law."

—FOURTEENTH AMENDMENT

"A man's property consists of the free use, enjoyment, and disposal of all his acquisitions, without any control or diminution, save only by the laws of the land."

—WILLIAM BLACKSTONE

"He who offers this thing called freedom as a soft option is a deceiver or is himself deceived. He who sells it cheap or offers it as a by-product of this or that economic system is a knave or a fool. . . For freedom demands infinitely more care and devotion than any other political system. It puts consent and personal initiative in place of command and obedience."

—ADLAI E. STEVENSON

"We achieve individual liberty through collective restraint."

—PHILIP F. LAFOLLETTE

136

Does freedom to act precede or result from freedom to express? Is free enterprise guaranteed by the Bill of Rights in the same way free speech, free press, free religion, and free assembly are guaranteed? Or is it a by-product of these freedoms? What is law anyway, unless a restraint on the freedom of individuals to do what organized society deems harmful to itself or to some of its members?

Perhaps Robinson Crusoe was the only man who did not need laws. He never complained about taxes or the bigness of government. But even he, when he found his man Friday, had to lay down some rules.

Henry Thoreau prized the solitude of Walden Pond. Today he might find his cabin near a public bathing beach. Even in the remotest wilderness he would find law and zoning regulations which would restrict what he could and could not do with his property. High up in the Rockies, far from any habitation, a sign beside a tiny trickle of a stream reads "Do Not Contaminate—City Water Supply."

Increasing the Range of Choices

In one sense the title of this chapter embraces the whole study of law, both civil and criminal. Government is organized society, to which all must belong and to whose rules all are subject. In the context of the Bill of Rights, however, our concern is to ascertain how government through law can increase the range of effective choices of action open to an individual.

The right to acquire, to own, and to dispose of property obviously affects an individual's range of choices. Long ago, in the 18th century, William Blackstone, the great English jurist whose Commentaries are still studied in law school, rejected one concept of private property. This he described as the "sole and despotic dominion . . . in total exclusion of the right of any other individual in the universe."

Instead, he defined property in the quotation heading this chapter, "free use, enjoyment and disposal . . . without any control or diminution, save only by the laws of the land." The phrase "due process of law" in the Fifth and

Fourteenth Amendments as applied to deprivation of property, clearly embraces Blackstone's definition. Due process, as it relates to life and liberty, requires extensive treatment in later chapters.

Because constitutional restraints are generally expressed in terms of "government shall not" it is often thought that the role of government in respect to individual freedom is wholly negative. This is not necessarily so. Certainly public education increases the opportunities of an individual to make significant choices in his life. This is seen as governmental units—local, state, national—develop such less traditional programs as adult education, homemaker and agricultural extension services, technical and vocational education, vocational rehabilitation, etc.

Likewise the public highway systems and the municipal airports across the land enlarge the choices of individuals as to where they can go and where they can live. Public hospitals and health programs for the prevention and treatment of disease and mental illnesses help restore to individuals their ability to make choices.

Physicists have long since abandoned the concept of Newton that the total quantity of matter is unchangeable. Still widely held, however, is a sort of Newtonian notion that whatever the government gains in power the people lose. Whether this is true or not depends largely on the purposes and methods by which government exercises power. People can use government to increase their power.

Now some might contend that any consideration of economic activity and property rights has no place in a discussion of liberty and justice for all. These might be answered by quoting Anatole France to the effect that the rich and the poor have the same liberty to sleep under the bridge!

Hard Choices

Others would maintain that property rights and freedom from economic restraints are the sole source and substance of liberty. Adlai Stevenson reminds such that freedom is no by-product of this or that economic system. "He who offers this thing called freedom as the soft option is a deceiver or is himself deceived."

This is to say that hard choices are involved in determining the proper role of government in promoting individual freedom.

Those who believe we could increase our freedom if only we could get rid of "big government" often quote Thomas Jefferson. He said, "The government governs best which governs least."

What is "least" in terms of modern life? Shall we repeal the Sherman Anti-Trust Act of 1889 and its successors because these anti-monopoly laws forbid combinations in restraint of trade? Can we maintain our complex, industrialized, urbanized, mobile system with as few laws as were in effect in Jefferson's Virginia? Should we assume rules governing relations between individual buyers and sellers are adequate when one party may be a giant, impersonal corporation?

To ask these questions is to show how the Jeffersonian statement begs the issue. We must still determine what is the role of government—federal, state, and local—in maintaining both freedom and order in our society under conditions which exist today. Many examples may be cited as to problems to be solved. Here are a few.

A hundred years ago a workman was free to contract to work on a job—provided he took the risk of becoming injured or killed. He, in effect, waived his right to sue for damages under common law. Of course, his freedom was only theoretical if his alternative was to go hungry. The cost fell on him and his family—or more probably on private and public charities who aided his widow and children—not upon the employer or his customers.

Shortly before 1900 laws were passed requiring employers to take safety precautions. Then came laws declaring that an employer could not avoid suits for damages even though the employee was presumed to assume the risk. In the first two decades of this century came workmen's compensation laws, requiring an employer to pay money awards to any injured workman regardless of whose fault it was. Employers, of course, protect themselves against this liability through insurance, and add the premiums to the cost of doing business.

The Social Cost

Thus while an employee lost some of his theoretical freedom of contract and the employer lost his freedom from the financial obligation for accidents, legislation actually enlarged the total freedom of choice. Legislation provided a more rational distribution of the social cost of the hazards inherent in modern industrial development.

The rationale of much of the legislation involving labor, management, buyers, and sellers depends upon a similar recognition. The nature of modern methods of production and distribution necessitates that government must act to enlarge the effective liberty of many people, even at the cost of specific—and more often than not—*theoretical* freedom of some. Specialization of skills and the organization of industry into large components require more rule-making, more discipline, less independence, and less opportunity for personal "man-to-man" confrontation.

Minimum wage and maximum hours legislation, social security, etc., etc. enlarge effective choices to action.

To meet the challenge of the impersonalization of distribution of goods and services, government enforces pure food and drug laws, weights and measures laws, truth in fabric laws, security exchange regulations, truth in advertising regulation, etc., etc.

The situation is far different from that faced by Tom Jefferson when he could personally determine the quality of what little he bought which was not produced on his own plantation.

When he talked about less government, he was probably thinking about the laws which gave special privilege to some particular group. Such laws are enacted even to this day— as anybody who follows the proceedings of state legislatures and Congress is well aware. There is a difference, however, between such laws today and those enacted under the "mer-cantile system" which had, more or less, prevailed up until Jefferson's day.

And "Public Good"

The difference is in the reasons given for the legislation. Today every proposal is offered in the name of the public good; then laws were frankly designed to regulate trade in great detail and give certain segments of the national economy a monopoly advantage. It was in argument against such a system that Adam Smith, English economist, wrote his *Wealth of Nations* in 1776, in which he called for a free play of forces in the market place.

If, to equalize the unequal for the public good government must intervene, it should at least conform to certain standards and methods. This is the essence of due process. Even so, however, value judgments must be made among conflicting claims of freedom.

An enterprising manufacturer builds a paper mill in an area where lush timber resources have never been touched. He gives employment to many who bring new life and progress to what was almost a ghost town. The mill dis-charges its waste into a stream the frontiersmen called Clear Creek—only it isn't clear any more. The stench and the foam kill the trout which were the fishermen's delight. The polluted water even smells up the wash of the women of the town—whose husbands work in the mill. (We'll overlook the fact that their detergents cause a foam in the irrigation ditch down-stream.)

Should government intervene? And, if so, on behalf of whose freedom—the free choice of the manufacturer to acquire and use property, the freedom of the fisherman to choose the fish in an unspoiled stream, or the right of the housewife to a clean-smelling wash? Is this a conflict between property rights or human rights? Or are these concepts merely different ways of looking at the same thing? Is the value judgment to be made on the basis of a nose count, with the freedoms of the greatest number getting the highest priority?

These are admittedly difficult questions. Without attempting to answer them certain standards and methods may be suggested by which government, if it intervenes, may enlarge the opportunities for effective choices and thereby increase liberty by positive action.

Proper Public Purpose—Proper Means

The first question to be answered is this:

Is this action for a proper public purpose carried out by proper means?

Public power may be legitimately used only for public purposes. One illustration of this is seen in the laws on eminent domain. A governmental unit can condemn property necessary for a highway, a public school, a public park, etc.— paying the owner just compensation of course—but it could not force the owner to sell to a church which wanted his property for expansion or to any other private association or individual. The "proper means" in the power of eminent domain are spelled out by law as to notice, hearings, determination of value, and appeal to the courts.

Incidentally, the U. S. Supreme Court upheld the Illinois Supreme Court to the effect that this power of eminent domain could be used even though its actual result was to accomplish what the law forbade doing directly. After twice defeating bond issues to create a public park, voters of Deerfield, Ill., an upper middle class suburb of Chicago, voted to condemn the area of a subdivision for park purposes. It was learned the developer, who had laid out streets and utility lines and completed a few homes, was going to sell some to Negro families. A municipal ordinance barring sale to Negroes—or any other class—would have been invalid.

It is easier to define a "proper means" than it is "proper purpose." In general "proper means" would mean passage of a law—or ordinance—by a duly constituted legislative body, or an administrative rule by an official or agency, both rule and agency being duly authorized by law. Judicial review should be permitted.

One way of approaching the isue of "proper purpose" would be to say that any interference with a private individual or group must be justified by a reasonably determined public interest. If you say this is a vague and "rubbery" statement you are so right.

It is certainly not a mathematical formula. Conflicting liberties of choices cannot be weighed on a pair of scales. Yet it is obvious that all freedoms are not of equal value. The paper mill owner will lose a comparatively small part of his property rights if he is required to treat his wastes before discharging them into the stream—or store them in an abandoned mine. By such a requirement, the public interest in maintaining a natural resource unspoiled for multiple use of present and future generations is served.

Determination of what is public interest which justifies interference with individual choices is a political matter. Different parties and interest groups disagree. Decision on an issue is not often reached on the basis of a philosophical appraisal of competing rights, but almost always on the basis of the relative strength of the power blocs involved. That is why the phrase "reasonably determined" is so important. In this context the phrase implies that the determination is made, not by the interests directly affected, but by deliberation of a body representative of the public at large. It also means that any of those affected may appeal to the courts for further determination of whether the interference with private rights for public goods meets the standards set in the constitution.

Openness on Equal Terms

A second question to be asked in examining the role of government to positively expand liberty by increasing the range of effective choice is this:

Is the course prescribed by law open to all who meet its standards on an equal basis?

This question is particularly significant in relation to the regulations regarding associations of individuals and regarding licensing of individuals and groups.

As previously noted, time was in English law when a company, or corporation, was formed by the granting of a special charter by Parliament. As the value of associations of individuals with limited personal liability became evident in the industrial revolution, general laws regarding incorporation were enacted, in America as well as in England. A vast body of corporation law has grown up.

The point is that, as far as government is concerned, any group of individuals can organize a corporation and avail themselves of the privileges and immunities which the corporate form of organization affords. Success in competing with existing corporations, of course, is a different matter. And, as any state legislator can tell you, pressures are always being exerted to enact further legislation to make it more difficult for newcomers to enter a field. The argument always, of course, is that it is in the public interest—an argument which legislators must carefully examine.

As an example out of many which might be cited: The initial capital which is required before an insurance company, a bank, or a savings and loan association can start business is raised by the legislature on the theory that the customers will be better protected. Yet institutions already in existence are allowed to continue with less than the increased capitalization.

Corporations, of course, are of many kinds, only some of which are business enterprises organized for profit. Laws have been enacted providing for various types of associations —ordinary commercial companies, investment trusts, financial institutions of various types, cooperative associations and non-profit philanthropic social, educational, religious, and scientific organizations, etc. Thus government can, and does, encourage individuals to associate together to increase their effective range of choices.

Individuals, however, do not have to ask government before entering into private associations.

Role of Licensing

Licenses or permits are required before a person—or an association—can engage in many occupations and endeavors, but the requirement of a license by government must be considered as the exception.

Whether the license is issued by the health department, the zoning board, the sanitation service, the police department, the motor vehicle division, or any of the professional and trade boards, it must be justifiable as contributing to the public good. Such a license ought to be available to anybody who meets the qualifications—which, in turn, should be reasonable.

It is easier to state this standard than to achieve it. It is obviously in the public interest that one who engages in a profession, be it medicine, law, dentistry, etc., meet certain qualifications of knowledge and skill or that tradesmen—barbers, pharmacists, plumbers, electricians, undertakers, hairdressers, etc.—meet requirements which will protect the health and safety of the public. In the case of occupations like real estate salesmen, accountants, collection agents, etc. the public purpose is to assure responsibility.

Yet the licensing function of government is sometimes used to limit the competition in the profession or occupation by making it difficult for a newcomer to get a license. Legislators can testify to the pressures which come from this or that occupational group to require licensing of that particular occupation or to raise standards required of those not already in it. And the board which administers the examinations and licensing is oftimes composed only of members of that profession or occupation.

It may not be typical, but in a western state the number of practicing dentists has remained almost static while the population has significantly increased. A majority of applicants for dental licenses failed the dentistry board examination although all of them had graduated from recognized dental schools—some with high honors. At the same time the state dental society asked appropriations be made to start a dental school at the state university.

However emphatically the philosophy that government should not restrict individual initiative is proclaimed, time and again government action is used to protect vested interests from the competition of newcomers.

Dispersal of Decision Making

The third question in establishing criteria for determining how government can expand freedom of choice asks:

Is there opportunity for the widest possible participation and is the power dispersed in decision making which affects liberty of action?

Applied to the problem of licensing the answer might, or might not, be the inclusion of persons outside the profession or trade on the licensing board.

The answer might well be in the right to appeal decisions to the courts for determination of whether the examination procedures were fair and equitable.

Certainly the legislative body—be it city council, county commissioners, state legislature, or Congress—which creates administrative boards and bodies should be truly representative. Furthermore, it should establish the policy framework within which the administrative agency makes its rules.

The line between laying down policy and implementing that policy with rules of procedure is always difficult for legislative bodies to draw. Yet, under the complex and specialized society in which we live, all decisions cannot be left to the specialists and experts. Many of them must be.

For example, the legislature (or the school board) may decide that a course on American government or history should be required in the Ninth and Twelfth grades. If it prescribes, however, exactly what the courses are to contain and how they are to be taught, it is getting into hot water. Those are decisions educators are better prepared to make.

In making decisions both minorities and majorities should have rights of participation. Those holding the minority view should have the right to explain and argue for their position.

Hopefully their purpose is to convert enough to their view to make it a majority, but even though they know their hope is vain they still have a right to express themselves.

When, however, does their arguing become an obstructionist tactic to thwart the will of the majority by preventing action? Most legislative bodies have rules regarding the closing of debate, usually by two-thirds vote, or by a set time limitation. The majority has the right to be able to act on an issue.

The United States Senate, of all deliberative bodies in the world, is the most jealous of the perogative of the individual member to continue debate. Though it has the two-thirds rule, it is used on the rarest of occasions to end a filibuster.

The right of participation in decision making can also be applied to non-governmental "private" associations. Indeed, this is an important way to get dispersal of power in decision-making. Relations between members and such organizations, voluntary and semi-voluntary, will be discussed in Chapter 19.

Checks and Balances

Highly centralized governments may not be necessarily totalitarian, but certainly every totalitarian state—Communist, Facist, Nazi—has had its decision-making power concentrated at the top.

By contrast, the American system is, of course, based on a system of checks and balances. The legislative, executive, and judicial powers are separated, and each branch has means by which it can check the other. All must conform to provisions of the Constitution.

Moreover, the federal system gives certain powers to the Federal government and those not enumerated in the Constitution to the states. Almost without exception states have been most generous in conferring decision-making powers on local authorities—counties, cities, towns, school districts, sanitation districts, recreation districts, and a host of other special districts.

In theory and in practice, we in America have a great dispersal of decision-making. Indeed, in a day of instant communication, rapid transportation, great mobility of people, and wide urbanization many of our problems arise from the inability of single governmental units to cope with situations. The problem of dealing with organized crime is one example. An inadequate local tax base to maintain good schools is another.

Cooperative action between the state and local units, or between the federal government and the states—as in the interstate highway program—may be necessary and desirable.

Nonetheless, the more decision-makers the greater variety of decisions, and a greater range of choices are available.

America has profited by the great diversity which has permitted wide experimentation among the various governmental units and outside of government. It may be more difficult to maintain as much dispersal of decision-making power to deal with the magnitude and complexities of modern problems. Yet a measure of our freedom is the degree to which we are able to do so.

Freedom to Bear Arms

In one area of action, the Second Amendment has been used to justify the right of any citizen to keep and use any type of firearms, without permit or registration or other type of regulation.

A complete reading of the amendment indicates, however, that its purpose was not so much to guarantee the right of each individual to "shoot it out"—although that had its place in a frontier society—as it was to guarantee the collective right of a community to protect itself.

Amendment II reads: "A well-regulated militia, being necessary to the security of a free state, the right of the people to keep and bear arms shall not be infringed."

A militia, of course, is a citizens' army authorized by a unit of government—not a private army such as the groups which are reported to be drilling against the day when they expect the Communists to take over. The framers of this amendment did not want the Federal government to have power to disarm the states as English kings had sought to disarm the people.

One authority points out it refers to arms necessary to a militia "and not the dirks, pistols, and other deadly weapons used by the lawless."

Most states—to which the Second Amendment does not apply—prohibit the carrying of concealed weapons and require a permit or registration of at least certain types of guns. Since the assassination of President Kennedy, Congress has been considering legislation regulating the mail order sale of firearms in an effort to keep them out of the hands of children and criminals.

Opposition to such legislation, however, has been strong —in spite of the Dallas tragedy. Typical of statements by opponents is this from the National Rifle Association:

> "One is forever being told, 'You don't need to protect yourself, that's the job for the police.' What kind of talk is this for America? Are we becoming a nation of defeatists; devoid of personal pride and content to rely entirely on our police for protection? Are we ready to deny to ourselves and to our children their American heritage—the right of personal protection and the pleasure of shooting and hunting for recreation?"

Although the courts have had little opportunity to construe the Second Amendment, the foregoing discussion would indicate it is neither a dead letter nor its meaning fully agreed upon.

Freedom to Move About

Travel is action highly prized and greatly used by us Americans. Long ago the courts established the right to move from state to state was one of the "privileges and immunities" of national citizenship. During the Depression California sought to prevent indigents from settling in that state, but the U. S. Supreme Court said "no." Neither American citizens nor resident aliens could be stopped from coming into a state. Neither can a welfare recipient be deported from one state back to the one from which he came.

The right of an American to travel abroad, and to return, has been recognized as protected by the due process clauses, but with significant exceptions. One cannot be denied a passport because of one's political beliefs, even membership in the Communist Party. A passport may be denied, however, in circumstances of "grave national emergencies." For instance, travel to Belgium in 1915 was banned because of famine, to Ethiopia in 1935 because of war, to China in 1937 because of unrest.

In 1965 the high court majority held the Secretary of State could impose restrictions on travel to certain areas for "foreign policy considerations affecting all citizens." Louis Zemel of Connecticut sought to visit Cuba as a tourist to make himself "a better informed citizen." The court majority denied him because, it said, the Castro government seeks to export revolution through travelers. To which dissenting Justice Douglas replied, "The First Amendment presupposes a mature people, not afraid of ideas."

Native-born citizens may lose their American citizenship by voluntarily serving in a foreign army, marrying an alien, voting in a foreign election, obtaining foreign citizenship, or voluntarily renouncing their American citizenship. But absence abroad to evade the draft is not sufficient to deprive one of citizenship. Francisco Mendoza-Martinez frankly admitted he went to Mexico to avoid the draft during World War II. Upon his return to the United States in 1947 he pleaded guilty to draft evasion and served a prison sentence. Five years later the Justice Department sought to declare him an alien and deport him, but a majority of the Supreme Court held the law upon which the action was based provided punishment without trial.

Naturalized citizens cannot have their citizenship revoked simply because they are temporarily absent from America, even as long as three years. Their rights are no different than natural-born citizens—unless they obtained naturalization through fraud. Aliens generally have been accorded the same due process rights as apply to citizens, although, it appears according to court decisions, Congress can make new rules for deportation which apply retroactively. In other words, the prohibition against *ex post facto* laws do not apply to aliens, who are considered "visitors" to our shores.

Part III

THE RULE OF LAW

14

What Is Justice?

"Justice is the fixed and constant purpose that gives every man his due."
—INSTITUTES OF JUSTINIAN
SIXTH CENTURY A. D.

"It is less evil that some criminals should escape than government should play an ignoble part."
—JUSTICE OLIVER WENDELL HOLMES

"The almanac of liberty for the free world is filled with episodes where the means are outlawed, though the ends sought are worthy. The greatest battles for liberty have indeed been fought over the procedure which police and prosecutors may use."
—JUSTICE WILLIAM O. DOUGLAS

Justice has many faces. Old Testament prophets spoke of justice as righteousness. Jesus emphasized the spirit of the law rather than its letter. The Greeks related justice to moral philosophy—the matter of proper relationships between individuals and between the individuals and the state. Roman

154

law developed the concept of justice as giving "every man his due." The English judicial system evolved the idea of equity alongside that of justice, to allow fairness to be applied in a concrete situation, as well as regularity and consistency in the administration of law. Nobody has ever surpassed Shakespeare's familiar portrayal in *The Merchant of Venice* in depicting the tension between mercy and the purely legalistic justice.

One of the purposes set forth in the Preamble to the Constitution is to "establish justice," but nowhere did the Founding Fathers define the term.

Instead, the Constitution and the Bill of Rights set up numerous safeguards against specific abuses which in England and Colonial America had produced injustice.

What do ancient practices of star chamber proceedings, torture to obtain confession, drawing and quartering, etc., etc., have to do with law enforcement problems modern Americans face today—lawlessness on the streets, riots in the cities, increases in crime, more sophisticated means of violence, etc., etc.?

Do not the procedural safeguards of the Bill of Rights— as now interpreted by the courts—hamper law enforcement, allow the guilty go free or off easy, and restrict the rights of law-abiding citizens? Do the courts pay too much attention to technicalities, too little to protecting society?

In the chapters of this section the restraints the Constitution and the Bill of Rights place on government in administering the law will be explored. At the outset it should be recognized that the procedures that justice demands are inextricably interwoven with substantive claims of justice— that without justice, liberty and equality become meaningless.

In his *Almanac of Liberty,* Justice Douglas recounts how William Penn had been tried on the charge of causing "a great disturbance" of the peace by conducting worship of the persecuted Quakers on a London street—after their meetinghouse was closed by police. The jury, in spite of threats and coercion by the court, found Penn not guilty.

Thereupon the judge sent Penn to jail for contempt of court.

"The judge," comments Douglas, "was a victim of the hysteria of his day."

He continues:

> "Short cuts are always tempting when one feels his cause is just. Short cuts have always been justified on the ground that the ends being worthy, the means of reaching them are not important. Short cuts, however, are dangerous. If they can be taken against one person or group, they can be taken against another.
>
> "Our greatest struggle has been to provide procedural safeguards that will protect us against ourselves and make as certain as possible that reason and calm judgment will not be swept away by passion and hysteria. Experience shows that it is the William Penns of the world, not the criminals, who suffer most when the procedural safeguards for fair trials are relaxed."

An Inventory of Safeguards

Those who wrote the Constitution and the Bill of Rights were procedure-minded. A catalogue of safeguards they established to protect the individual in the administration of justice include the following:

Privilege of *habeas corpus* (Article I, Section 9) —the right to be brought before a magistrate to determine legality of detention.

No bills of attainder (Article I, Section 9 and 10) —laws punishing a man without hearing or trial.

No ex post facto laws (Article I, Section 9 and 10) —laws making a crime an act which was not illegal when committed.

Independent judiciary (Article III, Section 1) —federal judges serving "during good behavior" without diminution in salary.

Trial by jury in criminal cases (Article III, Section 2, Amendment VI) —

Strict definition of treason and no attainder of treason (Article III, Section 3) —no punishment extending to heirs of traitor.

No unreasonable searches and seizures (Amendment IV).

Grand jury indictment in federal cases (Amendment V).

No double jeopardy (Amendment V) —being tried twice for same crime.

No compelling of self incrimination (Amendment V).

Due process of law guaranteed (Amendments V and XIV).

Speedy, public trial, specific charges, confrontation of witnesses, compulsory process for obtaining favorable witnesses, assistance of counsel (Amendment VI).

Jury trial in civil cases (Amendment VII) —applies in federal courts, may be waived.

No excessive bail (Amendment VIII).

No cruel and unusual punishments (Amendment VIII).

These procedural safeguards were originally mainly restrictions on the new Federal government, although the Constitution prohibited states from adopting *ex post facto* laws or bills of attainder. Most states had then, and have now, similar procedural safeguards in their state constitutions. Through the due process clause of the Fourteenth Amendment, forbidding states to deprive any person of life, liberty, or property without due process of law, the Supreme Court has extended many of these safeguards to criminal prosecutions in state courts. Among the most recent of such decisions are those extending the right of assistance of counsel, for instance, of which more will be said later.

Fair Play the Essence

This term "due process" merits special attention. It, indeed, is the capstone which holds in place the whole arch of

justice. It is another name for legal, judicial, and governmental fair play. Like "justice" it is almost undefinable.
Indeed, to define it with precision is to limit it—and that
the Founding Fathers, the lawmakers, and the courts have
been loathe to do.

Over a hundred years ago, just before the Civil War,
the U. S. Supreme Court expounded on this point:

> "The Constitution contains no description of those
> processes which it was intended to allow or forbid.
> It does not even declare what principles are to be
> applied to ascertain whether it be due process. It is
> manifest that it was not left to the legislative power
> to enact any process which might be devised. The
> article (Fifth Amendment) is a restraint on the legis-
> lative as well as on the executive and judicial powers
> of the government. . ."

On what criteria then is "due process" to be determined?
First, all legal, judicial and legislative actions must conform
to the provisions of the U. S. Constitution. Next, the settled
usages and modes of proceedings existing in the common and
statute law of England, unless modified by American law, are
guides in determining "due process." The interpretations of
the courts down through the years also provide guides for
deciding what is fair procedure, or due process, in a specific
situation.

Back in 1628 when Englishmen wrested a bill of rights
from the King, the terms "due process of law" and "the law
of the land" were used almost interchangeably to denote the
requirements that must be met before any man could be
punished or deprived of property.

No less essential today when modern technology greatly
complicates the problems of maintaining individual privacy,
apprehending crime, protecting the innocent, and guarding
against subversion are the procedures of due process of law.

15

The Right of Privacy

"The right of the people to be secure in their persons, houses, papers, and effects, against unreasonable searches and seizures, shall not be violated, . . ."
—Fourth Amendment

"They (the makers of our Constitution) conferred, as against government, the right to be left alone—the most comprehensive of rights and the right most valued by civilized man."
—Justice Louis D. Brandeis

"Eaves-droppers, or such as listen under walls or windows or the eaves of a house, to hearken after discourse, and thereupon to frame slanderous and mischievous tales are a common nuisance and . . . are . . . punishable by fine and finding sureties for their good behavior."
—Blackstone's Commentaries

"You had to live—did live—in the assumption that every sound you made was heard and, except in darkness, every move scrutinized."
—George Orwell in his novel "1984"

159

"The poorest man, in his cottage, bids defiance to all the forces of the Crown. It may be frail; its roof may shake; the wind may blow through it; the storm may enter; the rain may enter; but the King may not enter; all his forces dare not cross the threshold of the ruined tenement."

—WILLIAM PITT IN 1776

What is the state of this "most valued right," to be left alone, in America today? Does government protect this right from infringement by others—the common nuisance of common law referred to by Blackstone? Or does the "right of the people to be secure" (Fourth Amendment) refer only to searches and seizures relating to possible criminal activity.

Be the modern home cottage or mansion, there is no danger that the king will enter. But the telephone solicitor may enter; the wiretapper may enter (illegally, perhaps, but pervasive), the junk mail may enter; the computer cards may enter—without us ever knowing.

Beyond a man's home—his castle—his personal privacy is even more subject to invasion—on the job, in his car, at school. Even his innermost thoughts are probed by so-called lie-detectors and psychological tests. Orwell's predictions are outdated in the second decade before 1984, for infra-red cameras can take pictures in the dark!

Some will say that the so-called "right of privacy" is not really a civil liberty; that the unreasonable search clause of the Fourth Amendment is coupled with provision for search warrants; that at most invasion of privacy refers to commercial exploitations of one's home, portrait, or possessions.

Historically such a view has merit. The Fourth Amendment was directed at a specific abuse, indeed the same abuse Wiliam Pitt was denouncing in the speech to Parliament quoted above. This abuse was the practice of government officials to make searches and seizures on the basis of "general warrants." These papers allowed them to go anywhere any time to seek evidence of illegal, or allegedly illegal activity.

Search and Seizure, Reasonable or Unreasonable

The Fourth Amendment specifies ". . . and no warrant shall issue, but upon probable cause, supported by oath or affirmation, and particularly describing the place to be searched, and the persons to be seized."

Only since 1961 has the requirement of such search warrants applied to states.

The Supreme Court reversed the Ohio conviction of Dollyee Mapp because police had broken into and searched her apartment without a warrant. It held that such a search by state officers deprived her of liberty without due process of law, contrary to the Fourteenth Amendment. As noted, that phrase "due process" is not subject to precise definition —indeed, courts have deliberately refrained from limiting it to an exact meaning since its application varies greatly from case to case. In general, due process means fair procedure.

Two decades earlier the Court had held that a state could not direct its officers to intrude without a warrant. If they did so on their own, however, any evidence obtained would be admissible in court! On that occasion, the Court declared that the security of one's privacy against the arbitrary intrusion by police is basic to a free society.

Unreasonable or Reasonable

Yet the protection of one's privacy has been generally construed narrowly, literally, and sometimes tortuously. The intrusion must be physical. A wiretap made by driving a spike in the wall or planting a device in a room would probably be held to be such an intrusion. But such methods are hopelessly old fashioned.

Not until 1966 was any attempt made to place legal curbs on the use of any number of electronic devices which can pick up sounds without physical contact. Since all of these use the same basic principles of transmission of waves through the ether as radio and television, the Federal Communication Commission decided it had jurisdiction over such devices. It issued a regulation making their use illegal. How the FCC can enforce its ban remains to be seen, but at least here is a beginning which courts may use to bar evidence thus illegally obtained.

Law books contain literally hundreds of citations covering decisions on searches and seizures. A few of the topical headings will indicate how complex the right of the people to be secure in "their persons, houses, papers, and effects" has become. Here are a few: Abandonment of papers, antitrust proceeding, arrest as a pretext to search for evidence, automobiles, bank records, condemnation of food and drugs, congressional investigations, dwellings, fingerprints, health inspection, hotel rooms, mail matter, military authorities, odors as a basis for probable cause, offices, physical examination, property seized under void warrant, tax proceedings, telegrams, etc., etc.

The courts have drawn fine lines—and sometimes apparently circuitous ones—in distinguishing between reasonable and unreasonable search and seizure and in defining "effects."

One exception—and only one—is legally recognized to the rule that a search warrant must be obtained in advance from a judicial authority and sworn to as to probable cause. This exception is a search or seizure made during the course of a valid arrest. The police, of course, must have the right to "frisk" the person arrested to disarm him of weapons and to protect themselves. They may also seize evidence of crime or the fruits of crime. The extent to which they may go through a house in search of such evidence has been restricted in recent court decisions. Courts, generally, have been more lenient in accepting the legality of searches of automobiles, offices, and buildings not homes. Business places as well as automobiles, however, would seem to come within the Fourth Amendment protection against unreasonable searches and seizures of one's "effects."

The protection is against government officials. Private individuals—be they professional investigators or neighborhood busybodies—are not restrained from intruding on the privacy of others by this amendment. Indeed, as recently as

1962 the California Supreme Court held in one case it was illegal for police to spy into restrooms through ventilation screens or special devices. But the next year a lower court held spying into dessing rooms by a store detective was not unconstitutional because the detective was not a government agent! Incriminating evidence by "private eyes" who either plant hidden cameras or break into the bedrooms of estranged spouses is almost standard in divorce proceedings in certain states.

Electronic Snooping

"Electronic eavesdropping . . . is pervasively employed by private detectives, police, labor spies, employers and others for a variety of purposes, some downright disreputable."

So said Justice William J. Brennan in an angry dissent in a case involving the use of a miniature recording device hidden in the clothing of a U. S. Internal Revenue agent. He declared:

"The court has by and large steadfastly enforced the Fourth Amendment against physical intrusions into person, home, and property by law enforcement officers. But our course of decisions, it now seems, has been outflanked by technological advances of the very recent past."

The majority upheld the conviction of a restaurant owner in 1963 for offering the agent a bribe during a conversation in his restaurant. The secret recording was admitted as evidence as if it were the testimony of a third person who had listened and corroborated the agent's testimony.

Justice Brennan expressed the belief that by condoning electronic surveillance by federal agents, by permitting the fruits to be used, "we shall be contributing to a climate of official lawlessness and conceding the helplessness of the Constitution and this court to protect rights fundamental to a free society."

Justice William O. Douglas, who with Justice Arthur J. Goldberg, joined the dissenting opinion earlier declared: "The right to be let alone is the beginning of all freedom."

A Common Law Right to Privacy

The right to privacy goes back further than the Constitution. Indeed, Blackstone's comment on the common law on eavesdropping—quoted at the beginning of this chapter—was actually used to obtain conviction in an early case of electronic snooping in a state which had no law on the subject.

In 1936, a politician, a reporter, and a private detective planted a microphone in the Colorado governor's office, with a wire running to a private phone in the capitol's press room. Three months later they were discovered, along with 75 phonograph records and numerous stenographic notebooks detailing all that had transpired in the governor's office. The political opponents had hoped, of course, to "get something" on the new governor. They didn't. Instead, even though Colorado had no law against wiretapping or electronic eavesdropping, they found themselves convicted under an ancient common law against gossip-mongers.

The scientific development of electronic monitoring devices has advanced amazingly since 1936. Transistor powered microphones are so small they can be disguised as a tie-clasp; so powerful they can pick up voices a block away. Yet the law on the issue involved has progressed but little beyond Blackstone. Two-thirds of the states have enacted laws against wiretapping, but many of these are vague and difficult to enforce. Some distinguish between making physical connection with a telephone line and more sophisticated means of intercepting sound waves. In some instances the only ban imposed by state law is on the use of the results obtained as evidence in court. Electronic snooping is still used as means of obtaining leads which can be followed up for "legitimate" evidence. Some states except law enforcement officials, with or without court direction or order.

Federal court decisions provide little clarification. Back in 1928 in a case involving a bootleg ring, Chief Justice William Howard Taft interpreted the Fourth Amendment most narrowly and literally. Although the government's evidence consisted of 775 typewritten pages of conversation overheard on eight wiretapped telephones, Chief Justice Taft declared:

> "There was no searching. There was no seizure. The evidence was secured by the use of the sense of hearing and that only. There was no entry of the houses or offices of the defendants."

Justice Louis Brandeis vigorously expressed the dissent of four minority justices. In addition to the quotation at the beginning of this chapter, he commented:

> "As a means of espionage, writs of assistance and general warrants are but puny instruments of tyranny and oppression when compared to wire-tapping."

"Dirty Business"

More recently Justice William O. Douglas called wire-tapping "dirty business." But the *Olmstead* decision of 1928 was not reversed until 1967. Rather the courts had turned their attention to interpreting the provisions of the Federal Communications Act, passed by Congress in 1934, which ostensibly bans interception and divulgence of any communication, unless authorized by the sender.

The interpretation of this section and the practices of both Federal and state officials has produced what Robert F. Kennedy, former attorney general, called "legal chaos". The Department of Justice, including the Federal Bureau of Investigation, has held that to be illegal, information obtained by wiretapping must be both *intercepted* and *divulged*. Thus the FBI and other Federal agents employ wiretaps, taking care only to see that the evidence gained is not used in court. A series of Supreme Court decisions have made wiretap evidence inadmissible in Federal courts, but admissible in state courts if permitted by state law—even though illegally obtained. However, state officials using such evidence are breaking the Federal law.

Former Attorney General Kennedy, and others before him, have proposed bills clearly outlawing wiretapping by public officials or private individuals, but making certain exceptions. Upon receiving specific court approval, the FBI could use wiretaps in cases involving national security and such high crimes as murder, kidnapping, and "organized crime." State officials could also wiretap for these high crimes. That new legislation on wiretapping and electronic eavesdropping is needed cannot be disputed, but suggested exceptions to the ban raise the fear that a new law will legitimatize more invasion of privacy.

Wiretapping—How Effective?

Why should law enforcement officials be deprived of full use of the most modern scientific apparatus and methods in tracking down spies and saboteurs or professional criminals adept at using the most sophisticated methods of escaping detection?

Those who oppose permitting electronic eavesdropping under any circumstances advance both philosophical and practical reasons.

On the philosophical level, the argument against snooping by planted microphone or bugged telephone is the same as the ancient one against general warrants. Any wiretapping reveals all the conversations over the tapped phone or in the spotted room, not just what pertains to the suspected crime or is spoken by suspected criminals. What could be more general? Doubtlessly the agents of the king argued that they could not find the king's enemies or the suspected culprit unless they could go into every house in town and search for evidence anywhere. But the Founding Fathers said warrants had to describe the place to be searched and the persons to be seized—and even then, a warrant was to be issued only upon probable cause, sworn to by oath or affirmation. By its very nature electronic eavesdropping cannot be specific.

As a matter of practicality, such methods have not proved very effective. Cosa Nostra, the giant crime syndicate affiliated with the Mafia, operated in New York with impunity—as it did elsewhere—although since 1936 that state has permitted the police to make wiretaps on court order!

A study of court-authorized wiretaps in New York City for 1953-54 showed 1617, or almost half of the 3588 taps, were public telephones—either pay phones or in hotel rooms. Unlike normal search and seizure, wiretapping cannot be limited to specific calls or persons.

This issue of authorizing wiretaps by court order is far from settled. Attorney Generals from 45 states responded to inquiries from a Senate subcommittee on six constitutional rights. Thirteen called for wiretapping authority, six opposed such a move, but 26 refused to express an opinion! Thus the demand for the tool of wiretapping in investigating and apprehending crime is hardly overwhelming!

A powerful argument against electronic surveillance is that tape recordings, or transcriptions by wire or records, are thoroughly unreliable. Words, phrases, sentences can be erased and the remainder retaped so even the expert cannot tell it was not the original.

"Liberty and justice for all is not only an American concept but is also our answer to Communism" could be retaped to come out "Liberty and justice for all is not an American concept but is Communism." What an opportunity for blackmailers, whether the tapes are doctored or not!

Privacy Invasion by Government

During a probe of so-called leaks of "confidential" documents to the Senate Internal Security Subcommittee by the State Department's chief security evaluations officer, his superior admitted they had tapped his phone and watched his waste paper basket to obtain evidence against him.

Otto F. Otepka was dismissed from the State Department for allegedly giving confidential documents to the U. S. senators on the sub-committee and encouraging them to ask embarrassing questions of his superiors. Disregarding the issue of whether administrative officials are justified in withholding pertinent information from Congress—as if it were a security risk—the methods of spying on an associate appears totally inappropriate. After denying that Otepka's office phone was bugged, two of his immediate superiors later admitted they had put a wiretap on his line and resigned!

The device they employed was supposed to pick up any conversation in the room. Because of electrical interference it recorded only phone conversations. So the superiors abandoned the tap after 48 hours and resorted to searching for "incriminating" evidence in the contents of his wastebasket.

Following a probe by another Congressional committee of electronic surveillance by government agencies, as well as by the non-governmental sector of society, some federal officials issued orders against any such spying. One may wonder how much went on in their agencies before such orders, and how much may still go on in other agencies.

In Administrative Agencies

Indeed, numerous questions may be asked as to the extent the Fourth Amendment restrictions on unreasonable search apply to government officials other than those enforcing the law.

How far can internal revenue agents go in probing bank records and other business papers in searching for possible discrepancies or fraud in income tax returns? How about the investigative powers of other regulatory agencies? Do welfare officials have the right to enter clients' homes without an appointment—or at unreasonable hours'? Instances have been known where welfare department investigators have gone into homes of mothers receiving aid to dependent children late at night—to check to see if a man was living in the home. That fact would make the mother ineligible for ADC grants.

Or what about health or building inspectors entering a dwelling? Some decisions place the public good above the right of privacy. Yet in the rare instances where a householder is unwilling to admit a well-behaved inspector at reasonable hours, a search warrant can be obtained from a judge or magistrate authorizing entrance.

How far can a legislative investigative committee go in requiring that certain papers or effects be produced—or sending its investigators after them? The actions of Congressional investigating committees relate much more to due process than the issues of search and seizure of the Fourth Amendment. This aspect will be dealt with more fully as to methods, purposes, and limitations of such committees in Chapter 16, "Punishment without Crime."

In 1880 a unanimous decision of the U. S. Supreme Court declared Congress possesses no "general power of making inquiry into the private affairs of the citizen." Congressional committees may require answers to questions pertinent to obtaining information on which proposed legislation is to be based. But they may not use this power to extort assent to invasions of homes and to seizures of private papers.

In spite of such court rulings, former Rep. J. Parnell Thomas, chairman of the House Un-American Activities Committee—who later served a jail sentence for corruption— declared:

> "The chief function of the Committee . . . has always been the exposure of un-American individuals and their un-American activities."

"Exposure" is the opposite of "privacy"!

Privacy Invasion by Private Individuals

To what extent, and by what means, should and can government protect an individual's privacy from invasion by other individuals and groups? The shocking extent of this invasion by the non-governmental sector of society has been documented in such best sellers as Vance Packard's *The Naked Society* and Myron Brenton's *The Privacy Invaders*.

The answer to the question is still largely to be worked out in legislation and legal decisions. The constitutional basis for the right of privacy lies largely in the due process guarantees of life, liberty, and property of the Fifth and Fourteenth Amendments rather than in any specific language.

Brandeis' 1890 Concept

Long before modern gadgetry made electronic snooping possible, a legal concept of the "Right to Privacy" had been developed. Indeed it was Louis Brandeis and his partner, Samuel D. Warren, who, as young lawyers, first used this term.

"The Right to Privacy" was the title of their brilliant article in the December 1890 issue of the *Harvard Law Review*.

Warren, a Boston Back Bay socialite, had been irked at the way a Boston newspaper had reported "in lurid detail" his marriage to a U. S. Senator's daughter six years before and their subsequent entertainings. The *Harvard Law Review* piece was the distillation of six years of research by two of the keenest legal minds of their age.

Brandeis, the stalwart defender of civil liberties on the Supreme Court bench, is foreshadowed by this formulation of "the right to privacy, as a part of the more general right to the immunity of the person,—the right to one's personality."

Heretofore, cases involving the unauthorized use of letters, paintings, lectures, etc., had been decided on the basis of property rights, even though the property might consist of the intangible product of one's mind. Brandeis and Warren, however, maintained the inviolability of personality was protected by common law. It, they saw, "secures to each individual the right of determining, ordinarily, to what extent his thoughts, sentiments, and emotions shall be communicated to others."

Since 1890 a few states, beginning with New York, have enacted specific laws on privacy. Others, such as Georgia, have interpreted court precedents—which is the way common law is made—as protecting the right of privacy. Still others recognize no such right.

Commercial Exploitation

Where recognized legally the right of privacy is defined quite narrowly. Morris L. Ernst, distinguished civil liberties attorney, with Alan U. Schwartz, in their book, *Privacy, the Right to be Left Alone,* conclude:

> "It is violated whenever something unique about an individual—his face, his name, or even his dog's likeness—is taken by another without his consent and revealed to the public gaze in order to enrich the appropriator."

Another authority, Harriet F. Pilpel, summed up the current status of the legal right as follows:

> "By and large, today the right of privacy has been interpreted to prevent only, or at least primarily, commercial exploitation of a person's name or picture to sell something other than the facts about him presented as such. Generally speaking a fictionized or dramatized version of the facts is held to be a species of commercial exploitation."

Preventing commercial exploitation appears a rather slender reed to protect individuals from the unwarranted intrusion by others into their private lives.

Note that Mrs. Pilpel's statement, which appeared in *Publishers Weekly,* recognized the right of news media to use one's name and picture as news.

Brandeis and Warren were disturbed because a new gadget—flash powder—permitted "instantaneous photography" whereby portraits could be taken without the permission or knowledge of the subject.

Their 1890 article referred to a case in which a Broadway actress, whose role required her to appear on the stage in tights, asked the court to restrain a photographer from making use of a picture of her he had snapped from a box—without her knowledge. She won because the defendant didn't show up!

Modern Means of Exposure

What would these advocates of the right to be left alone say of the gadgetry of the present day—candid cameras, still or moving, silent or sound, sizable or miniaturized, professional or amateur? Or what would they think of the ever-scanning TV eye, or the electronic eavesdropping devices discussed earlier?

Would they approve of the use of the so-called lie detector which, in effect, bares the soul by recording emotional reaction through changes in pulse, breathing, and temperature of an individual as he responds to questioning? In the hands of a highly skilled professional the lie detector may have its usefulness, although its creditibility is not such that its records are admissible as evidence in court. Some authorities place its creditibility at 17 percent, rather than the 70 percent claimed. Yet lie detector tests in some industrial plants and business establishments are given employees and prospective employees almost routinely—and by those not professionally trained in psychological testing and interpreting.

Would they approve of information of a personal nature collected, compiled, filed, and exchanged on computer cards and address plates in credit agencies, insurance companies, private detective organizations, direct mail solicitors, periodical circulation departments, etc., etc.?

Truly our attitudes toward privacy have vastly changed since 1890. Americans generally welcome publicity. Consent, of course, ends a claim against invasion of privacy. Most persons are willing to give consent even though they may not know that their privacy is being invaded. Witness the popularity of "candid camera" television programs, for example. Only when some property right or prospect of gain is interfered with are most of us concerned. (Libel or defamation of character is another matter.)

A Georgia judge, in a case upholding the right of a man to object to the use of his photograph in an insurance ad, commented:

"The right of one to exhibit himself to the public at all proper times, in all proper places, and in a proper manner is embraced within the right of personal liberty. The right to withdraw from the public gaze at such times as a person may see fit, when his presence is not demanded by a rule of law is also embraced within the right of personal liberty. Publicity in one instance and privacy in the other is each guaranteed."

Times have changed mightily since that was written sixty years ago. Yet the principle enunciated remains sound in re-emphasizing the primacy of one's personality—that the right to be left alone is the beginning of all freedom.

Another "Zone of Privacy"

A third aspect of the right of privacy has been added to the ones of freedom from surreptitious surveillance and from unwarranted public exposure of one's name, picture, or intangible possession for commercial exploitation. This is the right to privacy in intimate personal relations.

In 1965 the U. S. Supreme Court declared unconstitutional Connecticut's 1879 birth control law which forbade the use of contraceptives by anyone, including married couples.

"We deal with a right of privacy older than the Bill of Rights," said the court in citing half a dozen amendments to establish "a zone of privacy created by several fundamental constitutional guarantees."

In one of the rare instances of judicial history it cited the Ninth Amendment's reference to rights other than those enumerated which are retained by the people and which cannot be disparaged or denied. This protection of unenumerated rights reinforces the First Amendment's right of association, the Fourth's stricture on search and seizure, the Fifth's guarantee against self-incrimmination, and the Fourteenth's due process clause. Even the Third Amendment's ban on the quartering of soldiers in a home without the owner's consent—a practice long obsolete—was cited to bolster the concept that privacy within the home is an ancient right.

This decision involved a married couple and the physician who advised them regarding birth control. Its ramifications in establishing the right of privacy in other circumstances involving conduct of an intimate nature cannot, at this time, be foreseen.

1967 Privacy Advances

Although involving more than the right of privacy, the unanimous U. S. Supreme Court decision in its 1967 declaring unconstitutional all laws barring marriage of persons of different races strengthens this concept of a zone of privacy into which the state cannot intrude.

The same term saw, finally, the clearcut reversal of the 1928 *Olmstead* decision (see pages 164,165). In overturning the New York wiretap and electronic eavesdropping law, the Court brought all bugging within the Fourth Amendment's ban on unreasonable search and seizure, regardless of whether or not physical trespass occurred.

Other decisions made clearer the requirement that in the absence of an emergency, fire, health, and other government inspectors must have a warrant to validly inspect private property.

16

Innocent Until Proven

"Political liberty consists in security, or at least, in the opinion we enjoy security. This security is never more dangerously attacked than in public or private accusation." and it is the ". . . goodness of criminal law upon which the liberty of a subject principally depends."

—Montesquieu, Spirit of the Law

"No free man shall be taken or imprisoned . . . except by lawful judgment of his peers or by laws of the land."

—Magna Carta, 39th clause

"The greatest dangers to liberty lurk in insidious encroachments by men of zeal, well-meaning but without understanding."

—Justice Oliver Wendell Holmes

"If the government becomes a lawbreaker, it breeds contempt for the law; it invites every man to become a law unto himself."

—Justice Louis D. Brandeis

Is the administration of justice in mid-20th Century America not so much a search for truth as it is a "forum for legal nit-picking"? What kind of justice do Americans want— strict enforcement of every law for everybody (e.g. the speed limit) or just the more blatant violations? Is there one standard of justice for the rich, another for the poor? Or, rather, is justice most difficult to come by for the citizen who is not indigent, and therefore not entitled to court-appointed counsel, but who cannot afford the cost of all the legal maneuverings open to a high-priced battery of lawyers?

These are questions that are being asked. Many, including a large segment of the bar, believe that U. S. Supreme Court decisions of the Sixties protecting rights of defendants in criminal cases have swung the pendulum too far; that the rights of society to be secure against the attacks of criminals "who walk our streets with increasing boldness" need greater protection.

The first question was asked by a newspaper columnist after a state supreme court had reversed the conviction of a man accused of engaging in a gun battle with police after an armed burglary. The judge had failed to warn the jurors not to read the newspapers while the trial was in progress. One paper reported the defendant was an ex-convict. This was true. Yet this fact could not be brought out in the courtroom before the jury, because it would be prejudicial. It might have influenced the thinking of one or more jurors.

Underlying this situation is the most basic assumption of our system of law, evolved out of a thousand years of Anglo-Saxon jurisprudence. This assumption is that a man is presumed to be innocent until proven guilty beyond a reasonable doubt. The ramifications of such assumption will be explored in this and the following chapters. While it primarily involves criminal law, it also impinges on the rights of individuals to be free from social censure and "character assassination" in non-criminal situations.

To Protect the Innocent

Corollary to the presumption of innocence is the axiom that the purpose of law is to protect the innocent fully as much as to apprehend and punish the guilty. Historically, many of the protections of due process developed in situations where the persons charged were not guilty of what would be considered a criminal act today, but because they offended the King, the Church, the Parliament, or the Court. It may be argued with considerable justification that the Founding Fathers were primarily concerned with preventing the kind of harassments the colonists had experienced from the agents of the Crown when they wrote the procedural safeguards into the Constitution. They built a bulwark against prosecution and persecution for political crime. This bulwark also protects the innocent from the awesome power of government in any accusation.

For centuries in England trial by ordeal or trial by combat were accepted means of administering justice. If the accused, on the third day, was cured of burns caused by plucking a rock out of boiling water or grasping a red hot iron, it was a sign of his innocence. If he chose trial by combat, the accused was acquitted if he slew his accuser, or made him cry "craven" or fought until the stars came out. Trial by forced confession persisted until very recently even though it is as illogical a method of determing guilt as belief in miraculous intervention to protect the innocent.

Apprehending the Suspect

To quote history or learned judges on the majesty of the law's procedural safeguards affords small comfort to the victim of a street mugger who is freed by an appeals court because the police held him incommunicado until he confessed.

The citizen who protests when a traffic cop writes him out a ticket charging him with a moving traffic violation may have a different concept of his rights. Obviously most Americans consider themselves law abiding—even if they fudge a bit on the speed limit or in reporting charitable contributions on their tax returns. They consider the police their servant paid to watch the other fellow rather than watching themselves.

Under what circumstances may a policeman "arrest" a person? "Arrest" means taking a person into custody, usually taking him to a police station. Some authorities would say a person is "under arrest" only when he is formally charged with committing a crime, but they do not have the preponderance of the law on their side. Police may make the charge on the spot, often by checking a ticket specifying violation of a certain section of a law or ordinance. Or the charge may be made when the person is "booked" at the police station. Sometimes a person may be held "for investigation" or "on suspicion" without being formally charged. To maintain that such a situation is not an arrest is a subterfuge to avoid the ban on "arrest for suspicion".

Here is an actual incident. A pair of patrolmen cruising in an integrated middle class neighborhood about 2:30 a.m. noticed a 25-year-old Negro walking to the back of a car. After he reluctantly identified himself he refused, according to them, to tell why he was in the neighborhood at that hour. They jailed him "for investigation."

Later he was brought to trial on charges of "wandering about at late and unusual hours." This part of a vague vagrancy statute common in many municipalities would probably be held unconstitutional if carried to the highest courts.

Here, however, the constitutionality was not the issue. The young man told the municipal judge he had just taken his date—a blonde—home from a late drive-in movie and had showed the police the ticket stubs and empty popcorn container.

His attorney, who had recently been the administrator over all the police in that city, declared police officers have no right to stop citizens unless they have "reason to believe a crime is committed or about to be committed." Since his client was guilty of no crime he therefore was under no obligation to talk to the officers.

The cops said they were only doing their duty and had "every right" to question the young man at that hour in the morning.

In dismissing the case the judge observed citizens could save time and embarrassment by answering questions asked by police.

Are any of these three views totally correct?

Chief Justice Warren, in the history-making 1966 *Miranda* decision on police interrogation restrictions declared:

> "It is an act of responsible citizenship for indi-divuals to give whatever information they may have to aid in law enforcement."

He said that general on-the-scene questioning as to facts surrounding a crime or other general questioning of citizens in the fact-finding process is not affected by the rules police must follow when a person is "in custody."

Arrest Without Warrant

Obviously a law enforcement officer can make an arrest if he sees a crime being committed. No warrant is needed. Neither is one needed to prevent a person whom he can reasonably asume may be connected with a crime from getting away.

The person apprehended, however, is not required to answer any questions except to give his name and address. The protection against requiring one to incriminate himself applies at this stage as well as at the booking station and during trial. On the other hand the officer is justified in using whatever force is necessary to make an arrest. Resisting an officer is a crime in itself.

Prudence, therefore, would suggest that a citizen be reasonable even though he believes the officer wrong. Yet very often incidents such as the one described involve persons who believe the police "have it in" for them because of age, race, area, or economic circumstances.

Problems of police power did not originate in any recent "crime wave", real or imagined, or the "delinquency of modern youth", or the new found militancy of minority groups, although these factors may accentuate them.

The officer of the law is the embodiment of the power of government, an awesome thing when contrasted with the puny power of the individual. That is why so many safeguards are thrown about the exercise of police power—including the requirement that a warrant is needed to make an arrest except under the emergency conditions just discussed.

In explaining why judicial officials should determine whether a warrant should be issued, Justice Douglas once commented:

> "The right of privacy was deemed too precious to entrust to the discretion of those whose job is the detection of crime and the arrest of criminals. Power is a heady thing; and history shows that the police acting on their own cannot be trusted."

"Suspicion" and "Investigation"

Nowhere in the United States is "suspicion" a crime. Or as Justice Douglas puts it:

> "Arrests for suspicion are not countenanced by the Bill of Rights. The Fourth Amendment allows arrests —as well as searches—only for 'probable cause'."

Even though recent decisions of the Supreme Court have clarified some of the procedural requirements in criminal cases, judges vary widely in applying these decisions to specific situations. It is no wonder that police officers, seeking to apprehend the criminal under conditions often requiring quick and decisive judgment, would prefer not to be hampered with fine distinctions of due process.

What could be easier than to pick up a suspect and question him? Or if there are numerous persons around whose records indicate they could be involved, why not throw out a dragnet to bring them all in for interrogation? These are not questions which are easily answered. A partial answer is that the professional criminal or the repeater knows his rights, knows his way around the police station and the courts. He will insist on his rights. Not so with the first offender, the emotionally distraught, the fearful, the young, the ignorant, the mentally or ethnically disadvantaged. Such persons may be completely innocent—or extenuating circumstances may justify a reduced or changed charge.

Such considerations are matters for judicial determination rather than police judgment. That is why rules of criminal procedure require a preliminary hearing—or arraignment—in felony cases before a magistrate "forthwith," "within a reasonable time," or some such wording. The rules vary from state to state, and between the federal and state courts. In addition to determining whether enough evidence exists to warrant holding the accused for a trial, the arraigning magistrate customarily sets bail, informs the accused that he need not make any statement but anything he says may be used against him, and informs him of his right to counsel.

In theory, this procedure is designed to assure adherence to the idea that a man is considered innocent until proven guilty. In practice, however, most of the violations of this basic idea occur before this preliminary hearing.

"In Custody" Procedure

Numerous issues which have been disputed among law enforcement officials, attorneys, legal scholars and civil libertarians as to what can and ought to happen during the crucial period before arraignment were settled by the 1966 *Miranda* case decision.

It involved appeals from four prisoners from different states who had confessed after police interrogations of varying lengths. It follows by two years the much-criticized *Escobedo* case (of which more later) which established the right of an accused to ask for and see his lawyer even in the police station before being brought before a magistrate for arraignment.

The Warren Court, though by a bare majority, decided:

—The Fifth Amendment protection against self-incrimination begins when a person is taken into custody.

—The Sixth amendment right to counsel also takes effect at this point.

—The poor or indigent accused has the same right to counsel as the one who can afford to hire one.

—Questioning by officers at the police station—or even in the police car—must be preceded by effectively informing the suspect of his right to remain silent, his right to counsel, and that anything he says may be used against him.

—The suspect can waive his rights only "knowingly", "willingly," and "intelligently." He does not do so by remaining silent.

—If he indicates in any manner, or at any stage in the process that he wishes to consult with an attorney, the questioning must cease.

—If he asks for an attorney, the interrogation must cease until the attorney is present. The attorney must be present at all subsequent interrogations unless the suspect consents to go it alone.

—The suspect may break off answering questions at any time.

—If a suspect expressly says he does not want an attorney and closely follows with a statement, that constitutes a voluntary confession admissable in court. Evidence of lengthy interrogation, incommunicado incarceration, or threats, trickery, or cajolery negates the voluntariness of waiver.

—A suspect may be held for a reasonable time, without access to an attorney, while investigation in the field is carried out—but he cannot be questioned during this period.

Effect on Law Enforcement

What will this far-reaching decision—which one liberal lawyer says "puts Escobedo in a dress suit"—do to law enforcement?

Will it, as Justice White wryly observed in his dissent, in an unknown number of cases return "a killer, a rapist or other criminal to the streets and the environment which produced him"? Or will it, as Warren suggested, apply to state and local police the rules long used by the Federal Bureau of Investigation and England's Scotland Yard?

Some chiefs of police and district attorneys say the decision will make little difference since they themselves follow essentially the same designated procedures. Others believe it will "dry up" confessions and make convictions more difficult. A few libertarian lawyers doubt that it goes far enough, in that it does not require the presence of an attorney at the point where an ignorant and uninformed person most in need of protection first confronts the law. In this view the accused, frightened and facing alone a skilled questioner in a strange room, needs advice from an attorney to decide whether he should waive his right to counsel!

Justice Warren devoted six pages of his 61-page opinion to detailing tactics and tricks advocated in police manuals to deprive the accused of every psychological advantage, ranging from not questioning the suspect in his own home where he "is more keenly aware of his rights" to maintaining "an oppressive atmosphere of dogged persistence." He commented:

> "This atmosphere carries its own badge of intimidation. . . The . . . practice of incommunicado interrogation is at odds with one of our nation's most cherished principles—that the individual may not be impelled to incriminate himself."

Confessions are not being dried up by application of the *Escobedo* ruling requiring warning the accused of his rights, which foreshadowed the 1966 *Miranda* decision. This was the consensus of the National Association of Attorney Generals at its 1966 session. Further refuting the dire forecast that police are being handcuffed are California statistics showing district attorneys obtained convictions in 85.6 per cent of felony cases in the first half year after the warning rule went into effect compared to 85.4 per cent convictions during the year prior.

Such evidence is not surprising in light of psychological insights that many one-time offenders want to talk, remorsefully desiring to "get it off their chests." Such persons will continue to confess, even though an attorney may be present. In other cases the "new" procedural rules will require police to do more thorough sleuthing for corroborating evidence, which is needed anyway. Indeed, Justice Warren commented in each of the four cases before the high court, the prosecution had ample evidence to prefer criminal charges without the confessions.

Right to Counsel Extended

Two significant conclusions may be drawn from the *Miranda* decision:

1. The procedural safeguards long taken for granted in the court room, be they that of an arraigning magistrate or the Supreme Court, must now be heeded in the back room of the police station.

2. The distinction in practice between the affluent (rich or merely middle class), who can pay for an attorney, and the poor, who cannot, has all but been erased.

This latter issue had been left unsettled in the *Escobedo* case. Danny Escobedo, accused of murdering his brother-in-law, had secured an attorney who gained his release on *habeas corpus* proceedings. Eleven days later he was re-arrested and questioned at the police station. He asked for his attorney who was sitting in an adjoining room. The attorney repeatedly sought to see his client. Both were refused. Escobedo confessed after several hours of interrogation.

The majority of the Supreme Court reversed the conviction based on this confession. It held that where a police investigation is no longer a general inquiry into an unsolved crime but begins to focus on the accused for the purpose of eliciting a confession, the Sixth Amendment guarantee of the right to counsel comes into play. Justice Potter Stewart expressed a dissenting view that only when "formal, meaningful judicial proceedings" have been instituted does the constitutional right to assistance by counsel take effect.

Some prosecutors and law officers complained that the logical conclusion of this decision would be the requirement that a defense attorney accompany a patrolman on his beat! The answer is that police must confine their interrogation of a suspect to a general inquiry prior to putting him under restraint. Many persons will be excused at this point, but if one is held, further questioning is out until he is apprised of his rights.

Ramsey Clark, deputy attorney general in the Johnson Administration, recently observed,

> "Court rules do not cause crime. People do not commit crimes because of decisions restricting police questions or because they think they might not be convicted."

"Booking"

The *Miranda* and *Escobedo* cases go a long way in drawing the guidelines between voluntary confessions, always admissable as evidence, and those which are not. By inference they also answer questions of delays in "booking" or charging the suspect with a specific offense.

Traditionally, at this point, he is permitted one phone call—to a relative, friend, or attorney. That tradition is not always observed.

In the past, booking has been delayed for hours or even days. A 1959 study of a random sample of two thousand arrest slips in the Chicago Police Department files showed that half the prisoners had been detained 17 hours or longer before being charged. One out of 40 had been held for at least three days before being arraigned. Some of these delays may be justified—to check out alibis and make other outside investigations. With the new limits on questioning suspects in custody, however, a major reason given for delays is eliminated.

Many—perhaps most—of these picked up by police are released without ever being charged. These are lucky, for if a person is booked it means, technically, he has a police record even though he is later acquitted. To expunge this record is very difficult, usually requiring a court order. Particularly in the case of young persons the existence of such a record can be harmful to their future. It has been suggested that expunging of arrest records where there is no conviction ought to be automatic. Some employers ask job applicants if they have ever been arrested—or even if they have been questioned by police. Some employers refuse to hire a person who answers "yes." Here certainly, is punishment without crime.

Coerced Confessions

The 1966 decisions culminate a thirty year trend. Not until 1936 did the U. S. Supreme Court reverse a state conviction because of coerced confessions. One Brown and two co-defendants were sentenced to death solely on "evidence" obtained in the following manner. The quotation is from th opinion of two Mississippi Supreme Court judges who dissented from that state court's majority upholding the conviction:

> ". . . The last two named defendants were made to strip and they were laid over chairs and their backs were cut to pieces with a leather strap with buckles on it, and they were likewise made by the said deputy definitely to understand that the whipping would be continued unless and until they confessed, and not only confessed, but confessed in every matter of detail as demanded by those present; and in this manner the defendants confessed the crime, and as the whippings progressed and were repeated, they changed or adjusted their confessions in all particulars of detail so as to conform to the demands of their torturers. . ."

In 1963 in a closely divided decision, the U. S. Supreme Court reversed the conviction of a prisoner based on his confession because he had been held incommunicado for sixteen hours. He was not allowed to call his wife or an attorney until he "cooperated" by confessing to armed robbery of a filling station.

Four justices disagreed that the circumstances made this a coerced confession. This decision appears, however, merely to extend to a state court the so-called "McNabb-Mallory rule" long recognized in federal courts.

"Without Unnecessary Delay"

In 1943 the U. S. Supreme Court upset the conviction of five Tennessee mountain moonshiners, the McNabb brothers, for the murder of a revenue officer in the course of a raid on their whiskey still. The reversal was made because they had been arrested and questioned relentlessly for a long period before being taken to a U. S. Commissioner or other judicial officer for preliminary hearing. Their conviction was based not on confessions, but on incriminating statements made by them during that period.

Andrew Mallory, a Negro of limited intelligence, did confess to raping a white tenant in the basement of a Washington, D. C. apartment house where he lived with his janitor brother. He was held at the police station only about eight hours. After denying his guilt during questioning by four officers for more than an hour, he agreed to take a lie detector test. Several hours later this polygraph test was given and after an hour and a half of questioning by the polygraph operator he said he was responsible. Only then, at 10 o'clock in the evening, was he taken before a U. S. Commissioner to be arraigned.

In 1957 the U. S. Supreme Court unanimously reversed the conviction, holding the confession was inadmissible as evidence. It held the arrest violated the rule of Federal Criminal Procedures requiring that an arrested person be taken before a judicial officer "without unnecessary delay." Without the confession, however, the arrest was made without the "reasonable" or "probable" cause required.

Such decisions prompted U. S. Court of Appeals Judge J. Skelly Wright to say:

"Coerced confessions have received the condemnation of current Court. Under the Anglo-Saxon system of criminal justice a defendant has a right to remain silent, not only at the time of trial, but, most importantly, after his arrest before trial. The Supreme Court has been at pains to condemn, as uncivilized and as a reproach to our system of criminal justice, not only physical pressure, but psychological pressure as well, designed to force an accused to confess."

On the other hand, Justice Frankfurter said in one case:

"The public interest requires that interrogation and that at a police station, not completely be forbidden, so long as it is conducted fairly, reasonably, within proper limits with full regard to the rights of those being questioned."

Thirty Minute Delay

One Sunday evening Leroy Spriggs was arrested after a brawl in which a man was wounded by a shotgun blast.

He was taken to a Washington police station. There he refused to answer questions.

Then the officer filling out the arrest slip said:

"The hell with it. If you don't want to tell me anything you don't have to. The man you shot knows you shot him—the man who was with him knows you shot him—and I have a completely disinterested witness who knows who shot him and she is the one who gave me your name . . ."

Whereupon Spriggs confessed and gave more details. All of this occurred within a 30-minute period after his arrest before he was arraigned before a magistrate. At his trial he repudiated his confession.

Upon appeal, the District of Columbia Court of Appeals, by a 2-to-1 vote, reversed his conviction on the ground that there had been an "unnecessary" delay in his arraignment, even though there was other evidence, besides his confession, of his guilt.

If the fracas had been on the other side of the avenue, in Maryland, little would have been heard of this rather common type of case. In the District of Columbia, however, where U. S. courts have general police and criminal jurisdiction, decisions and procedures may forecast guidelines federal courts may lay down for state and municipal courts throughout the nation—under the Fourteenth Amendment.

The policeman had warned Spriggs he did not have to talk. No intimidation or coercion was alleged. Perhaps the court today would have used the *Miranda* rule on right to counsel rather than the *Mallory* rule on unnecessary delay. The *Spriggs* case taxes the ingenuity of law enforcement officials to devise procedures which will stand up in court.

Remedies Against Improper Police Acts

Where there is a wrong there is a remedy. This is a lawbook axiom.

When a person believes he is wrongly detained he has the ancient right of *habeas corpus.* Justice Douglas says since England enacted her famous *Habeas Corpus Act* in 1679, it has become perhaps the greatest of all civil rights. It is a procedure whereby a jailer is required to deliver a prisoner before a court so that the legality of his detention may be determined.

Usually when a person is held before arraignment it takes an attorney, on the outside, to file such a writ. In many instances prisoners who believe their conviction was illegal petition a court for a habeas corpus hearing—sometimes, as will be seen in the following chapter—with far-reaching results.

Another remedy, though rarely successful, is a civil suit for false arrest. If the officer so sued had reasonable grounds for suspecting the individual might have violated the law, the arrest was not false even though the suspect is readily cleared.

A Federal civil rights law enacted nearly a century ago and rarely used has proven to be an effective remedy on several occasions in recent years. It provides for a civil damage suit in Federal court against a state or local official who deprives a person of his civil rights "under color of law."

In one such case a miner driving to work was stopped by a state patrolman for failing to dim his headlights. The patrolman, who was acquainted with the miner, beat him with a blackjack and took him to the justice of the peace. The JP refused him bail or to release him unless he plead guilty to charges of drunken driving. Faced with loss of his job unless he reported for his shift, the miner did plead guilty. Later he sued both the patrolman and justice of the peace under the Federal civil rights law. The substantial monetary judgment awarded in Federal district court was upheld on appeal.

Here is a rare instance where the allegations of mistreatment by an officer of the law was proven to the satisfaction of the court.

Illegal Police Practices

The term "police brutality" evokes strong emotions. Such an accusation oftimes brings sharp retorts by law enforcement officials that "police brutality" is a figment of the imagination, or that such a charge is leftist inspired, or it occurs only in isolated rural communities, or that it is not as prevalent as when the Wickersham commission made its report on "third degree" methods in the early Thirties.

On the other hand, almost any attorney with an extensive criminal defense practice will claim instances where officers have used unnecessary force in making an arrest, in the patrol wagon, in the police station.

Minority spokesmen, particularly for the Negro and Spanish-surnamed, are certain some policemen are unnecessarily rough toward low-income minorities. "Police brutality" to these, however, denotes more than a rare beating. It means, to them, a harrassment by the police, especially toward young people, to which those living in white middle class neighborhoods are not subjected. That a policeman is the only "whitey" those in a racial ghetto may see regularly does not improve the image.

Treatment of civil rights demonstrators in some Southern communities and some northern cities present a special circumstance. The television cameras showed the evidence for millions to see. Yet the use of police dogs on children and nightsticks on young people are the exception rather than the rule.

Ignoring such special situations, what can be done to meet the charges, real or alleged?

First is a recognition that law enforcement officers have a difficult job. Putting a 200-pound resisting drunk into a patrol car is not easy. Risking assault or even death almost daily is not easy. Taking the torrent of profanity and abuse which may come from a suspect—or even from by-standers, is not easy. Walking a slum beat at night, where jamming of people together in itself increases the incidence of crime, is not easy.

Then comes the recognition that generally police work is not a highly paid profession. Its beginning salaries are not such as to attract the ablest and best educated young men— yet a cop has to be a pretty good sociologist, psychologist, even something of a lawyer. Few join the force out of any idealistic motivation to help society. Some may glory in the exercise of authority which a police badge bestows. A small number may even find sadistic satisfaction in inflicting pain, physical or psychological, on others. It is these, perhaps well under ten percent, who make the issue of "police brutality" pertinent.

Yet some enlightened city administrations over the country have taken giant strides to improve police operations. Salaries and other benefits are being offered to make law enforcement work a desirable career. Men with broad educational backgrounds may look forward to successive promotions in supervisory positions. Pre-service and in-service training includes courses in community relations stressing causes and methods of dealing with minority tensions. In Chicago at some police stations, neighborhood workshops are held regularly so the people and officers may get acquainted and exchange ideas. Chicago also has integrated its police force more than any other major city. Fourteen percent of its policemen are Negroes, with a number of them in supervisory positions.

Citizens Review Boards

One proposal that meets almost universal opposition on the part of law enforcement authorities is the establishment of citizens' police review boards. While varying somewhat, the essential purpose of such a board is to provide a place, outside the police department, where a citizen who believes he has been aggrieved by a police officer may bring charges. The board, or its staff, then investigates. It may hold hearings and make findings, which may or may not be mandatory.

All of the larger police departments have their own internal machinery to investigate and discipline infraction of their rules. They consider any review of police procedures outside this semi-military structure an unnecessary and unwarranted intrusion on the orderly process of law enforcement. Those favoring independent review agencies maintain that internal disciplinary machinery almost always operates to protect individual officers from charges of malpractice.

Where an independent review board has operated successfully, particularly in Philadelphia, police opposition has largely disappeared. Indeed, it operates to clear policemen of unfounded charges. Only a small percentage of complaints result in recommendations for disciplinary action by the police department. Somewhat more often, although still infrequently, a word of apology or an exchange of explanations between the patrolman and the complainant is all that is required.

What kind of law enforcement do Americans want? Part of the answer may lie not in proving or disproving the existence of "police brutality" but in the knowledge that any person, whatever his race or economic circumstance, can complain and have his complaint heard.

Bail

No chapter headed "Innocent Until Proven" would be complete without quoting part of the Eighth Amendment:

"Excessive bail shall not be required . . ."

Bail is the bond or surety given to guarantee that the accused will appear for trial. Right to bail is denied usually only to persons accused of murder, sex, or narcotic cases. Ordinarily the accused is entitled to make bail at the time of his arraignment.

Does a person without property or funds to post bail have to remain imprisoned until the time of his trial? Historically this has been the case, even for the routine crimes which clog the court dockets. At least half of those accused of crime in metropolitan cities cannot post bond. Neither they nor their relatives have the property to pledge as surety, nor do they have the premium, ten percent of the bond, to pay a professional bondsman.

Reform of the archaic bail system has been discussed for years. In 1961 the Manhattan Bail Project was started in New York City by the Vera Foundation, financed by a chemical engineer named Louis Schweitzer. Each morning Vera staff members investigated those arrested on felony charges the previous 24 hours and recommended to the judges whether or not each defendant was a good risk for release without bond.

Of more than 1,000 accused persons released without bond during the four years of the project only nine, less than one per cent, failed to show up for trial. The average of those jumping bail is around four per cent.

Since 1964 this system of "pre-trial parole" has been adopted as an integral part of the New York City court system. Other municipalities and states are adopting this or similar plans. "Personal recognizance bond" is another term with essentially the same meaning. In Illinois as an alternative to professional bondsmen, the accused is permitted to deposit ten percent of the face of the bail bond with the court. Then if he shows up for trial, he gets back 95 percent of his deposit. Thus $1,000 bail would cost him only $5, instead of $100 from a professional bondsman. "Hard core" criminals, of course, may be required to post traditional bail.

For the poor any requirement of bail under the traditional system is excessive. For the taxpayers, pre-trial parole saves countless millions in the cost of keeping persons in jail and providing relief for their families.

In signing the 1966 law extending similar discretion to Federal judges to release persons without bond in non-capital cases if deemed trustworthy, President Johnson hailed the bail reform act as opening a "new era" in the American system of criminal justice.

The Manhattan Bail Project showed 60 percent of those given pre-trial parole were acquitted or had their case dismissed. To jail such because they could not furnish bail, as has been traditional, would not only illustrate one standard of justice for the rich and another for the poor, it would also demonstrate how to encourage resentment toward the law.

Calling the traditional bail system in the United States "cruelly unrealistic, outrageously discriminatory, staggeringly expensive." Sylvia Porter, syndicated business columnist, pointed out that it is "a monstrously costly and unnecessary" burden on the taxpayers as well as being "a sickening illustration of one type of justice for the rich, another for the poor". Because from a half to three-fourths of persons accused of crime cannot raise bail, our communities must build jails to house them, maintain them in brooding, degenerating idleness and oftimes support their families.

Bail was devised so a person presumed to be innocent until proven guilty beyond a reasonable doubt would not be punished until so proven. In practical operation traditional bail procedures have not achieved that purpose. Current reforms are long overdue.

Police Powers

Several 1967 Supreme Court decisions clarified or amplified powers of police. They may seize "mere evidence" as distinguished from the "actual fruits of crime" while in pursuit of a suspect; make a warrantless arrest based on an informant's tip; search a car seized without warrant; use the testimony of undercover agents who enter a defendant's home under false pretenses or use recording devices.

17

Fair Trial

". . . Nor shall any person be subject for the same offence to be twice put in jeopardy of life or limb;

"nor shall be compelled in any criminal case to be a witness against himself;

"nor be deprived of life, liberty, or property without due process of law. . ."

—FIFTH AMENDMENT

"In all criminal prosecutions, the accused shall enjoy the right to a speedy and public trial, by an impartial jury of the state and district wherein the crime shall have been committed, which district shall have been previously ascertained by law,

"and to be informed of the nature and cause of the accusation;

"to be confronted with the witnesses against him;

"to have compulsory process for obtaining witnesses in his favor,

"and to have the assistance of counsel for his defense."

—SIXTH AMENDMENT

195

"In suits at common law, where the value of the controversy shall exceed twenty dollars, the right of trial by a jury shall be preserved, and no fact tried by a jury shall be otherwise re-examined in any court of the United States, than according to the rules of the common law."

—SEVENTH AMENDMENT

"Excessive bail shall not be required, nor excessive fines imposed, nor cruel and unusual punishments inflicted."

—EIGHTH AMENDMENT

"Not the least significant test of the quality of a civilization is its treatment of those charged with crime, particularly with offenses which arouse the passions of a community."

—JUSTICE FELIX FRANKFURTER

"Some of our judges have the notion that the way to go down in history as a great judge . . . is to devote all of their attention to the Bill of Rights—overlooking the fact that the Constitution Preamble says that the purpose of it all is to promote the domestic tranquility and public welfare."

—FRED IMBAU,
PROFESSOR OF CRIMINAL LAW

"In the past generation, we as a people, have been moving forward towards a better, a greater, and a nobler conception of the dignity of man, a more comprehensive conception of the rights of man."

—JUSTICE ABE FORTAS

Whether you believe with Prof. Imbau that the courts have overemphasized individual rights at the expense of public welfare or with Justice Fortas that we are moving forward, you must concede that the first Congress which formulated the Bill of Rights was most specific in detailing the elements of fair trial.

Not only were four of the ten amendments concerned with explicit trial procedures, but declaration of the right to trial by jury in the state where the offense was committed was repeated, even though embodied in the Constitution itself.

These elements of fair trial were, true enough, confined to federal courts, but most state constitutions did, and do, have similar protections. In recent years the due process clause of the Fourteenth Amendment has extended the protection of most of these safeguards to state courts where they do not already exist.

Each of the specific provisions of the Fifth through the Eighth Amendments resulted from historical abuses by the courts, either in England or in the Colonies, or both. That they are still relevant today can be amply illustrated. The Founding Fathers would have been shocked at Prof. Imbau's statement, for they recognized that specific safeguards were needed to insure domestic tranquility and the public welfare.

"Speedy Trial"

A "speedy" trial is one without unreasonable delay. It is not to be so speedy as to prevent either the defense or the prosecution from preparing their respective cases. Felony cases where the accused was tried and sentenced within a 24-hour period have been sent back for retrial by an appellate court. More often a trial is delayed for months because of crowded court dockets and postponements sought by prosecution or defense counsel for any number of reasons—some valid and some flimsy. A saying goes "justice deferred is justice denied." Yet few, if any, judicial decisions have been reversed on the grounds a "speedy trial" was denied. Rather the remedy has been a *habeas corpus* action to force a court hearing and release of the accused on bail.

"Public Trial"

Requirement of a "public" trial presents more problems. "The accused shall enjoy the right . . ." says the Sixth Amendment. Obviously the requirement is for his protection—to prevent secret trials such as the infamous "star chamber" proceedings of Seventeenth century England. It does not confer a right for all of the public to enjoy a spectacle.

Mickey Jelke, a wealthy playboy, was convicted in the Fifties on widely publicized vice charges. Because of the obscene and sordid character of the prosecution's case against Jelke, the trial judge excluded the general public from the courtroom during this salacious testimony, while admitting any friends and relatives the defendant desired to protect his interests. This conviction was reversed on the ground that the trial was not public if only a limited class of people was allowed to attend, particularly if no member of the press is included among those privileged to attend.

On the other hand the appellate court rejected the contention of newspaper publishers that the press and the general public had a right to insist that Jelke's trial be open to anybody. The press' interest can be no greater than that of the public or the defendant, according to this decision. Judges have always been allowed to clear a courtroom where delicacy and gentility, or even sanitary conditions, warranted the exclusion of spectators.

If Jelke's trial had been held in an open and highly publicized atmosphere, could his lawyers then successfully have appealed on the ground that this notoriety deprived him of due process of law? The possibility that he could win reversal of his conviction either because the public—including the press—was excluded or because it was free to hear all testimony is not fantasy. Six months before the assassination of President Kennedy, the U. S. Supreme Court overturned a murder conviction because a television station broadcast—three times—a pre-trial interview between the accused and the sheriff. Commented the court:

> ". . . To the tens of thousands who saw and heard it, in a very real sense this *was* Rideau's trial—at which he pleaded guilty of murder. Any subsequent court proceedings in a community so pervasively exposed to such a spectacle could but be a hollow formality."

Publicity and Fair Trial

If Lee Harvey Oswald had lived, would any trial he could have had been anything less than a "hollow formality"?

The problems of publicity—pre-trial and during trial—by press, radio, and television are complex.

Sam Sheppard was in a different position from Mickey Jelke. His trial on charges of murdering his wife was so public "bedlam reigned at the courthouse" in a "carnival atmosphere" said the U.S. Supreme Court in ordering a new trial twelve years after his conviction.

The Court placed much of the blame on the trial judge who permitted extra chairs to be packed inside the courtroom bar for newsmen so the defendant and his lawyers had to withdraw in order to engage in confidential conversation and jurors were constantly confronted "eyeball to eyeball" by newshawks. The screaming headlines practically naming Sheppard as the killer before the trial and front page editorials which called for "the same third degree to which any other person in similar circumstances is subjected . .." were not lost on the Court.

In a warning which may help considerably to resolve the conflict between rights of free press and fair trial, Justice Clark, for the Court, wrote:

> "From the cases coming here we note that unfair and prejudicial news comment on pending trials has become increasingly prevalent. . . Given the pervasiveness of modern communication and the difficulty of effacing prejudicial publicity from the minds of the jurors, the trial courts must take strong measures to ensure that the balance is never weighed against the accused."

By an Impartial Jury

Implicit in the comment about a trial for Rideau—or Oswald—being a "hollow mockery" is recognition of the right to an "impartial jury."

The constitutional guarantee extends to Federal courts, but all states provide for jury trial for serious crimes and felonies. Even for such misdemeanors as traffic offenses, in most local jurisdictions an accused may demand and get a jury trial—although the jury may be composed of less than twelve and need not reach a unanimous verdict.

The right to be tried by one's peers goes back to the Magna Carta and beyond. It is basic to the Anglo-Saxon system of justice.

How can a jury be picked that is impartial? Particularly in cases where the whole community, which in many instances includes the whole region or the whole nation, has learned about the crime through modern methods of communication.

"A juror," Justice Tom Clark once said, "who reads or sees it, who sees the blood-chilling pictures of the victim, lurid confessions, the ugly weapons, the bloodstained garments, the widow and orphans, may be unable to put them out of mind and decide guilt or innocence on the basis of the evidence properly produced in court."

Someone might reply such judgment underrates the integrity and capacity of the average American to assume a judicial frame of mind when given responsibility for decision. Attorneys accustomed to questioning prospective jurors say those most conscientious will excuse themselves out of an excess of caution, while those most guilty of prejudice are least likely to admit it.

Jury Prejudice

The editorial writer who wondered if the administration of justice in mid-20th Century America is "not so much a search for truth as it is a forum for legal nit-picking" inadvertently bolstered the case for maintaining a jury system untainted by prejudice in so far as humanly possible.

The Colorado Supreme Court "unanimously decided the right to a fair trial had been denied a man—regardless of how guilty he was—because a Denver trial judge neglected to tell a jury not to read press reports of the trial and one juror read such a report."

Continuing to quote the editorial writer:

"The juror thus may have been prejudiced. He learned outside the court room that the defendant had committed at least one major crime in the past.

"The judges don't really know if the juror was prejudiced. Nor do I.

"But I'll bet there was a little prejudice against the defendant elsewhere. I bet the merchant who looked down that gun barrel and, in the anguish of fear, turned over the contents of his cash register, was prejudiced.

"I bet the police officers who risked their lives against a salvo of bullets were prejudiced."

Precisely because those victimized are so prejudiced must the jury be convinced, beyond reasonable doubt, through evidence presented in court that the defendant was the one who actually committed the crime.

Here a new trial was ordered. In cases, however, where defendants in civil rights murder cases are acquitted by juries whose impartiality is questionable, no retrial is possible.

Exclusion of Negroes, of the Spanish-surnamed, or other minorities from jury panels by law has long since been ruled unconstitutional, although it is not required that such actually sit on a specific jury. Yet all-white juries in communities with sizable Negro population still persist. By custom, only names of white citizens manage to get in the box from which the names of prospective jurors are drawn by lot. Can such a jury be impartial in cases where emotional racial issues are involved? In some states convictions have been reversed because persons with Spanish-surnames have been systematically excluded from jury lists.

Women on juries have been in an anomalous position in some states. Florida, for example, limits jury service by women to those who register for it.

When the Sixth Amendment was written, the first Congress was mindful that one of the complaints in the Declara-

tion of Independence was that King George had transported
Colonial citizens across the seas for trial. So federal offenses
must be tried in the state and pre-determined district where
committed.

On the other hand, change of venue, meaning transfer
of a case from one court to another, is permitted in state
courts where inflamed passions or other prejudicial situations
would make it impossible for the accused to get a fair trial.

Right to Counsel

Other procedural safeguards in the Sixth Amendment—
the right to be informed of specific charges, to be confronted
with unfavorable witnesses and to cross examine them, and
to subpoena favorable witnesses—constitute a heritage against
ancient English abuses rarely violated in American criminal
proceedings. Whether such rules of fairness ought also to
apply to quasijudicial hearings of administrative agencies and
legislative hearings is another question—for another chapter.

The extent of the right to counsel, however, constitutes
one of the hottest controversies among jurists and lawyers
today. In the previous chapter the right of a suspect to
request and secure counsel at the point where he is accused
was discussed. Here this right is considered in relation to the
trial itself.

Since Gideon blew the trumpet, courts, the law-enforce-
ment officials, the lawyers, and the prison wardens have been
confounded with confusion. This Gideon is Clarence Earl
Gideon, four times convicted of crime and imprisoned for a
good share of his life. The fourth time, however, he knew
he was not guilty. His trumpet call that a man could not get
a fair trial without a lawyer reached the ears of the United
States Supreme Court. After hearing arguments it agreed
with his contention that there can be no equal justice where
the kind of a trial a man gets depends on the amount of
money he has.

More formally, Gideon, from his cell in the Florida
penitentiary petitioned the Supreme Court to review his

conviction on the ground that, at his trial, he asked the state court for the aid of counsel and was denied. In June, 1962, the Supreme Court decided to hear the case involving the right of an indigent defendant to have a court-appointed counsel. It appointed Abe Fortas, later to sit on that highest bench himself, to prepare Gideon's appeal. The following March the court unanimously reversed Gideon's conviction, declaring, in the words of Justice Hugo Black, "Any person haled into court who is too poor to hire a lawyer, cannot be assured a fair trial unless counsel is provided for him."

Counsel for Indigents

Twenty-one years before, Justice Black had been in the minority opposing a decision that only cases punishable by death, or where the issues were so complex, or the defendant demonstrably harmed by denial of counsel, required state courts to furnish a lawyer. Even this opinion broke the tradition that the Sixth Amendment right to counsel meant a person was entitled to secure a lawyer if he could—not to be provided one if he could not afford it.

The *Gideon* case greatly extended the right to counsel. It particularly affected thirteen states, including Florida, which had no guarantee of the right to counsel in their state constitutions. In Florida alone over 5000 prisoners were serving time on convictions after trials in which they had no counsel. Practically all of them petitioned for retrial—with counsel. Over a thousand were released unconditionally either because they had served a large share of their sentences or because records and witnesses were no longer obtainable. Nonetheless only about four per cent of those released had returned with new convictions the first year or so—compared to an average of twenty percent of parolees who return to prison.

The second trial of Clarence Gideon demonstrates why the right to counsel is important. Gideon had been charged with burglarizing a poolroom across the street from where he lived. Missing were four bottles of wine, twenty-four cans of beer, and twelve bottles of pop as well as an undetermined amount of change from the jukebox. Gideon admitted being in and out of the poolroom, that he had been drinking heavily, and that he remembered nothing about that weekend. At the first trial, the state's chief witness testified he had seen Gideon in the poolroom, come out the back door and call a cab.

At his second trial his court-appointed attorney brought out testimony that the eyewitness had indicated to a nearby grocer he was himself the chief suspect but he "thought" Gideon was the one who did it. Furthermore, none of those who saw Gideon call a cab saw him carrying anything. The second jury acquitted him. His attorney simply probed for facts, which in his case did not establish beyond reasonable doubt he was guilty of the petty larceny.

Public Defenders

As a result of the *Gideon* decision Florida established a public defender system to provide counsel for those unable to pay for lawyers. Public defenders, salaried officials serving under varying arrangements, have been employed in some cities and states for many years but their use has been limited. An alternative more widely used is the court appointment of an attorney, usually but not always, paid from public funds, for a particular indigent defendant faced with serious charges. Appointed defense attorneys in federal courts serve without fee, although bills setting up a federal defender system have been before Congress.

With recent decisions, such as *Gideon* and *Escobedo,* indicating all criminal suspects are entitled to counsel—and earlier than the actual trial—the public defender system may be expected to become more widespread. That government employees both prosecute and defend an accused person is not incongruous, as might appear, for the purpose of attorneys is not a contest of wits but the means to get at the truth. No judicial system ever devised has proven as effective at doing just that as the adversary system developed by Anglo-Saxon jurisprudence.

One problem arising under either public defender or court appointed counsel is determining who can afford to pay and who cannot.

An argument raised against the public defender system is that the defender, or one of his assistants, may treat many cases perfunctorily. Except when unusual circumstances are evident, the accused is advised to plead guilty, it is charged.

This scarcely squares with the assertion that the requirement a suspect be informed of his right to counsel each time he is interrogated will dry up confessions and guilty pleas. Nobody questions the fact that a majority of convictions—for crimes large and small—result from pleas of guilty.

On the other hand the Nevada attorney general, Harvey Dickerson, predicts that eventually all confessions, whether voluntary or not, will be abolished. He expresses doubt that removing confessions from admission as court evidence would hamper law enforcement officials or prosecutors in obtaining convictions.

Probably most police and district attorneys would disagree vehemently. Yet the "criminal elite"—members of crime syndicates, dope peddlers, vice lords and such—inevitably know and use their right to refuse to say anything at any stage without their attorneys at their elbows. It is those charged for the first time who are most likely to be ignorant of their rights—the very ones who need the protection of due process and fair trial.

Protection against Self Incrimination

Attorney General Dickerson referred to the *Griffen* case in his comment about confessions. *Griffen* completes the trio of names—*Gideon, Escobedo* and *Griffen*—by which the United States Supreme Court has tightened the guidelines for fair trial. In the *Griffen* case it invalidated a California law which permitted a judge or prosecutor to comment on the failure of a defendant to take the witness stand on his own behalf. Such comment, in effect, denied his right not to incriminate himself.

Only since 1964 has the Fifth Amendment provision that no person "shall be compelled in any criminal case to be a witness against himself" been held to apply equally to state cases through the due process clause of the Fourteenth Amendment.

"We must condemn," Justice Tom Clark wrote earlier, "the practice of imputing a sinister meaning to the exercise under the Fifth Amendment. The right of an accused person to refuse to testify, which had been in England merely a rule of evidence, was so important to our forefathers that they raised it to the dignity of a constitutional enactment. . .

". . . We scored the assumption that those who claim this privilege are either criminals or perjurors. . .

". . . A witness may have a reasonable fear of prosecution and yet be innocent of any wrongdoing. The privilege serves to protect the innocent who otherwise might be ensnared by ambiguous circumstance."

Extent of Fifth Amendment Protection

While the Fifth Amendment states the protection against self-incriminations applies to criminal cases, it is interpreted to extend to grand jury, legislative, and administrative investigations which could lead to criminal prosecutions. It applies to production of documents as well as giving testimony which might incriminate an individual—but not to records of corporations or associations. It applies to answering questions innocent in themselves which might lead to incriminating ones.

If one chooses to testify he cannot choose which questions he will answer and which ones he will not. If he answers some he must answer all. That is why attorneys often advise their clients not to answer any questions at all.

Congress and most state legislatures have passed "immunity laws" which require a person to testify in certain situations but protect him from criminal prosecution resulting from his testimony. Contempt convictions under such laws have been held constitutional. Nonetheless, many jurists and attorneys are concerned lest the guarantee that one cannot be compelled to testify against one's self be too narrowly restricted.

Basically the protection against compelling one to testify against himself is inherent in the presumption that a man is considered innocent until proved guilty beyond reasonable doubt by evidence properly presented.

Once the high court ruled inadmissable evidence gained in a narcotics case by pumping a man's stomach after he had swallowed the pills when apprehended. This was held to be compelled self-incrimination.

But pricking a person's finger to obtain a blood sample to test its alcohol content does not constitute similarly compelled self-incrimination even though one may be too badly injured—or too drunk—or refuses to give consent. This is the gist of a 5-4 decision in 1966. Obviously the Court was concerned with the growing problem of traffic accidents and its relation to drunken driving. Circumstances do alter interpretation of constitutional law! Justice Brennan in the Court's opinion, however, indicated "minor intrusions into an individual's body" must be "under stringently limited conditions."

No Double Jeopardy

When his conviction was reversed, Clarence Gideon thought he would go free. He was wrong. The Supreme Court remanded his case for a new trial, in which he was acquitted. This second trial did not constitute double jeopardy, prohibited by the Fifth Amendment.

It is settled American law that there is no bar to re-trial where a conviction is set aside because of an error in proceedings leading to the conviction. If, however, Gideon had been acquitted in his first trial, he could not have been tried again on the same charges.

One can, however, be convicted in both state and federal courts on the same set of facts where state and federal laws cover the same crime. In the late Fifties defendants were convicted under Illinois law for conspiring to dynamite telephone company property. Then they were convicted under Federal statutes for having conspired to destroy communication lines "operated and controlled" by the United States government. Justices Black, Warren, and Douglas dissented in this case. In another case decided the same day, an Illinois state conviction of robbing a savings and loan association was upheld although the defendant had been acquitted in a Federal court of the same offense, robbing a Federally-insured institution. These three justices argued that the double jeopardy clause applied to the states as well as the Federal government, that double prosecution was "so contrary to the spirit of our free country" as to violate the then prevailing view of the limit of the Fourteenth Amendment.

Theirs probably would be a majority opinion today rather than that of Justice Frankfurter who held "a long, unbroken, unquestioned course of impressive adjudication" upheld a second trial after an earlier acquittal by another government for the same offense.

Punishment and Fines

What constitutes "cruel and unusual punishment" or "excessive fines"—both prohibited by the Eighth Amendment?

The answer today may well be quite different from that when this amendment was adopted. Indeed, over a half century ago, in 1910, the Supreme Court asserted that its application was not to be limited to "an experience of evils" known at the time of its adoption.

A man in the Philippines, then a territorial possession of the United States, had been sentenced to fifteen years imprisonment for making false entries in public records, and condemned to carry a chain attached at the ankle and hanging from the wrist. This constituted cruel and unusual punishment regardless of whether such practices would have been condoned in the 18th century.

The ban on cruel and unusual punishment was designed primarily to prevent maiming and other bodily indignities, all too common in the 17th and 18th centuries. In recent years it has been extended to punishment for drug addiction by recognizing addiction as an illness demanding treatment rather than mere incarceration. A more severe penalty for a lesser crime than for a more serious one has been held cruel and unusual. Likewise a fine so heavy a person discharging it by serving time in jail would be imprisoned for a lifetime and more has been held to be excessive.

Proponents of abolition of capital punishment argue the time has come to reassess the death penalty as cruel and unusual, even though a succession of court cases run to the contrary. No longer is a man hanged for stealing sheep as in 17th century England or a woman put to death for witchcraft as in Colonial New England. Times do change. Modern insights in psychology, criminology and other behavioral sciences do make a difference. Other, and perhaps more compelling arguments on capital punishment than it offends the Eighth Amendment, will be considered in the final chapter, dealing with "frontier issues."

Juries in Civil Cases

Right to a jury trial in civil cases, or suits at common law, guaranteed in the Seventh Amendment, applies to federal courts only. In appeals from such cases the appelate courts cannot question the facts as determined by the jury—only whether some error has been made in applying the law.

Most civil cases, by far, are tried in state courts. In forty-four of the fifty states trial by jury is guaranteed without distinction between civil and criminal trials, and for civil cases in two of the states. In many states juries of less than twelve are permitted in civil actions, while several permit civil verdicts on three-fourths or five-sixths of the jury vote.

In civil cases trial by jury is waived much more frequently than in criminal cases. To break the logjam of congested court calendars, it has been suggested that trial by judge alone be substituted for jury trial in civil cases. This is the practice in England, except for cases involving charges of fraud or dishonesty. Perhaps that works in England with 50 highly competent judges, but the suggestion would tamper with the very bulwark of the federal and state bills of rights. Decisions of some two or three thousand judges, at various levels, elected or appointed under varying degrees of political consideration and of judicial ability, do not afford as great a guarantee of justice as the deliberation of juries of one's peers, however unpredictable they may sometimes seem.

In an America on wheels a large proportion of civil lawsuits are personal injury claims resulting from traffic accidents. To modernize our system of fair trial, including the right to a jury trial, to accommodate these cases requires as great ingenuity as, perhaps, designing and building a system of freeways for this traffic.

The Mentally Ill and Juvenile Offenders

It was a great advance when those who were mentally ill or insane and offenders of tender years ceased to be treated as ordinary criminals, subject to all the rigors of criminal procedure.

Juvenile delinquents and the mentally ill are considered under modern concepts of law not to be fully accountable for their acts. Therefore proceedings against them should not be directed toward determining their "guilt beyond a reasonable doubt." Rather "fair trial" in these special categories should be designed to prescribe a course of action which will best help them, as well as protect society.

That is the theory of both the juvenile court system and the mental commitment laws. The practice, however, is too often far different from the theory. Grave abuses can follow, in the name of the welfare of the juvenile or the possibly ill, of the procedural safeguards of fair trial developed in our Anglo-Saxon adversary system.

Although the treatment of the mentally ill has miraculously advanced in the past decade through the use of wonder drugs and modern therapy, it is still possible in most states for a person to be locked up on the complaint of a relative, a doctor, or even any citizen on the ground he is dangerous to himself and society.

Each year 200,000 persons are locked up against their will because they are judged "insane". An increasing number, however, voluntarily commit themselves to mental hospitals for treatment. Obviously a person demonstrably violent or engaging in overt anti-social acts must be restrained, even before a formal hearing. In most instances, however, a hearing may be held before even a temporary commitment for observation and treatment.

Here the question becomes whether the hearing is real and meaningful or whether it is routine and perfunctory. In many instances a judge may hear dozens of cases in a day, merely signing an order on the say-so of a physician who may or may not have any psychiatric training.

Obviously the word of the person alleged to be mentally ill cannot be accepted at face value, for delusions of persecution is one of the most common forms of mental illness. Yet cases where a spouse seeks to put his or her partner away, or a relative seeks to get control of a person's property by becoming the court-appointed conservator are not uncommon.

Fair Sanity Hearings

Numerous suggestions have been made to assure due process in commitment procedures. Insanity laws are being changed in numerous states, embodying some of these suggestions. The very fact that the term "insanity", a legal and proper designation, is not recognized by the medical profession illustrates some of the problems encountered in framing such laws.

A man has a right to be at his own sanity hearing with advance notice so he can arrange his defenses, say proponents of a model law. A psychiatrist might counter that in some cases this would be a traumatic experience harmful to the patient.

The model code would guarantee the right of counsel to the defendant in a sanity hearing unless he formally waives that right. Two doctors with psychiatric training would have to certify his need for hospital care. His lawyer would have the right to question the doctors. Doctors of the patient's own choosing could also testify for him.

In some states a defendant in a sanity hearing has the right to appeal the findings to a court with a lay jury within a specified number of days. How near to the dark ages the laws have been is indicated by the terms used until recently —"lunacy hearing" instead of "sanity hearing", for example.

More dramatic in effect has been the amazing reduction of the number of patients in mental hospitals, up to fifty per cent in some states. Modern treatment and out-patient care is responsible for most of the reduction, of course, but periodic re-examination required by new laws has restored more than a few "forgotten" patients to their community. Some of these should never have been committed in the first place; others had been "restored to reason" through treatment.

The existence of laws providing due process may mean they need not be applied. An attorney told a doctor at New York's famed Bellevue Hospital he was going to represent a patient at a hearing the next day for a long-time commitment. Whereupon the doctor said "Consider him released." The patient was being held under New York's 10-day "hold and treat" law.

A "bill of rights" proposed in a bill before Congress on the hospitalization of the mentally ill in the District of Columbia specifies that mental patients would not, unless adjudged incompetent, lose their rights to vote, execute documents, or buy and sell property, etc. Property rights, in particular, are often the cause of family altercations which augment, or even produce, mental instability.

Criminal Insanity

What has been said thus far applies to mental illness not connected with criminal acts. The phrase "innocent by reason of insanity" conjures up another set of difficult questions. Where is the line dividing responsibility for criminal action from unaccountability because of an abnormal mental condition? Who determines this line and how? What, indeed, is abnormal, criminal insanity, mental illness—or whatever term you prefer?

These are questions which divide the legal profession from the medical profession. More than that, lawyers argue among themselves. Psychiatrists also reach sharply different conclusions on the same case. Laymen on a jury where an insanity plea is the defense must decide which experts, giving diametrically opposite opinions, to believe. Legislators in various states wrestle with attempts to write statutes which will recognize the conclusions of modern science while protecting society from possible laxity toward those prone to anti-social acts under the excuse of insanity.

Historically, the inability to distinguish right from wrong has been the test for criminal insanity. That is the well known McNaghten rule, named after a case in England which marked a great advance from the earlier practice of persecuting the insane because they possessed devils. This test is still the law in most states.

The Durham rule, in effect in New Hampshire and, by court decision, in Washington, D.C., holds that a person is not criminally responsible "if his unlawful act was the product of mental disease or mental defect." This more nearly accords with the accepted medical findings that severe and dangerous mental sickness may exist side by side with ability to tell right from wrong. Determination of whether a mentally ill individual can refrain from doing what he knows is wrong is a medical judgment, not a moral one. Acceptance of this view—if it comes—may result in modifications in laws governing criminal insanity that are neither strictly "McNaghten" nor strictly "Durham."

Reversing the assumption that an offender prefers the "not guilty by reason of insanity" plea is the case of a short-check artist who sought to plead guilty. The judge, however, found him not guilty by reason of insanity and committed him indefinitely to a mental institution. It took a U. S. Supreme Court decision to get him out. Its opinion held a law requiring mandatory commitment for those acquitted of a crime by reason of insanity applied only to those voluntarily pleading insanity as their defense. Otherwise a judge could commit a person for a far longer period than the penalty specified for the crime—without the procedural safeguards of a full sanity hearing.

An even more bizarre—and shocking—use of insanity laws to circumvent justice is the case of a Virginia trash collector. At 3 A.M. a lunacy commission hearing sent him to an institution for the criminally insane. On the commission was a psychiatrist who had earlier employed a "mental telepathist" to hover over the graves of a murdered family to try to throw light on the unsolved murder. On the advice of the telepathist, alone, to look for a man whose business was either junk or garbage, this trash collector was questioned by police. When they failed to turn up any evidence, the psychiatrist prevailed on the man's wife to sign commitment papers! Fortunately an attorney for the American Civil Liberties Union filed a *habeas corpus* petition. Whereupon the hospital authorities conceded the man was not indeed insane and released him.

Justice and Juveniles

"We don't have juveniles in this county. If they're old enough to steal, they are old enough to go to jail," a county judge is quoted as saying. He had sentenced two 14-year-old girls to a year on an industrial farm as vagrants—at a hearing where neither an attorney nor their parents were present. Later an attorney persuaded the judge to place them on probation.

It was a great advance when Illinois, in 1899, adopted the first juvenile court law. Its fundamental purpose, as described by a bar association at the time, was

> "that the state must step in and exercise guardianship over a child found under such adverse social or individual conditions as develop crime. . . It proposed a plan where he may be treated, not as a criminal or one legally charged with crime but as a ward of the state. . ."

Today all states have juvenile court laws. In most instances, however, children's court hearings are only a part of a judge's total judicial responsibility. Specialized courts dealing exclusively with juvenile delinquency, dependence, and neglect are found generally in large population centers. The upper age limit of jurisdiction varies, with 16 to 18 being the prevailing range.

The essence of the juvenile hearing is that it is not a criminal trial, but a determination of whether a child is delinquent and, if so, the best course of treatment for its rehabilitation. The judge is supposed to act as a parent might in meting out discipline.

Analogous to the tension between the psychiatric and legalistic approaches to insanity is that between the social work and the "fair trial" aspects of juvenile delinquency proceedings.

Informality of hearing, absence of the adversary atmosphere with strict adherence to rules of evidence, decision on the basis of "preponderance of evidence" rather than "proof beyond reasonable doubt"—in theory these protect the interests of the child. In practice, however, the absence of due process safeguards may give rise to abuse, particularly when a judge may dispose of several cases a day.

Sometimes a probation officer rather than a judge metes out punishment. The chief probation officer in one county arrested a 17-year-old for saying, "Jesus Christ" to a housewife and fined him $25 for blasphemy. Three days later he fined the youth another $25 on the same offense and committed him. When an attorney called the court there was no record of the commitment.

Suggested Improvements

A pamphlet published by the U. S. Department of Health, Education, and Welfare suggests that juveniles taken into custody be taken to their homes for questioning—or some other place approved by the parents. It reminded the police that the child should be instructed as to the significance of his own statements, informed of his rights to remain silent, and told that he may contact his parents and attorney.

Some juvenile court judges insist that parents be present at a hearing. One even appoints counsel in serious cases, not so much as an advocate but to advise the child and parents as to their legal rights. Social work-oriented professionals complain an attorney at a juvenile hearing injects the litigious aspects of a criminal trial into the hearing, subjects an already emotionally-disturbed child to further trauma through cross-examination, and contributes little to developing the facts. Indeed, in a large proportion of cases, there is no question about the allegations involved.

Obviously, circumstances vary greatly according to the age of the child and the seriousness of the offense. Teenagers with their own cars, with little parental supervision, who pull hold-ups, or vandalize, or assault persons are subject to incarceration for considerable periods in reform schools—by whatever name they bear.

Should such culprits be denied their due process rights—prompt arraignment, bail, confrontation, production of witnesses in their favor, advice of counsel, even a jury—merely because the proceedings are held not to be a criminal trial? The problems of maintaining the sociological values of the juvenile court system and the constitutional rights of those affected need continuing examination.

Publicity and Juveniles

Most states provide that names of juvenile offenders may not be published. In 1961 Montana opened the door to the public on juvenile felony cases. Non-felony cases are still heard in closed court.

The district judge who helped write the law and is its most ardent advocate claims it is working well, that it has reduced the extreme violence so "a woman can walk the streets of Helena at night and no one will bother her." Judge Lester H. Loble maintains that publicity is the twin enemy of crime, along with fear of punishment. Among the gains he says, "the delinquent parent becomes conscious of what his child is doing" and the good youth does not get blamed for what a hoodlum does because publicity makes known the culprit.

Such views are shared by few social work professionals— nor indeed by Judge Loble's colleagues in Montana. He is practically the only judge who has made use of the law, and the number of juveniles appearing before him has declined because juvenile authorities file their cases before other judges.

In its 1966 term the U. S. Supreme Court passed on the first juvenile court case reaching it in the sixty years such courts have existed. It ruled the District of Columbia Juvenile Court must give a minor a hearing and permit him to have counsel. It also agreed to hear an appeal from the Arizona State Supreme Court which held a juvenile did not have to be given notice or legal representation. If the court decides this case as it did the District of Columbia case it will overturn laws and procedures in all states where juvenile proceedings are considered "civil" proceedings rather than criminal trials requiring constitutional safeguards for the children involved.

"A legal fiction, presenting a challenge to credulity and doing violence to reason," is the way the California Supreme Court has described the theory that juvenile cases are merely "civil" matters.

Juvenile Rights

In its 8-to-1 decision in the *Gault* case from Arizona in June of 1967, the U. S. Supreme Court held that children in juvenile courts are entitled to *at least*, (1) to notice of charges, (2) representation by counsel, including court appointment if indigent, (3) to the protection of the privilege against self-incrimination, (4) and to the right of cross examination. Thus the prediction made above in the first printing of this volume has materialized.

18

Punishment Without Crime

"The mere summoning of a witness and compelling him to testify, against his will, about his beliefs, expressions, or associations is a measure of governmental interference. When those forced revelations concern matters that are unorthodox, unpopular, or even hateful to the general public, the reaction in the life of the witness may be disastrous. Those who are identified by witnesses and thereby placed in the same glare of publicity are equally subject to public stigma, scorn and obloquy."

—CHIEF JUSTICE EARL WARREN

"Guilt by association is a dangerous doctrine. It condemns one man for the unlawful conduct of another. It draws ugly insinuations from an association that may be wholly innocent."

—JUSTICE WILLIAM O. DOUGLAS

"The Fifth Amendment is an old friend and a good friend. It is one of the great landmarks in the struggle to be free of tyranny, to be decent and civilized. It is our way of escape from torture, it protects man against any form of the inquisition."

—JUSTICE DOUGLAS

218

"Those who wrote the Constitution well knew the danger inherent in special legislative acts which take away life, liberty, or property of particular persons because the legislature thinks them guilty of conduct which deserves punishment."

—JUSTICE HUGO L. BLACK

"Time was when the investigations were justified by Congress' need for information as a basis for wise legislation. Now they often serve chiefly as a wailing-wall for the penitent and a whipping post for the recalcitrant."

—TELFORD TAYLOR

Exposure through legislative investigations is a powerful weapon. Indeed, it has proved a means of inflicting the punishment of "public stigma, scorn and obloquy" (quoting Justice Warren) as well as loss of jobs where conviction in a criminal court would be well nigh impossible.

Nearly a century ago the U. S. Supreme Court laid down limitations on the investigative powers of Congress. The House of Representatives had appointed a select committee to investigate the failure of one of the financial enterprises of Jay Gould and his banking associates. One of them refused to answer the committe's questions and was jailed for contempt. He sued for false arrest. The Supreme Court decided that the House had engaged in "a fruitless investigation into the personal affairs of individuals"—fruitless in the sense "that it could result in no valid legislation on the subject" of the inquiry.

The legitimate function of legislative investigation is to obtain information useful in writing laws. In practical operation, however, the authority of Congress to make investigations has rarely been restricted because of a questionable relationship to this function.

Recent Investigations

In recent years major legislative investigations have been concerned with loyalty and security—or perhaps more accurately with disloyalty and "Un-Americanism." Merely to list famed investigations of the past, however, is to indicate that the problems of due process and constitutional rights in this area are not confined to subversion and the Cold War.

The list is almost endless. Some of the more famous Congressional probes of this century include that of the "Money Trust" before the First World War, the Teapot Dome scandal of the Twenties, the Munitions and Stock Exchange investigations of the Thirties, the Labor-Management, TV Payola Scandal, and the influence-peddling investigation involving Sherman Adams and Bernard Goldfine of the Fifties. The quarter-century span of the House Un-American Activities Committee and the slightly shorter era of the Senate Internal Affairs Sub-Committee of the Judiciary Committee, of course, surpass in continued operation and scope all of the other investigations.

Out of numerous investigations have come new laws, particularly legislation creating regulatory bodies. The Interstate Commerce Commission and the Security and Exchange Commission are two examples. Such administrative agencies —and their numbers increase with the growing complexity of modern life—are given quasi-judicial power to make and enforce regulations. Not an insignificant part of this regulatory function is investigation of those subject to regulation. The protection of the due process rights of individuals against bureaucratic infringement is akin to the safeguards which should prevail in legislative investigations.

What is said of Congressional investigations and Federal agencies applies with equal force to state legislative investigations and administrative agencies. Some of the most flagrant instances of "exposure for exposure's sake" and "public inquisition" have resulted from state legislative investigations.

Inquisition or Investigation?

Robert Shelton, Grand Dragon of the United Klans of America, boasted that the publicity given the Ku Klux Klan by the investigations of the House UnAmerican Activities Committee would double the membership of that organization.

Regardless of how ridiculous his boast sounded, just what was accomplished by the long heralded "exposure" of the Klandom by HUAC? Shelton, as did the rest of the Kleagles, Klods, and Klucks took the Fifth Amendment when questioned by Chairman Edwin E. Willis of Louisiana and Rep. Charles Weltner of Georgia. That was their right, as it is of every American to refrain from incriminating himself, to be considered innocent until proven guilty beyond reasonable doubt.

About all that comes out during the dull series of hearings were allegations, made in the form of questions. "Is it not true that . . . etc.?" Many of the allegations concerned the mulcting of funds for the personal use of Klan officials, from collections and sales of paraphernalia, profiteering in sheeting robes, made by informers within the organization. Little light was shed on the terrorism, the destruction of life and property, and the collusion of law enforcement officials in condoning such unlawful activities.

If the Federal Bureau of Investigation—an agency of the Justice Department—has informers within Klan membership, why should not their knowledge of illegal activity be made the basis of grand jury indictments and arrests? While, in some instances, local law enforcement in some Southern communities has proven itself paralyzed on racial issues, practically all of the alleged crimes brought before HUAC could be prosecuted under Federal law—using the mails to defraud, embezzlement in interstate commerce, depriving a person of his civil rights under color of law, etc., etc. If new laws are needed to curb illegal activities of the Ku Klux Klan, that need was not brought out in the HUAC hearings.

"Investigation of Propaganda"

Indeed, the UnAmerican Activities Committee was faithful to its Congressional mandate—to investigate UnAmerican propaganda activities.

"Who can define the meaning of 'UnAmerican'?" asked Chief Justice Earl Warren. Since when has engaging in propaganda activities—respecting freedom of speech and press—been subject to restriction by Congress, contrary to the First Amendment, either by law or by investigation? That is a question being asked by civil libertarians.

True, a bare majority of the U. S. Supreme Court has held that because the Communist Party believes "in the ultimate overthrow of the Government of the United States by force and violence", investigation of advocacy or preparation for overthrow is a legitimate subject for a Congressional inquiry.

Should, then, the ridiculous cross-burnings and racist rallies of sheeted bigots be equated with a world-wide ideology as a threat to the nation? Perhaps the more vital issue is whether any threat, large or small, can be met by mere exposure by an investigating committee.

Typical of those who answer in the affirmative is columnist David Lawrence who once wrote:

> "There is only one way to combat the Communist Conspiracy, and that is by exposure. There is only one instrument by which that can be done without encountering technical barriers—the congressional investigating committee."

"Technical barriers" would appear to refer to the due process safeguards of the Bill of Rights. At least that is a view that permeates much popular thinking and certainly that which has been demonstrated by most of the congressmen who have served on these committees.

How Effective?

Opposing this thesis is the one which maintains that the record shows such investigating committees have been quite ineffectual in dealing with the Communist menace, or the threat of extra-legal activities by outfits like the Klan. Furthermore the net of exposure ensnares many innocents— subjecting them to punishment without crime.

Congress, in all of its attempts to curb Communism, has never made belonging to the Communist Party a crime. It is, however, a crime to knowingly conspire to advocate action to overthrow the government by force and violence. It is not a crime to attend or speak at a Klan rally, however ridiculous, but it is a crime, in many states, to appear in public hiding one's identity. It is always a crime to assault, to maim, to extort, to kill.

The very case cited by David Lawrence to bolster his contention that only congressional investigations can combat the Communist conspiracy refutes it—the Alger Hiss case. It was a libel case against Whittaker Chambers for accusations made outside the privileged committee room which produced the State Department papers, the crucial evidence showing Hiss an agent for the Communists. It was a grand jury investigation, under the rules of criminal procedure, which resulted in the conviction of Hiss for perjury.

It might be argued that had not the congressional investigating committee first "exposed" Alger Hiss the judicial procedures would not have followed. That assumption, however, must be predicated on another—that the Federal Bureau of Investigation and the Justice Department are incapable of doing their job of bringing evidence of law violation before a grand jury for investigation and indictment. Are men like Whittaker Chambers such prima donnas that they will present their evidence only in the publicity spotlight of a congressional investigation? If so, maintaining loyalty and security is in a bad way for America.

Claiming "The Fifth"

Even if it is granted that the House Un-American Activities Committee and the Senate Internal Affairs sub-committee have alerted the nation to Communist infiltration into government agencies and private organizations during the past twenty or thirty years, the pertinent question remains. It is: Are innocent persons punished without crime—without any of the procedural safeguards developed over hundreds of years in England and America?

"Are you, or have you ever been, a member of the Communist Party or of any organization cited as subversive?" That is almost the first question asked of every witness. If you claim the Fifth Amendment protection against self incrimination you are branded as a "Fifth Amendment Communist." "Obviously" if you will not answer "No" you must be a past or present Commie, according to those who so brand you.

But that conclusion is far from obvious! If you do not claim the Fifth Amendment at the outset, you waive it and must answer all subsequent questions. You cannot pick and choose.

During the depression of the Thirties and World War II when Russia was our ally, tens of thousands of Americans joined the Communist Party in the idealistic belief it might contribute to solving problems of the times. Hundreds of thousands joined organizations—including labor unions—in which Communists participated (and sometimes took over) on specific issues. In both instances such membership was perfectly legal. If you were one who was once a member of the Communist party and, like many, became disillusioned, and answered the key question, you could then be required to detail the circumstances and provide the names of others you knew as Party members who may or may not have come to regret their activities.

If you admit membership in one of the so-called Communist-front organizations—which you may or may not have known was infiltrated—you still are not out of the woods. Such admission might lead to further questions which blur the distinctions between technical party membership and action to further a Party end, the specific one of which— say reduction of working hours or promoting disarmament— is a legitimate one shared by many non-communists.

But, it is said, the privilege against self-incrimination is guaranteed only in criminal cases—and no crime is alleged. Hold on a minute! Perjury is a crime. Libel is a crime. Contempt for failure to answer a proper question may bring a prison term. Since 1940, under the Smith Act as interpreted by the courts, knowingly to advocate, or conspiring to advocate, the overthrow of the government by force and violence is a crime. In testifying about events and persons out of the past in response to adroitly-worded questions, who can be sure that he will not be snared into self-incrimination?

Historically, the protection against forcing one to accuse himself came out of an era when the chief crimes were heresies, oaths, and treasons against a king or governor. The protection was designed against inquisitorial proceedings. So the use of the Fifth Amendment before investigating bodies has strong historical precedents. Indeed, Presidents Andrew Jackson and Ulysses S. Grant are among the distinguished persons who claimed the privilege against self-incrimination when asked by Congress concerning certain of their acts.

Branding a witness with a "Fifth Amendment" label is not the only weapon HUAC and similar committees in state legislatures have in their arsenal for unfriendly witnesses. Indeed, even to be called before a committee (with subpoenas being given advance publicity) has cost scores of persons their jobs. Numerous others whose names have been dropped by a "friendly" witness have been fired by their employers, without ever being afforded an opportunity to present their side of the story or confront their accusers on cross examination. Loss of employment is indeed punishment.

Proper Investigatory Procedures

How can the historic right of Congress and State legislatures to investigate matters within their competence and jurisdiction be reconciled with the due process rights of individuals? The answer is in rules of procedure which though short of the formal legalism of the courts, protect individuals against the excesses which occur because committees are prone to operate with no rules at all.

In the Thirties a congressional committee investigating lobbying activities cited for contempt Edward A. Rumely for failure to produce the names of those who had purchased right-wing literature of the Committee for Constitutional Government in the amount of $500 or more. The law provided that contributors of $500 or more to lobbying organizations must be identified. Rumely therefore had such donors buy his literature. The Supreme Court unanimously held the First Amendment guarantee of free press protected the anonymity of such purchasers.

Count this a victory for the First Amendment! Even though five high court justices have considered the advocacy of the violent overthrow of the government so entwined with overt action as to be a proper subject of legislation, the *Rumely* decision serves as warning that neither Congress nor State legislatures can interfere with freedom of speech and press.

Three Americans went to the State Department in 1963 to ask that a temporary visa be granted to a Japanese law professor to make a 10-day speaking tour across the country on peace, particularly advocating the cessation of nuclear testing. Their petition was granted. A year later a sub-committee of HUAC called the three, Mrs. Dagmar Wilson, Mrs. Donna Allen, and Russell Nixon, to inquire whether the State Department had violated the intent of Congress in the McCarran-Walter Immigration Act in admitting a peace speaker to this country who was alleged to be "anti-United States" and associated with international peace groups which included members from Communist countries.

The inquiry, the sub-committee decided, was to be held in executive session.

"Ah, no," the American peace workers replied, through their counsel. Without admitting that HUAC had any right to inquire into their First Amendment right to petition for redress of grievances, they said they would willingly testify in public, but not in secret session.

Open or Closed Hearing?

This was the first time in the history of HUAC that witnesses had demanded a public hearing. Very often witnesses have sought executive sessions because, without knowing the evidence against them and unable to confront their accusers with cross examination, they would be subjected to pillorying on the basis of unevaluated allegations, oftimes from anonymous sources.

Indeed, the permanent harm, the destruction of one's reputation, that has resulted to many individuals by mere accusation by investigating committees, suggests the elemental fairness of executive sessions to screen "defamatory, prejudicial, or adverse information" to determine its reliability before exposing it publicly.

On the other hand, the peace workers were so confident they had nothing to hide they felt that the result of a secret hearing would only promote the inference of a sinister relation between their activities against nuclear testing and the international communist conspiracy. "Insinuation" like exposure, has been a weapon of punishment without crime.

Due Process Suggestions

Whether an investigatory hearing is in executive session or public—or, as is more customary, a public hearing follows a private one—due process would appear to demand:

That the person summoned be given adequate notice to give him a fair chance to prepare his testimony;

That he be apprised of the specific matters on which he will be queried;

That he be afforded the right to have counsel present, to advise him and to question, through cross examination, the truth of adverse information;

That he be permitted to testify or offer sworn statements on his behalf;

That he be given assistance of the investigating committee in compelling attendance of witnesses and production of documents reasonably necessary to rebut charges against him;

That no publicity be given to allegations concerning a witness prior to their development in an open hearing.

These, it will be noted, parallel the elements of fair trial in court proceedings. Some will argue that a legislative committee ought not to be bound by rigid rules of procedure like a court. These suggested safeguards, however, fall con-

siderably short of court rules of evidence. They would, however, curb the wild excesses of the past thirty years. Incidentally, early HUAC chairmen, like Reps. Martin Dies and
J. Parnell Thomas, frankly stated their purpose was to attack and discredit Franklin Roosevelt New Dealers as much
as to uncover real Communists. Each house of Congress makes
its own rules, and some improved procedures have resulted
from earlier criticisms. Courts will interfere with such rules
only when individuals prove infringement of their basic
rights.

Contempt Citations

Congress does have the power to cite for contempt, subject
to conviction in a court, for failure to answer legitimate
questions of a congressional committee. "Legitimate" is the
word here, as indicated by the earlier discussion of the
proper role of such committees.

A witness before a committee, assuming he has not invoked the Fifth Amendment, faces a terrific dilemma when
he is asked a question which he or his attorney believe is
beyond the right of the committee. If he refuses to answer
and is cited for contempt, the courts may or may not hold
his refusal is justified. If he answers, he may needlessly expose
matters which he has a constitutional right to keep private
and damage his reputation permanently.

Two solutions to this double-bind have been suggested
in Congress. One is application to a Federal court for determination of the propriety of an inquiry immediately after
it is questioned. The other would be creation of a supervisory committee of Congress to determine whether a contempt citation by an investigating committee is justified,
rather than a decision by the committee itself. In either case,
the witness would be permitted to purge himself of contempt
by answering questions determined to be justified.

The courts, rather than legislative action, may make the
first alternative obligatory. In barring enforcement of two
Louisiana anti-subversive laws, the Supreme Court in 1964,
pointed out that even if the prosecution were not successful,

there might be a "chilling effect" on freedom of expression from the mere fact of prosecution. No witness before a modern investigatory body put more forcefully reasons for refusing to answer improper, irrelevant questions than that contankerous printer, John Lilliburne, in 1638. He told the Star Chamber:

"Why do you ask me all these questions? These are nothing pertinent to my imprisonment, for I am not imprisoned for knowing and talking to such and such a man but for sending over books (from Holland) . . . I see you go about this examination to ensnare me; for seeing the things for which I am imprisoned cannot be proved against me, you will get other matter out of my examination; and therefore if you will not ask me about the thing laid to my charge, I will answer no more; but if you will ask me of that, I shall then answer and do answer for the thing for which I am imprisoned, which is for sending over books, I am clear, for I sent none."

The dissenter was fined and whipped, but he preached vehemently from the pillory where he was flogged. Three years later the House of Commons vindicated him and awarded a substantial sum for damages. How much Congress would owe if all who had been impertinently questioned and persecuted for "knowing and talking to such and such a man" were awarded damages for public pillorying!

Due Process in Administrative Agencies

What has been said concerning procedural rules of fair hearing before legislative committees has equal validity for administrative agencies.

Of bureaus, boards, and commissions, at local, state and federal level there appears to be no limit—and no end of types and methods of operation. Every citizen, at one time or many times, is involved in their operations and decisions.

Some are known as "quasi-judicial" bodies. Their procedures in hearings closely follow court rules, more or less.

Respondents are notified of the matters to be heard, are permitted counsel—who may or may not produce witnesses and records and confront other witnesses—make arguments and file briefs.

The Interstate Commerce Committee and its state counterparts which license common carriers and fix transportation charges are an example of long established quasi-judicial agencies operating according to well-fixed rules.

Others are less formally patterned after judicial bodies— nor should they be, if they are to perform the functions for which they are established. Generally they are set up to "protect the public interest" in fact-finding, in developing administrative rules for day-to-day operation, in granting licenses, and adjudicating violations. Those who complain of "bureaucracy" say the "bureau" becomes the executive, the legislature, the prosecutor, judge, and jury all rolled into one. While some truth may lie in the charge, the "bureau" must follow laws adopted by Congress or the state legislature, its members are appointed by the executive, and its findings subject to judicial review—at least as to procedures.

Fair Procedures

Usually no allegation of crime is involved, although failure to obey a "cease and desist" order of the Food and Drug Administration to stop selling filth-contaminated cereal or misbranded, dangerous drugs may lead to criminal prosecution. The same is true of false-advertising orders of the Federal Trade Commission, or violation of regulations of the Civil Aeronautics Board, National Labor Relations Board, Security Exchange Commission, Department of Internal Revenue, a State Board of Health, etc., etc.

It is not "punishment" in a formal sense to be denied a driver's license, or lose one's license to practice a profession because of infringement of rules of the particular professional licensing board, or to face suspension of one's broadcast license by the Federal Communications Commission, or to have the value of one's property diminished by re-zoning of the local zoning commission. Certainly, the effect in any of these instances may be more damaging than a fine and jail term.

Few would deny the protection of public interest in these and other areas is not only necessary but also highly desirable.

The problem is that of assuring fairness to all concerned. Categorical rules cannot be laid down. For example, in civil and some criminal proceedings, the defense attorneys are given access to documents the plaintiff attorneys intend to use in evidence. In a proceeding on alleged illegal pricing of milk before the Federal Trade Commission such documents may contain trade secrets and cost data that competitors would give their eye teeth to have made public. Should such proceedings be private? Should counsel for the respondent be allowed to cross-examine those bringing charges as well as his client to rebut adverse testimony? These are two of many questions more easily asked than answered in a very complex area of administrative law. "Due process in administrative agencies" is discussed here, inadequately and incompletely, chiefly to recognize an area of concern if justice for all is to be made real in modern society.

Subversive Activities Control Board

One administrative agency, however, requires further consideration. This is the Subversive Activities Control Board. This was the instrumentality set up by the McCarran Act in 1950, the outgrowth of the Nixon-Mundt bill, designed to ferret out Communist action, Communist-controlled and Communist-infiltrated organizations. The means employed was to require registration of each organization, after a hearing and an order by SACB, including a list of its officers, their aliases, and its periodic financial statements. If an organization so ordered failed to register, then each member was required to register under a penalty of a fine of $10,000 and imprisonment of five years for each day he failed to register. President Harry Truman called the tune in his veto message when he said:

"The idea of requiring Communist organizations to divulge information about themselves is a simple and attractive one, but it is about as practical as requiring thieves to register with the sheriff."

The act was passed over his veto, and 15 years later the U. S. Supreme Court unanimously agreed that nobody could be compelled to register because that would be self-incrimination. The basis of the McCarran Act lay in the concept that Communist organizations were agents of a foreign power. An administrative agency, the SACB, designed to find and punish persons on the basis of what they said and with whom they associated, has been no more effective in dealing with subversion than other past attempts at thought-control in American and English history.

How may the government protect itself from those in a position to imperil national security? Treason is explicitly defined by the Constitution as giving aid and comfort to the enemy, and the proof needed for conviction precisely set forth—the testimony of two witnesses to the same overt act or confession in open court. Laws against sabotage and spying are strict and enforceable.

Loyalty and Security

In the ideological struggle against Communism it has become important to keep persons who might provide information or assistance to foreign Communist powers from sensitive positions before they have the opportunity to do harm.

Such is the rationale of loyalty and security programs. In practice, however, loyalty oaths, security checks, and personnel files have been used to damage the reputation and livelihood of hundreds, even thousands, of persons. Here, indeed, is punishment without crime. Volumes have been written on the subject. Here it suffices to briefly indicate the areas of due process involved.

Loyalty oaths—or non-disloyalty disclaimers, have been widely but not wisely employed. No real subversive is going to hesitate to swear falsely. Those most conscientious are the ones troubled because some past association, innocent or which they thought was innocent at the time, may rise to plague them. A loyalty test oath differs from an ordinary oath of office. The latter is a pledge of faithful performance of duties in the future. A loyalty oath disclaims present or past conduct or opinions.

After the Civil War Missouri attempted to bar attorneys and others from practicing their professions unless they swore they had not been sympathetic to the South. That law was declared unconstitutional. In recent years various state loyalty oaths have likewise been stricken as being vague, discriminatory (e.g. required only of teachers, etc.) or infringements of First Amendment rights. Zechariah Chafee once compared the requirement of a loyalty oath to a husband at a dinner party requiring his wife to swear she had never been unfaithful!

If loyalty oaths are both ineffective and unconstitutional, what about security checks as a means of preventing employment in government positions of disloyal persons? Obviously employees with access to confidential information useful to our opponents in the world's ideological conflict must be trustworthy and thoroughly reliable.

Federal Loyalty Program

How can this be accomplished? Is any security check absolutely error-proof? Should all Federal employees be subject to the same rigorous scrutiny as those in sensitive positions? Should an employee or prospective employee be informed of "derogatory" information placed in his personnel file? Should he be given an opportunity to know who has given this information? To confront his accuser and rebut the accusation through cross-examination? To be restored to his position if unevaluated derogatory information is found to be without foundation?

These questions have been very real in the development of the Federal loyalty program since World War II.

When President Truman issued his executive order requiring security clearance for Federal employees he cited
its two-fold purpose. It sought to afford the maximum protection against infiltration of disloyal persons into the ranks
of Federal employees. At the same time Truman believed it
would provide "equal protection from unfounded accusations
for disloyalty."

In the light of experience, particularly during the heyday
of McCarthyism but even to the present, it is most doubtful
that Truman's second objective has often been achieved.
The effectiveness of his first purpose may also be open to
challenge. Damage to one's reputation, or even livelihood, by
accusation and suspicion can rarely be erased by eventual
vindication.

"Membership in an organization," declared Truman, "is
simply one piece of evidence which may or may not be
helpful in arriving at a conclusion as to the action which
should be taken in a particular case."

If such evidence was considered solely by a fair-minded
and judicious superior—if the raw material which FBI investigators or others place in a person's file about his associations, his friends, his expressed opinions remained confidential—if his whole record were evaluated with all the
safeguards of due process—then, and only then, could it be
said that the two-fold objective expressed by Truman was
accomplished.

Since the original executive order was issued, the loyalty
and security program has been expanded. It has been extended to cover not only Federal employees in sensitive
positions but to employees of firms with defense contracts—
contracts which have access to classified information. Some
firms and some states screen employees and prospective employees for loyalty irrespective of whether their work is
related to the security of the nation.

In 1953 President Eisenhower amended the security
order to state that any person who plead the Fifth Amendment was automatically a "security risk" and not eligible
for work on classified government materials. To defend such

an order on the technicality that such a person was not being punished is to reduce the whole history of the right against self-incrimination to a quibble.

Loyalty Checks in Non-Sensitive Positions

Even more shocking to due process is the action of private companies of discharging employees simply because they "took the Fifth" in refusing to answer questions of a congressional investigating committee. Such employees have little or no recourse. The United Steel Workers took the case of three such employees—working in plants having no defense contracts—to the union-management arbitration board—without success. Furthermore, the workers were refused unemployment benefits on the grounds that they had been fired for just cause.

Government employees in non-sensitive positions are not subjected to the federal security program. This is the guideline laid down by the Supreme Court in 1956 in reinstating an employee in the Health, Education and Welfare Department, who had been fired because of alleged sympathetic associations with Communists. The court said the employee's position did not affect national security.

Yet evidence is available that the U. S. Civil Service Commission may be seeking to get around this decision by invoking regulations permitting removal of an employee where his "conduct or capacity" is such as not to promote efficiency of the service. "Suitability" tests for probationary employees is another way to avoid this decision regarding employees in non-sensitive positions.

Questionnaires to non-sensitive technical and scientific probationers ask about such things as one's knowledge of his relatives' and friends' involvement with alleged Communist causes, of being on a left-wing mailing list, of being invited as a student to a progressive youth club meeting. Even if no use is made of the questionnaires, which allege no wrong-doing, the answers remain in an employee's personnel file in the department where he works.

Pre-Employment Records

The Civil Service Commission, however, settled a case out of court rather than have the U. S. Supreme Court rule on the question of whether the government had the right to fire an employee for acts committed before he entered federal service.

William Lyman Dew had served in the Air Force. Upon his discharge in 1955 he became a file clerk for the CIA (Central Intelligence Agency). To obtain the necessary secret security clearance to handle coded data he underwent a lie detector test. He admitted when in the Air Force in 1951 and 1952 he had smoked marijuana cigarettes on at least five occasions. In 1950, at the age of 18, while a freshman in college he had committed at least four homosexual acts, some for pay. He was permitted to resign his CIA job.

He secured a job as an airways operations specialist with the Civil Aeronatics Board, receiving one promotion and a performance rating of satisfactory. After 20 months, however, his CIA file caught up with him. Charges were filed but he resisted dismissal, securing federal district court orders permitting him to file a psychiatric report. The psychiatrist wrote that Mr. Dew functioned mentally and emotionally within normal range, that he appeared to be happily married and had accepted the responsibilities of parenthood, and that the incidents he had engaged in were isolated and primarily the result of curiosity.

In spite of this report, Dew was fired. He carried his appeal to the U. S. Circuit Court of Appeals for the District of Columbia. It upheld the CAB on the ground that the court lacked the background and experience to dispute the agency's judgment that Dew's removal would promote efficiency of the service. In a stinging dissent, Judge J. Skelly Wright declared if the ruling stood no civil service job would be safe. The pre-employment background of any employee whom some superior wanted to "get" could be searched to dig up something—even his innermost feelings and thoughts through use of lie detector tests.

"The mere threat," commented Judge Wright, "of this kind of inquiry would be sufficient in most cases to cause the resignation of the worker marked for dismissal. . ."

The Supreme Court agreed to hear Dew's appeal, but at this point the Civil Service Commission got the CAB to reinstate Dew with $12,000 back pay. This settlement, it was said, was made so justice could be done because Mr. Dew had been shown "fully rehabilitated and competent . . . and should not be scarred for life by a youthful mistake."

That evidence, of course, was what Dew and his attorneys had been trying to get the government to accept for eight years. Still unsettled, however, is the general issue of whether a government employee may be dismissed on the basis of pre-employment acts regardless of his present competency and trustworthiness.

Federal agencies vary greatly in the methods they employ in making security checks. Two of the bureaus dealing with the most sensitive areas of national security, the Atomic Energy Commission and the National Security Agency permit counsel, or a friend or relative, at interviews. The Civil Service Commission, the U. S. Information Agency and the Navy Department do not, while others discourage the presence of counsel.

Psychological Testing

Under guise of psychological testing, job applicants for State Department positions, the Labor Department's Job Opportunity Program, and the Peace Corps, among others, have been questioned about their religious beliefs, sex life, political attitudes of themselves and their parents, and the magazines they read.

Is there any real difference, one may ask, between such probings into religious and political and personal matters and the ancient inquisitions that our Bill of Rights was designed to prevent? Even in the name of national security or of helping an applicant to self adjustment such modern racks and screws are unjustified punishments without crime.

19

Due Process in
Private Organizations

" 'Due process' is, perhaps, the least frozen concept
of our law—the less confined to history and the most
absorptive of powerful social standards of a progressive
society."

—JUSTICE FELIX FRANKFURTER

"Democratic stockholders meetings are not an
empty abstraction. Without them you are denied a
voice over your own property."

—LEWIS D. GILBERT

"The law cannot create the spirit of self-government. It cannot compel union members to attend
meetings or hold their officers to a strict accounting—
The most the law can do is to secure the opportunity
for workers who wish to take an active part in democratic unions without undue loss of personal freedom."

—FORMER SOL. GEN. ARCHIBALD COX

"The basic rights of citizenship, within unions as within a democratic state, include the rights of free speech, free assembly, and fair elections. In addition, within the union context, it is essential that local meetings be held regularly and conducted fairly."
    —JOEL SEIDMAN, UNIVERSITY OF CHICAGO

What business does a chapter headed "Due Process In Private Organizations" have in a book about the Bill of Rights? Historically, very little. The internal affairs of social clubs and business companies, of religious associations and benevolent societies, were their own concern. Common law shied away from interfering with the rules by which they admitted, disciplined, or expelled members, or with the form of organization, be it democratic or not.

When, however, a social club acquired property or provided benefits (the earliest form of insurance) then the vested interest of the individual member began to be recognized. As developed in English and American law through generations, an individual had to exhaust all remedies within the organization before he could take his case to court.

Rights Within Organizations

As indicated in Chapters 11 and 12, the rights and limits on association have grown in significance as society has become increasingly complex. This chapter is concerned with the rights of an individual within an organization which, theoretically speaking, he is free to join and free to leave—but which may, in practice, greatly affect his economic situation, social standing, cultural acceptance, and good reputation.

"Conform or get out!" What could be a simpler rule for a private organization then that? But the "powerful social standards of a progressive society" demand fairness, not just simplicity.

Dr. Julian M. Firestone is a dentist in New York City. He prepared a talk on dental care for radio broadcast. In accord with the requirement of the American Dental Association he submitted his manuscript for clearance to the ADA's Ethics Committee.

Clearance was denied by this committee because, it said, some of his statements "were not in good taste and not designed to uphold the dignity of the profession. . . The reading of this proposed script was not in the best interest of dentistry and it should not be read over the radio."

Dr. Firestone's proposed talk criticized conventional standards of dental care, and urged improvements of the level of care offered the public. He brought suit and the judge held the ADA could not exercise prior restraint on what Dr. Firestone proposed to say.

His attorney pointed out the "monopolistic character of the association" and its complete control over the dental profession which gave it a quasi-governmental status. Non-compliance with its regulations could mean expulsion of a member, with resulting "loss of prestige and patients, loss of referral patients, loss of opportunity to use hospital facilities, loss of possibility of obtaining teaching positions, etc."

Thus the attempt of the dental association to censor statements of its members designed to reach the public was held equivalent to the denial of free speech by a governmental agency.

Suppose the critical dentist had been a stockholder in a corporation attempting to convince other stockholders to oust the current management; or a union member who sought to discredit union officers.

In the first instance, could not the stockholder be attempting to drive the price of the stock down so he could make a killing? In the second illustration, might not management have "planted" the dissident member to stir up trouble and weaken the union's position at the bargaining table? Would it make a difference whether the criticisms were made publicly or only to fellow members?

To raise such questions is to indicate how precarious is the ground upon which government treads when it enters upon the internal affairs of private organizations. It goes without saying private groups ought to maintain fair procedures and democratic processes toward their members—but what happens if they don't?

Although this area of due process is indeed a frontier issue, legal guidelines have been developing over the past thirty-five years in two specific areas—corporation law and labor relations.

Corporate Due Process

Annual stockholders' meetings of corporations seem a most unlikely place to look for a revitalization of democratic processes. Many Americans own corporation stocks, either directly or through insurance policies or investment in mutual funds.

Almost without exception, ownership of stocks is considered wholly as an investment, not as a sharing of responsibility in operating a business enterprise. If a company does well by its stockholders its stocks are a good investment, if not the recourse is to sell one's stock and invest elsewhere.

That image of American capitalism is fostered generally by management. Officers and directors, whether they themselves own a substantial share of the corporation, whether they own very little, or—in some cases—none at all, consider running the business, making the decisions, their sole prerogative. All they ask of a stockholder is that he sign a proxy statement giving them, the insiders, the right to vote his shares as they see fit.

Some stockholders assail this view. One of the most notable of these is Lewis D. Gilbert, who has made a career of going to hundreds of annual meetings of corporations in which he owns a few shares—insisting on his legal right to ask questions, to inspect the records of stockholder ownership, etc.

Gilbert, in his book, *Dividends and Democracy,* sees democratic control over the nation's business by increasing numbers of shareholders, perhaps attending annual meetings held in various cities via closed television circuits, as a modern extension of the New England town meeting.

"This, and not witch hunts, loyalty oaths, and disregard of the Bill of Rights is the way to fight communism. Increasing the number of public shareholders and their democratic control over the nation's business is the way to salvation, the check to communism, the cure for socialism," writes Gilbert.

Perhaps this is an overstatement, reflecting the single-minded zeal of a crusader who sees but one path to salvation. Nonetheless, changes in corporate practices have occurred through laws like the Securities and Exchange Act and by use of older laws generally flouted or ignored. In the three centuries of corporation history, proxy voting is a relatively recent development. In the seventeenth and eighteenth centuries English courts held a shareholder's vote was a responsibility he could not delegate to another. Not until near the turn of the 19th century in America did the idea that a stockholder had an obligation to attend an annual meeting completely die out.

Proxy Voting

State legislatures, around 1900, passed laws providing voting by proxy. Such laws both reflected and encouraged the change from the closed corporation whose ownership was restricted to a selected few to public ownership where anybody could buy or sell shares on the open market. Today, of course, many corporations are still owned by families or a select few, but many more are publicly owned. Few of those listed on the stock exchange are actually controlled by stockholders owning 51 per cent of the shares—or anything approaching a majority.

Out of the stock crash of 1929 and the Great Depression which followed came the demand for regulation which resulted in the creation of the Securities and Exchange Commission. The SEC has not prevented all of the abuses by which "insiders" milked and manipulated corporations for their own aggrandizement by methods revealed in the Pecora investigations of Wall Street. (Ferdinand Pecora was chief counsel of the U. S. Senate committee conducting the hearings.) The SEC, and the law which brought it into existence, has provided mechanisms by which stockholders may insist on due process—at least in the half of the American corporations listed on the stock exchanges.

Security and Exchange Commission Regulations

SEC regulations require companies to disclose to stockholders financial statements, including total compensation of its three top officers, the amount of securities held by officers and directors, and other information in proxy statements. Proposals of management to be presented at the annual meeting must be listed with a provision for a YES or NO vote.

Most important from the standpoint of due process is the so-called proposal rule under which a corporation must include any proper shareholder proposal, with provision for a YES or NO vote, in the proxy statement mailed at the corporation's expense to shareholders prior to the annual meeting. It has been called the "shareholder's bill of rights". The constitutionality of the rule, the right of shareholders to be heard, the right of stockholders to receive accurate information as to what transpires in annual meetings, has been upheld by the courts.

Neither the proposal rule nor other methods open to "independent" shareholders (i.e. independent of management) insure corporate democracy. Judge John J. Biggs, Jr. of the Third District United States Circuit Court declared in the case referred to, "A corporation is run for the benefit of its stockholders and not for that of its managers."

Nonetheless stockholders who exercise their rights to influence policy are still a rarity..

Suggestions for Better Procedures

Some of the means of improving due process in the conduct of corporate affairs which have been suggested are:

Cumulative voting—obligatory in 22 states and permissive in 21 others. By this means minority stockholders may concentrate their votes to elect as many directors as their shares are proportionate to the total number of shares. This means a minority can be represented on the board as it cannot be if its votes are split among the total number to be elected.

Public Annual meetings—this means opening the meetings to the press, particularly financial reporters.

A primary objective of independent shareholders, says Gilbert, is full disclosure of the facts.

"While management of a vast majority of publicly owned corporations realize that an annual meeting is a public meeting, at which the press is entitled to be present, there are occasional exceptions that remind us of the need for vigilance."

Use of stockholder lists—state laws and SEC regulations require that names of stockholders be available to any stockholder desiring to obtain them. It is costly, of course, to circularize all of the stockholders of a widely held corporation, but the right to do so is a safeguard that may sometimes be needed.

More information to stockholders—through understandable audits, post-annual meeting reports, regional meetings where stockholders may ask questions and hear explanations.

Union Due Process

Union members, even more than corporate stockholders, have a vital stake in the fairness by which the internal affairs of their organization are conducted. Selling one's stock in a corporation one does not like is easier than withdrawing from a union when one's livelihood is at stake.

Good union leadership seeks to increase membership participation—most often with frustrating results. No such frustrations are apparent in those unions—a small but significant part of the labor movement—which have been dominated by dictatorial, corrupt, and racketeering leaders. Apathetic members have been unconcerned about how their union was governed as long as the leaders could show results at the bargaining table.

The McClellan hearings on union corruption in the Fifties might be compared with the Pecora investigations of Wall Street in the Thirties in that both produced legislation seeking to correct the abuses uncovered. As previously noted the Security and Exchange Act grew out of the earlier probe. Senate hearings chaired by Senator John L. McClellan—

with Robert F. Kennedy as chief counsel—resulted in the Landrum-Griffin Act, formally the Labor-Management Reporting and Disclosure Act of 1959.

A significant difference is that organized labor had recognized the need to clean its own house of corrupt influences prior to the time the law stepped in to regulate the internal procedures of unions.

Ethical Practice Codes

Although the American Federation of Labor historically refrained from interfering with its autonomous member unions, when the AFL merged with the Congress of Industrial Organizations in the mid-Fifties to form the AFL-CIO, six codes of ethical practice were adopted. Five dealt primarily with questions of corruption and conflict of interest.

The sixth code urges that all affiliates guarantee the democratic rights of union members, including: democratic participation in union affairs; fair treatment in the application of union disciplinary regulations; the right to criticize union policies and leaders without undermining "the union as an institution"; periodic open conventions, at least once every four years; and free election of national and local union officials, with the terms of office not to exceed four years.

Dr. Joel Seidman, professor of industrial relations at the University of Chicago, points out between 1911 and 1949 the Hod Carriers union failed to hold a single convention, and for years Longshoremen as well as others went without local meetings. In the case of some Teamsters' locals, even a member of the majority group found any motion not acceptable to the chairman and his faction would be ruled out of order. No appeal to the courts was possible because such a member would have to exhaust all avenues of appeal within the union. That might take years, with the hierarchy upholding the chairman every step of the way.

The AFL-CIO Ethical Practices Code is advisory, not mandatory, on unions, although a handful which have been found guilty of gross corruption by its Ethical Practices Committee have been expelled from the AFL-CIO.

Obstacles to Union Democracy

Much of the code follows recommendations of the American Civil Liberties Union over the years for a "Labor Union Bill of Rights."

Yet even in proposing such a bill of rights the ACLU recognizes the obstacles to union democracy:

"Any demands for union democracy must be tempered with a clear recognition of the serious obstacles which face unions in maintaining democratic standards. Historically, many unions have had to struggle for survival against deadly attacks by employers who did not hesitate to use spies, bribery, intimidation, or even physical violence. Although large segments of management have fully accepted collective bargaining, anti-union practices are not dead and the old fears remain. Employers are not the only enemy, for rival unions may constantly threaten a union's very existence by raiding its membership or seeking to supplant it as bargaining representative."

Management representatives are seldom chosen by democratic procedures so even where collective bargaining procedes in good faith "management seeks discipline, efficiency, and productivity, and so frequently prefers a union which maintains a rigid control over its members to one which suffers instability and turbulence of democratic policy making."

The proviso in the AFL-CIO code limiting criticism of union policies and leaders "without undermining the union as an institution" reflect these considerations.

Unions vary greatly in degree and methods of permitting democratic participation, application of union discipline, and the right of criticism.

At one extreme the Upholsterers and the Auto Workers, perhaps others, have set up independent review boards composed of eminent citizens outside the union available to review discipline cases. Those unions, however, are among the ones which needed such appeal agencies least, for their structure provided for such hearing safeguards as the right to produce witnesses and cross examine accusers in disciplinary hearings.

On the other hand the McClellan Committee hearings disclosed shocking action to punish factional opponents to union leaders. For example, a member of an Operating Engineers local leading a reform movement was fined $650 and barred from the union for five years when he brought a court case against strong-arm men for beating him up. It was he who was charged with "bringing the labor movement into disrepute!"

Landrum-Griffin Act

Out of such revelations the Landrum-Griffin Act was passed. It provides for a so-called bill of rights for union members, filing of a union's constitution and by-laws, annual financial reports, disclosure of possible conflicts of interest of union officials and employees, restrictions on union trusteeships, and detailed rules for the conduct of union elections. These last two sections are called into play only upon complaint of union members.

Predictions that Landrum-Griffin would put unions out of business have hardly materialized.. Neither has it proven a cure-all for the ills it was supposed to correct. Indeed, some authorities hold that the Landrum-Griffin "bill of rights" add few, if any, remedies a member did not have if he took the time and expense of going to court after exhausting internal remedies. Courts generally, will act only to enforce an association's constitution and by-laws.

If a union member cannot obtain redress by internal procedures within four months, he can, under the Landrum-Griffin Act, appeal to the courts. Apparently, however, his union could expel him during that period.

Solomen Salzhandler was barred from taking part in the affairs of a New York Painters local union for five years for falsely accusing its president of larceny. The U. S. Appeals Court reinstated him in good standing, a decision which the U. S. Supreme Court declined to review. Thus the constitutionality of this part of Landrum-Griffin has been upheld. Nonetheless the conflict between a union member's right to criticize and judicial interference in the conduct of union affairs presents real dilemmas in effective collective bargaining.

While other provisions of the Landrum-Griffin Act have undoubtedly curbed flagrant abuses of corruption, mismanagement, and bad faith in certain instances, perhaps its greatest impact has been psychological. It served notice that where unions do not provide due process, the government will step in with regulations that may be unduly complex, restrictive, uncertain and difficult to administer. Indeed, many of the provisions of that law had already been accepted as the result of court decisions, state laws, and union codes themselves. Too many unions had waited too long and done too little internally to avoid legislative action to absorb "powerful social standards of a progressive society" (quoting Justice Frankfurter).

In an atmosphere created by the McClellan committee revelations, Congress passed a law designed to cope with practically any situation of union malfeasance anyone could imagine.

Democratic procedures and due process, however, are not merely creatures of legislative fiat. The role of government is, and ought to be, most limited in private organizations—even in those like unions which are given quasi-governmental powers.

Discrimination in Private Organizations

Recent civil rights legislation and activity suggest another field where concepts of private association may be profoundly altered—discrimination because of color, race, creed, or national origin..

A case before the Fifth Circuit Court of Appeals concerns the refusal of an all-white church in Jackson, Miss. to accept Negro parishioners.

If there is any area of private organization in which the courts have been reluctant to enter it has been in disputes within religious groups—and rightly so under the First

Amendment guarantee of religious freedom. Yet some of the bitterest organizational hassles arise in factional splits within a church or religious society. Upon occasion courts have had to determine who is entitled to the name, or the property, of a particular group—or which officials are to be recognized. Most denominations have their own bodies of church law and procedures for disciplining or expelling members or clergymen for stated reasons. Here the state ought not to interfere, yet in rare instances where due process within the organization has been denied, appeal has been taken to the court. Should then the courts say that a church must admit to membership one of different race or color provided he otherwise qualifies? Should a private beach or tennis club be so required? A state real estate board or a national organization of sports writers? Or a boys' club that appeals to the public for funds for its support? Or a union or trade association? Or a university fraternity?

Prohibition of discrimination by law is quite different from voluntary integration engendered by the good will of an association's membership. Any kind of exclusionary policy may damage the cultural atmosphere of a democratic society. Yet freedom of association and privacy in private organizations are freedoms which ought not to be ignored or lightly subordinated to the demands of other freedoms.

Suggested Guidelines

Perhaps some guidelines can be suggested to determine when non-discrimination should take precedent over the privacy of association.

One of these is whether an agency receives public funds for part or all of its support. Obviously such facilities should be open equally to all.

A similar guideline on tax exemption is not quite as clearcut. Churches, church-related schools, and charitable and other non-profit organizations often are tax exempt yet they wish to maintain a common bond which would exclude certain persons. Is there not a difference, however, between denying membership in a church society or social club and denying service in agencies—colleges, hospitals,—which they may sponsor?

A third guideline might be the solicitation of support for the private group. If the general public is asked to contribute to an agency directly or through a community united fund, can that agency then limit its service to those of certain ethnic or religious categories?

For many years, as one example, the United Negro College Fund has appealed for contributions to support institutions of higher learning for Negroes. However much in theory all Negroes should be able to receive equal educational opportunities in non-segregated colleges, as a practical matter, the traditionally Negro colleges will be needed for many years to come. Actually these private Negro colleges are open to any student, and some have become substantially integrated. Nonetheless the illustration demonstrates that simple clear-cut answers are not found when competing freedoms are involved.

Finally, a guideline which would seem to be elemental and clear concerns organizations which establish vocational or professional standards which affect the right of persons to engage in these vocational or professional activities, or determine eligibility to participate in recreational and cultural activities of public importance. In these instances a private organization exercises a quasi-official function.

As an illustration, the Amateur Athletic Union certainly has the right to determine the standards of those who perform as amateurs under its approval, but should it have the right to discriminate on the grounds of race or creed? If not, how are the rights of those aggrieved by discriminatory policies to be achieved? Almost always in the case of private organizations, some excuse other than discrimination can be advanced for exclusion, even though the real reason is patently apparent.

It is not easy to resolve the tension between the interest of such private organizations in controlling their internal affairs and the public's interest in keeping opportunities to participate open to all.

Part IV

FRONTIERS OF FREEDOM

20

In Early America

*"In framing a government which is to be adminis-
tered by men over men, the great difficulty lies in
this: you must first enable the government to control
the governed, and in the next place oblige it to control
itself."*

—THE FEDERALIST No. 51*

*"I . . . affirm that bills of rights . . . are not only
unnecessary, . . . but would even be dangerous . . . For
why declare that things shall not be done which
there is no power to do? Why, for instance, should it
be said that the liberty of the press shall not be restrained, when no power is given by which restrictions
may be imposed? . . . This may serve as a specimen
of the numerous handles which would be given to the
doctrine of constructive power, by indulgence of an
injudicious zeal for bills of rights."*

—ALEXANDER HAMILTON, THE FEDERALIST No. 84

---

* Attributed to either Madison or Hamilton.

"Let me add that a bill of rights is what the people are entitled to against every government on earth, general or particular, and what no just government should refuse or rest on inferences."

—THOMAS JEFFERSON
(TO JAMES MADISON, DEC. 20, 1787)

Why was not the Bill of Rights made a part of the Constitution by the Constitutional Convention—perhaps embodied in its preamble, as in some of the state constitutions?

The answer involves some fascinating history.

American colonists were very much aware of their traditional liberties as Englishmen. English courts had to be called upon around 1700, however, to make clear that all of the laws in force in England were also in force in the colonies. Some of the royal governors sent over in the century before the American Revolution were prone to forget or ignore such decisions.

Particularly after the passage of the Stamp Act of 1765, the colonists complained not only about "taxation without representation" by the far-off king and parliament in London. They also passed resolutions demanding trial by jury and the right of petition (Stamp Act Congress of 1765) and listed infringements and violations of rights, including one that "our houses and even our bed chambers are exposed to be ransacked, our boxes, chests, and trunks broke open. . ." (Boston town meeting, 1772).

Declarations of rights were drafted by the Continental Congress of 1774 and by the various colonies as they adopted constitutions when they became independent states.

By the time of the Constitutional Convention convened late in the spring of 1787 to replace the unworkable Articles of Confederation with a stronger federal union, all of the thirteen states had embodied, in one form or another, a statement of individual rights of citizens. Eight had separate declarations or bills of rights.

"Rights" and the Constitutional Convention

For four months the Constitutional Convention wrestled with the problems of forming a strong central government, hammering out the various compromises which resulted in the federal system with its division of powers between the states and the federal government, and among the three branches—executive, legislative, and judicial.

Little attention was given to the relations of the individual to the federal government, because it was thought that the national government operated only in limited, specified areas and that the states would be the guarantors of personal liberties.

As the convention progressed, however, some delegates became alarmed that the new United States was going to have such a strong central government that they thought the rights of individuals should be protected against it.

(Incidentally, debates of the convention were secret, so what we know of what went on for nearly a year comes from journals and diaries published after the Constitution had been adopted. Robert Allen Rutland has reconstructed what happened relative to statements on individual rights in the chapter, "The Federal Convention", in his book, *The Birth of the Bill of Rights*.)

One of these delegates was George Mason, who had been the author of the Virginia Declaration of Rights ten years earlier, which had become the pattern for similar declarations in other states.

Mason did not formally propose a bill of rights to the convention until a few weeks before it was ready to adjourn. Earlier other delegates had proposed certain statements of rights, but a big majority thought that the protection to the individual by the states was sufficient. Even James Madison, who later as a member of the House of Representatives was to draft the first Ten Amendments, apparently shared this view.

Typical of the reasoning of the majority was the reply to one delegate, Roger Sherman of Connecticut, to the demand for a statement, "That the liberty of the Press should be inviolably observed." He claimed such a provision was unnecessary because the "power of Congress did not extend to the Press."

Sherman also argued that where the rights of the people were involved, Congress could be trusted to preserve them. How naive history has proven him to be on this point!

In spite of the fact that the convention rejected all attempts to put a complete enumeration of individual rights into the Constitution, several specific provisions were inserted, such as:

> Prohibiting suspension of the writ of habeas corpus, except in cases of rebellion or invasion when public safety may require it. (Art I, Sec. 9, Par. 2)
>
> Prohibition of bills of attainder and ex post facto laws by either the federal government (Art. I, Sec. 9, Par. 3) or by the states. (Art.I,Sec. 10, Par. 1)
>
> Trial of all crimes, except impeachment, shall be by jury, in federal courts. (Art. III, Sec. 2, Par. 3)
>
> Treason shall consist only in levying war against the United States, adhering to their enemies, or giving them aid or comfort, and "no person shall be convicted of treason unless on the testimony of two witnesses to the same overt act in open court." (Art. III, Sec. 3, Par. 1)
>
> ". . . no religious test shall ever be required as a qualification to any office or public trust under the United States." (Art. VI, Par. 3)

Each of these restrictions had specific reference to situations which had either prevailed in England or in the colonies.

Regarding treason, Montesquieu said, "If the crime of treason be indeterminate, that line is sufficient to make any government degenerate into arbitrary power." Despots have called any criticism of themselves "treason" throughout the ages.

As for the prohibition of religious tests for public office, this was used as an argument against ratification of the

Constitution in Massachusetts because it might permit a Mohammedan to become president. The same writer, however, also lamented the lack of guarantees for a free press and freedom of speech.

The Virginia Declaration

In May, 1776, when the Continental Congress was pondering the issues which were to result in the signing of the Declaration of Independence, Virginia held a convention. Besides asking the Continental Congress to declare the colonies free and independent, it took steps to prepare a plan of state government and a declaration of rights. A large committee was appointed to draft the declaration. Many ideas were advanced. George Mason, neighbor of George Washington and seven years his senior, prepared a draft of what he thought the declaration should contain. With some additions and changes his draft became the Virginia Declaration of Rights.

Mason had read John Locke closely, but he expanded on Locke's favorite idea of "life, liberty, and property." The first clause of the Virginia Declaration deserves quoting:

"That all men are by nature equally free and independent, and have certain inherent rights, of which, when they enter into a state of society, they cannot, by any compact, deprive or divest their posterity; namely, the enjoyment of life and liberty, with the means of acquiring and possessing property, and pursuing and obtaining happiness and safety."

Since the Virginia Declaration was passed on June 12, it is a good assumption that Thomas Jefferson had seen this clause when he wrote that among "certain unalienable rights" are "life, liberty, and the pursuit of happiness."

The Virginia convention debated four days on the revolutionary first line, "all men are by nature equally free"! Conservatives raised the issue of what such a statement would do to the institution of slavery. The "immediate answer, and apparently satisfactory, was that slaves were not 'constituent members' of their society and therefore a general maxim could not apply to Negroes," observes Rutland.

Even Patrick Henry, who had exclaimed "Give me liberty or give me death," joined the opposition to attack the clause against ex post facto laws. According to a fellow delegate, Edmund Randolph, Henry drew "a terrifying picture of some towering public offender, against whom ordinary laws would be impotent." So the article saying "all laws having a retrospect to crimes . . . ought to be avoided" was defeated. Here is an illustration which shows that "rights" were not something handed down on tablets of stone, but rather hammered out in political debate. Sometimes the proponents of liberty were not very consistent.

The Virginia Declaration was circulated to political leaders of other colonies, although they were not strangers to the sources upon which Mason had drawn for his formulation. Virginia, however, was the largest colony and, as John Adams wrote Henry, was looked up to for examples. By 1780 all of the former colonies, except New Hampshire, had adopted constitutions. New Hampshire fell in line in 1784. In some states, a bill of rights formed a preamble, in others the rights were embodied in various sections of the constitution. Although some rights such as trial by jury and habeas corpus were considered a part of common law, the new states, without exception, put them in writing.

The declarations varied substantially from state to state, and the differences were more marked on religion than on any other issue. The Virginia Declaration said "all men are equally entitled to the free exercise of religion, according to the dictates of conscience."

The Pennsylvania declaration, for example, extended civil rights to all men who professed belief in God, but the Delaware Declaration limited "equal rights and privileges" to Christians. Maryland required a "declaration of belief in the Christian religion" for an office in the state. (As previously noted this requirement was struck down in 1962 by the U. S. Supreme Court.)

The Virginia Declaration statement on freedom of conscience did not end the religious controversy in that state. Dissenters, particularly Baptists and Presbyterians, objected to having to pay the established Anglican church. They found a champion in Thomas Jefferson. In the fall of 1776, the Virginia lawmakers exempted dissenters from making a contribution to the established church and repealed laws requiring church attendance and restricting religious opinions. Until 1780, however, marriages performed by dissenting ministers were not recognized. Then supporters of the established church attempted to push through a bill giving state subsidies to "teachers of the Christian religion"—meaning only those of the established church. Jefferson and the dissenting Virginians defeated this bill and in 1785 passed his own "Bill for Establishing Religious Freedom," which virtually completed separation of church and state. Thus Virginia joined Rhode Island, which had had religious freedom for 100 years.

Ratification and the Rights Battle

The United States Constitution had been adopted by the Constitutional Convention without any declaration or bill of rights. Mason, and two others, Elbridge Gerry of Massachusetts and Edmund Randolph of Virginia, refused to sign the completed constitution. Mason and Gerry, with others, became the leaders of the Anti-Federalists who worked against ratification by the conventions called in each state. The lack of a bill of rights was used as the chief argument against the new Constitution. Proponents of ratification, the Federalists, while defending the lack of such a statement because it was unnecessary, also argued that the real reason for opposition was economic. Some feared a strong central government which could regulate foreign and domestic commerce. The charge that the demand for a bill of rights was a cover-up may have considerable truth in it. Nonetheless the demand was real. Historian Herbert J. Muller says the Constitution was "drawn up by conservatives now fearful of the common people," was "attacked by the democrats of the time" and "is today revered by almost all Americans who assume it was a good popular document."

Thomas Jefferson, who was in Paris as minister to France during the Constitutional Convention, found much that he liked when he received a copy of the completed document, but he decried the lack of guarantees of personal liberty.

Religious denominations, particularly the Baptists, were fearful of the lack of a guarantee of religious freedom. Some Northerners did not like the compromises which recognized the institution of slavery.

The Federalists, however, carried the various state conventions, but in a few states by a very close margin.

Massachusetts, the sixth state to ratify, was one of these. The final vote was 187 for and 168 against. To secure even this margin for ratification, the Federalist members of the convention had offered a concession in the form of a series of amendments recommended to be added when the new government was set up.

This idea of putting the Constitution into effect and then adding to it appeared to offer a way of compromise. Jefferson lauded it as better than the move to hold a second Constitutional Convention. After the Massachusetts ratification, in February, 1788, the strategy of the Anti-Federalists was to have the state ratifying conventions demand the addition of amendments. Federalists accepted this compromise to assure ratification.

James Madison, though he was a strong Federalist and had argued against the need for a bill of rights during the ratification debates, became the leader in proposing such amendments in the House of Representatives during the first session of the new Congress in 1789.

Madison was young and a very practical politician. He had been defeated for U. S. Senator in the Virginia legislature by the manipulations of Patrick Henry, who mistrusted his campaign promises to work for a bill of rights. He then defeated James Monroe, an Anti-Federalist, in a race for representative from a district which the legislature had carved out (gerrymandered) to include strong Anti-Federalist sentiment. He had returned from the Continental Congress to campaign in the district and won over some of the Anti-Federalists, particularly some Baptists, with a promise to work for amendments, embodying "all essential rights, particularly the Rights of Conscience in the fullest latitude, the freedom of the press, trials by jury, security against general warrents, etc."

Madison wrote to Jefferson that "my own opinion has always been in favor of a bill of rights provided it be so framed as not to imply powers not meant to be included in the enumeration." He had not considered omission of a bill of rights as an error, but he did not agree with the belief that the federal government was prevented from interfering with the rights of individuals because it was a government of enumerated powers. Yet he preferred the tacit assumption of religious freedom by Congress to a statement which could, conceivably, be narrowly defined. He pointed out that the legislative majority in every state had violated these "parchment barriers" of declarations of rights whenever it served their interest to do so.

Yet, continuing his discussion in a long letter to his friend, he found two desirable ends in passing a bill of rights. One was that it might supply a standard of free government which would create a national tradition to "counteract the impulses of interest and passion." The other was to provide "a good ground for an appeal to the sense of the community" from the possibility of arbitrary acts of government, which, rather than oppressive majorities, might invade citizen's rights.

Jefferson, in reply, cited a third argument favoring a bill of rights—"the legal check which it puts in the hands of the judiciary." Thus Jefferson foresaw the potential role the Supreme Court could play as a protector of individual liberties. Doubtless, except for court interpretations, our Bill of Rights would indeed be a "parchment barrier."

The Congressional Debate

Whatever reservations Madison had on the value of a declaration of rights, he pushed for consideration of proposals in the House in June after the new Congress had been in session two months. Some wanted to further delay debate until such issues as import duties were settled. Madison argued, however, to the effect that a debate would show the good faith of the Federalists in accepting the idea. A great number of citizens who thought the guarantees essential to their liberties were apprehensive, but were ready to support the new government if an explicit declaration were forthcoming.

Madison read a draft which he offered, embodying general principles taken from the Virginia Declaration of Rights and incorporating some additional features proposed by various ratifying conventions.

Rutland observes:

"After canvassing the whole field of objections to a bill of rights, he declared that specific declarations of rights would be worthwhile because it offered 'tranquility of the public mind, and the stability of government'. Madison alluded to Jefferson's striking observation that the 'independent tribunals of justice will consider themselves in a peculiar manner the guardian of those rights . . . (and) resist every encroachment upon rights expressly stipulated . . . by the declaration of rights.' "

Madison's draft was turned over to a committee, of which he was a member, and was reprinted widely in the press. His proposals covered all of the ten articles which eventually formed the Bill of Rights. Some complained they went too far; others that more rights should be included. Madison candidly confessed to a friend that his proposals were limited to issues which would rouse the least opposition. "Nothing of a controvertible nature ought to be hazarded by those who are sincere in wishing for the approbation of two-thirds of each House, and three-fourths of the State Legislatures," he wrote.

James Madison was not the last "middle-of-the-road" American politician who was successful by pushing a compromise which was not really liked by both sides!

It was August 17 before the House, after considerable debate, finally acted on the committee's report. It sent seventeen proposed amendments to the Senate, out of 124 which were submitted to the committee, many far removed from issues related to rights of individuals.

Madison considered as "the most valuable on the whole list" the proposal, "No state shall infringe the equal rights of conscience, nor freedom of speech, or of the press, nor the rights of trial by jury in criminal cases."

The Senate, however, defeated this proposed amendment. It was to take a Civil War, the Fourteenth Amendment, and the interpretations of the Supreme Court of the mid-Twentieth Century before individuals were given protection of the federal courts against encroachments in these areas by the states.

The Senate combined the language of some of the amendments, and finally passed twelve. A conference committee of three Senators and three House members was appointed to compose the differences in language. The most significant change made by this committee was broadening the clause relating to religious freedom from "Congress shall make no law establishing articles of faith" to "Congress shall make no law respecting establishment of religion."

On September 25, 1789, Congress completed work on the amendments and they were submitted to the states for ratification. Two amendments were rejected, one relating to apportionment for the House and the other forbidding increasing salaries of members of Congress during the term for which they were elected. These hardly belonged to a bill of rights anyway.

Although the Virginia legislature was one of the first to consider ratification it became the last to ratify, discussing the amendments and postponing consideration for over two years. The extreme Anti-Federalists, led by Patrick Henry, thought they were too weak and would do more harm than benefit.

Meantime other states did ratify. Rhode Island finally came into the Union in May, 1790 and became the ninth state to approve the amendments. Vermont was admitted as the fourteenth state in 1791 and became the tenth to ratify the Bill of Rights. Its admission raised to eleven the number of states necessary to put the amendments into effect under the three-fourths requirement.

Finally, almost unnoticed, Virginia ratified the Ten Amendments on December 15, 1791, the anniversary of which we observe as Bill of Rights Day each year. On the 150th anniversary of the Bill of Rights ratification in 1941, the three original states which did not ratify, Massachusetts, Connecticut, and Georgia, passed ratification resolutions as a token gesture of celebration.

21

A Look Ahead

"Time works changes, brings into existence new conditions and purposes. Therefore, a principle to be vital must be capable of wider application than the mischief which gave it birth."
—U. S. SUPREME COURT IN 1910

"It must be remembered that legislatures are ultimate guardians of the liberties and welfare of the people in quite as great a degree as the courts."
—JUSTICE OLIVER WENDELL HOLMES IN 1904

"Liberty lies in the hearts of men and women; when it dies there; no constitution, no law, no court can save it."

Judge Learned Hand

"Liberty is something each age must provide for itself."
—JUSTICE ROBERT H. JACKSON

"There is no true liberty for the individual
Except as he finds it
In the liberty of all."
—EDWIN MARKHAM

Americans, no less than other members of the human race, are pressing on to frontiers that are bringing changes as far-reaching—perhaps as unforeseen—as were occurring when our new nation adopted the Bill of Rights 175 years ago.

Some now—as then—look back and decry the trend of applying new interpretation of law to new situations.

Should the United States Supreme Court recognize these new frontiers by developing new applications of the concepts of freedom and equality? Or should needed changes be left to legislative and executive action at Federal and state levels? These questions are involved in the argument between the philosophy of "judicial restraint" and the doctrine of "judicial activism". This conflict has been personified respectively by Justices Felix Frankfurter and Hugo L. Black, great and brilliant contemporaries, serving during the period when more decisions dealing with the Bill of Rights were rendered than in all our previous history.

Freedom's Growing Edge

Certainly since Earl Warren became chief justice in 1954 the high court has not hesitated to break new ground to make meaningful the ancient guarantees of liberty and justice for all, although the trend had been foreshadowed many years before. Some have argued that the Supreme Court has "twisted" rather than "adapted" the provisions of the First Ten Amendments and the Fourteenth, particularly the "due process" and "equal protection" clauses, to fit modern needs.

The end is not yet. Freedom must have a growing edge— else it shrinks. While court interpretations may continue to press forward on frontier issues, the role of national and state legislatures—and the opinion of the people—should not be minimized. Perhaps the time is at hand when judicial activism will take second place to legislative and executive action to expand the scope of freedom, as indeed it has in civil rights acts of recent years.

Along the growing edge of freedom are unsolved (perhaps unsolvable) conflicts and tensions which require assignment of priorities between or among competing rights. Most of these are extensions of old conflicts under new circumstances. Other problems arise from the scientific revolution society is undergoing. These include both physical changes being wrought by technology, cybernation, urbanization, or whatever terminology is applied, and the behavioral insights brought about by new sociological, psychological, and ethical understanding.

Some trends may be unfavorable to freedom, others favorable—and some both favorable and unfavorable. The primacy of the individual, his liberties, and the rule of justice are all bound up together in most frontier issues of civil liberties.

The trends which demand increasing attention in the years ahead may be grouped under four categories:

> The impact of mass communication on our sense of justice, on our susceptibility to indoctrination and manipulation, and on our ability to find diversity amid conformity.

> The impact of the new knowledge of the behavioral sciences on our attitudes toward treatment and/or punishment of the drug user, the alcoholic, the sex aberrant, the criminal offender—including the use of the death penalty.

> The impact of the danger about which President Eisenhower warned in his farewell address—that of becoming captive of the "military-industrial elite" in an era when there is neither declared war nor established peace.

> The impact of urbanization on individual rights, particularly those of the poor and those of the affluent, but also affecting the rights of the big majority of those Americans who are neither poor nor affluent.

Many of the issues raised are not new. Some have been presented in previous chapters, but here the emphasis will be on the new circumstances which may require radical departure from accepted norms.

Mass Communication

Of the questions raised by the impact of electronic journalism and electronic surveillance upon the administration of justice, perhaps the simplest one to deal with is the old issue of "free press versus fair trial."

The courts in recent years have laid down guidelines which place responsibility on both the news media and the officers of the court—prosecuting and defense attorneys and the presiding judge—to refrain from publicity—pre-trial or during the trial—which will create an atmosphere prejudicial to the right of the defendant to be judged on the evidence presented alone.

Within this frame of responsible action the news media can satisfy the public's right to know—but not its appetite for sensationalism nor the mendacious appetite of the media to build circulation or listenership. Occasional overstepping of this responsibility in specific cases means reversal on appeal. Wholesale irresponsibility, however, could bring on stringent restraints similar to those in England, where the news media are practically limited to giving the name of the defendant and the charge until the trial is over.

Although the Supreme Court overturned the conviction of Billie Sol Estes because his trial was televised, this does not mean that television cameras and press photographers will always be barred from all court rooms in all situations. Reporters with pads and pencils have—with the acquiescence of the trial judge—made a circus out of a criminal trial (quoting the Supreme Court in its *Sheppard* decision). Reporters using unobtrusive modern electronic tools could operate in the court room, under rules of procedure to be worked out jointly by bar and press, which would preserve court decorum and fair trial.

A municipal court judge of Bellflower, California, Roberta Butzbach, said of an ordinary criminal trial televised in her court, with consent of the defendent, before such practice was banned by a Judicial Council rule:

"The universal comment was that once the trial began, the presence of the news media was forgotten. All the dire predictions and suppositions as to the manner in which people would behave in such a situation simply did not happen. There were no attempts to play Hamlet or outdo Bob Hope."

Television—Controlled or Controller

Public enlightenment resulting from the televising of Congressional hearings demonstrates how electronic journalism can be an influence in promoting democracy. It also poses an unresolved question: Who is going to determine what is going to be telecast and when?

When the TV networks preempted daytime "soap operas" and "quiz shows" to present such a hearing (or was it the first rendezvous in space?), the stations were deluged with protests from angry viewers who missed their habitual programs. Public affairs presentations on prime viewing time are diminishing in number, however much they improve in quality.

All of these opinions, whether well founded or not, suggest that mass media are geared to mass appeal alone. Perhaps it is inevitable when costly television production is underwritten by advertisers who must compete with one another for the largest possible viewing audience to justify their expenditures, the result is directed to the lowest common denominator of public taste. One successful series breeds others like unto it on competing networks.

Can mass communication media cater to selective tastes and be commercially successful? The growth and improvement of educational television suggests selective audiences do exist. One might see hope in the development of 70 UHF (ultra high frequency) channels in addition to 12 VHF (very high frequency) stations that more stations would lead to much greater diversity in programming—except that the more radio stations there are on the air, the more sameness there appears to be.

What is the role of government in electronic mass media? That is the question involving civil liberties. Should the FCC demand that so much "prime time" (the evening shows with the maximum number of viewers) be devoted to "public service" or non-network programs? Should it force the broadcast industry to adopt the British system whereby the advertiser buys spots on a commercial station but has no voice in the content of the program between spots? (That system is used on some American network news programs, but most entertainment programs are produced and bought by advertising agencies for specific sponsors.)

Should government agencies, including universities and school systems, subsidize more educational TV stations? Should federal and state governments have their own stations to telecast official proceedings? Should stations solely, or primarily, broadcast for the interest of their own members— religious organizations, cultural groups, political parties, etc? (They all publish their own periodicals.)

Is it necessary that every station provide diversity and balance in its programming, or only that the programs available from all the stations in a community cover a full range?

Can the political ideas of Americans be manipulated by electronic mass media as their buying habits are influenced by the drip, drip, drip, of commercial advertising? Is the time at hand when only candidates who can "project a favorable television image" can hope to be elected to office?

Or will the electronic mass media—and its viewers— mature to a point where danger of indoctrination and manipulation will be minimal? Can any such assumption excuse lack of action now to encourage freedom and diversity of expression in the most potent area of modern mass communication?

Critics of the Federal Communications Commission assert that it has been too hesitant in fulfilling its mandate under the law to insure fairness, diversity, and balance in programming.

Defenders of the FCC point out that when it goes beyond steps assuring widest possible access to broadcasting, through numerous and diverse licensees and owners, it is in danger of becoming a censor. It is up to competition among numerous private parties to provide a wide range of program material.

Its critics reply that to set standards by which a station must devote a certain proportion of prime time to public affairs, cultural, and educational programming in no way dictates the content of any specific program. Generally too much government control limits freedom of expression, but in the very nature of electronic mass media, positive action by a government agency is essential if the deadening conformity of mass commercialization is not to prevail.

Issues in this debate will not be resolved by Supreme Court decisions, nor probably by any new legislation. Hopefully, experimentation by the administrative agency and by the broadcast industry will bring new answers—perhaps unexpected ones.

Regulating Surveillance

In an allied field of electronics—surveillance by listening devices and computerized information-gathering—new legislation as well as perhaps new court decisions is needed.

Against the right of privacy are to be weighed the interests of public disclosure and of private and public authorities. Surveillance by modern techniques is not going to disappear because it is legally banned. Nor is information gained by an employer necessarily detrimental to the interests of his actual or prospective employees—in fact, it may be very helpful to them. Likewise modern methods of detecting crime may protect the innocent as well as find the guilty.

The problem posed for the future is not only to weigh the priorities of these competing rights and responsibilities, but also to find the proper means and degrees of regulation and control.

"The right to speak, to publish, to worship, and to associate," writes Alan Westin of Columbia University Law School, "cannot survive in the age of scientific penetration of house, auto, office, and meeting room, unless the courts and public mores install a curtain of law and practice to replace the walls and doors that have been swept away by the new instruments of surveillance."

Freedom of communication, he points out, clearly means the right to discuss with intimates in confidence, and prepare positions in private for later presentation in public.

Should the "curtain" be penetrated by government agents only under certain, specified circumstances—and then with proper safeguards—such as defense of national security or the saving of human life as in kidnapping cases or threats of extortion? In the latter cases permission of one of the parties to the communication would be forthcoming anyway.

Use of electronic eavesdropping, polygraphs, or psychological testing might be limited among private individuals and organizations to those who knowingly and willingly consent. Volunteering for scientific experiments, educational purposes, or new product testing might provide instances where intrusion of the "curtain", otherwise forbidden, might be permissible.

If use of surveillance mechanisms in public areas—to catch shoplifters in stores, for example is to be used at all, should not placards clearly stating the area was being watched by closed-circuit television or whatever be required? The extent and manner of use of such devices in factories and shops might well be points in collective-bargaining agreements between management and labor.

Factors which may inhibit the electronic invasion of the privacy curtain include at least these:

> Most companies do not use polygraphs (lie detectors) to curb employee thefts but rely on more traditional methods of inventory control, gate inspections, etc.
>
> Fewer companies use personality (or psychological) testing for employee selection and advancement than in the Fifties. This demonstrates the contention that techniques of evaluation which do not pry into the protected areas of personal life and private belief are at

least as reliable criteria of performance as techniques which do seem more personal.

Scientific counter-measures are being developed which can give protection against electronic-snooping.

Professional standards of ethical conduct for professions dealing with the collection and use of personal data—doctors, lawyers, psychologists, accountants, etc. —can discipline those who violate the privacy of clients.

Beyond such restraints lie the moral consciousness of public opinion which ultimately results in policy decisions by private and public organizations, in the writing of laws and in decisions of the courts.

In this whole new area of technological impact on human behavior, so much remains to be discovered and evaluated, so many borderline problems are unexplored, so many competing values are involved that the challenge of this frontier of freedom cannot be overstated.

Treatment or Punishment

Is a drug addict a "criminal" or a sick individual in need of confinement and treatment. Is a chronic alcoholic who presents himself in public to be repeatedly "thrown in the tank" as a petty misdemeanant—or is he too, basically ill and in need of treatment? How is society to deal with the use of psychedelic drugs, such as LSD, non-narcotic and non-habit forming, yet certainly behavior-changing? Can, or ought, all laws against deviant sex behavior—homosexuality, adultery, etc. be strictly enforced? If not should the laws be changed? Is the criminality of any individual so inexorably and irretrievably established that society ought to put an end to his life?

New knowledge and new techniques of the behavioral sciences certainly have much to contribute to the answers for each of these questions. As frontier issues of civil liberties these questions raise a re-evaluation of the claims of justice. Punishment presumes wilful intent to wrongful action. De-

terrence and rehabilitation assumes treatment of the person—
not his crime.

In each of the questions posed a not-so-new issue is also
denial of equal protection of the law.

It is the wino on skid row who is picked up and convicted—not the alcoholic who is sheltered in a comfortable
home or goes off and on to a resort sanitarium. Likewise the
narcotic user who is affluent can be shielded—as revelations
concerning a handful of entertainment celebrities attest. The
addict who commits other crimes to pay for his costly habit
is most likely to receive a prison sentence. Admittedly only
a very small percentage of sex acts between consenting adults,
defined as criminal, are prosecuted—and it is the mentally
and culturally disadvantaged who are most likely to get
caught.

Capital Punishment

Evidence that the victims of capital punishment are almost exclusively from the most disadvantaged groups is ir-
refutable. Even though the poor defendant has the most
conscientious court-appointed counsel at the trial and appeal
level, and the middle income defendant can employ an attorney of average competence, such counsel cannot equal the
batteries of high-priced attorneys, psychiatrists, and other
experts available to the affluent. Such experts can take years
to exhaust every possible remedy available to one under
penalty of death.

In the last 35 years 53.7 per cent of persons executed
have been Negroes although Negroes comprise only 10 per
cent of the population. A study in Ohio—a northern state—
shows 78 per cent of Negroes convicted of capital crimes were
actually executed as compared with 51 per cent of the whites
so convicted.

James V. Bennett, former Director of the Federal Bureau
of Prisons, although favoring retention of the death penalty
for certain crimes, writes:

"Today it is chiefly the indigent, the friendless, the Negro, the mentally ill, who are doomed to death. Or the young."

In addition to a denial of equal justice, it may be argued that the death penalty denies due process because only those biased in favor of the death penalty serve on juries where the death penalty is a possibility, those against it being customarily excluded. It may be argued due process is denied because rather than risking the death penalty, the accused may accept "a deal" to plead guilty in exchange for life imprisonment—even though a fair trial might result in acquittal or conviction on a lesser charge. The irreversibility of conviction after a man is executed (few women have ever been executed in modern America) also is a denial of due process. Numerous errors in capital convictions have been documented.

Perhaps the classic example is that of the case in which a man convicted of murder escaped hanging because the jury foreman had written his own name rather than that of the accused in the blank space on the execution order! Sometime later another man confessed.

If capital punishment actually deterred crime, these arguments based on denial of equal justice and denial of due process, as well as the one that it constitutes cruel and unusual punishment, might be disregarded. Little real evidence can be produced to prove the deterrent value of the death penalty and considerable evidence shows the contrary.

In 1963, 8,404 acts of murder and non-negligent manslaughter were committed in the United States. That year 21 persons were executed throughout the country. In the same year in California 208 persons were convicted of murder, of whom 24 were sentenced to death. Only one person was executed and he had been on death row for a decade.

Trial delays, use of technicalities, appeals to highest courts, amnesty and commutations—all attest to the hesitancy to execute a person. Aside from the fact that most murders are committed in passion—or by a deranged person if actually premeditated—the long delays between trial and execution and the 400-to-1 chance a murderer will not be executed demolish any deterrent effect the death penalty might have.

Increased neuropsychiatric knowledge demonstrates that persons legally sane may have organic brain conditions that completely dominate their behavior. Such knowledge, together with new technology and new techniques, also demonstrates that rehabilitation can be achieved in many cases. Even where an individual cannot be completely released into society, his behavior patterns can be changed. In any case what justification has society for snuffing out his life, bringing about the only condition beyond change?

In the light of all the evidence it is not surprising that the use of the death penalty has been declining at an accelerating rate the past decade or two. The questions remain whether legislative action will hasten the decline, or whether future court decisions, each in a specific case, will determine that equal justice, the due process, or no cruel and unusual punishment clauses have been violated by imposing the death penalty. Perhaps both trends may occur.

Drug Addiction

In the areas of drug-addiction and alcoholism the impact of the behavioral sciences on legal trends is even more marked.

In 1962 the U. S. Supreme Court held that a California law making it a crime to be "addicted to the use of narcotics" was unconstitutional as a cruel and unusual punishment. Justice Stewart compared the "status" of being a drug addict to that of being mentally-ill or a leper. Justice Harlan said the law authorized punishment for the "bare desire to commit a criminal act." Overt acts—the use, possession, sale, or giving of narcotics—are still punishable as crimes.

Carried to a logical end, however, does not this trend suggest that dope addicts be treated under civil proceedings as persons requiring therapeutic care and control, rather than being sentenced to and released from purely penal institutions? If so, then all of the due process problems presented in the treatment of the mentally ill will be present.

Use of LSD and other behavior-changing but non-narcotic drugs is so new that solutions to problems involving individual rights can hardly be anticipated at this time. The claim of free exercise of religion may be advanced by LSD devotees as it has by the Indians who use peyote in their religious ceremonies. Spiritual experience through hallucinatory perception is claimed for both.

Alcoholism

Chronic alcoholism is the fourth largest public health problem in the United States, but the police and the courts routinely treat it as though it is a crime, not an illness. Such treatment is being questioned in numerous test cases. Does a chronic alcoholic who becomes drunk in public possess the criminal intent necessary for criminal prosecution? Is it cruel and unusual punishment to impose criminal sanctions on one who exhibits a symptom—drunkeness—of what is actually a disease—chronic alcoholism?

From a practical standpoint society has not solved the problem by repeatedly arresting and confining mainly skid row drunks—comprising 10 per cent of all chronic alcoholics. Yet such arrests constitute about one-third of all arrests in the country. Society may well be forced to take a different approach to the problem, perhaps because of future court answers to the questions posed, or perhaps because it finds therapeutic treatment a more effective means of control..

Sex Offenders

In considering the impact of behavioral sciences on the new sex mores of our society, care must be taken to distinguish between the moral and the legal aspects of the problem. Society, of course, must protect itself—particularly its young—against the sex psychopath, the molester, the rapist, the exhibitionist, the panderer, the professional prostitute. Here the emphasis on psychotherapy and other treatment, including indeterminate sentencing, is rightfully replacing purely punitive action.

Our laws which make acts between consenting adults in private criminal are rarely enforced but operate to encourage blackmail and other types of crime. The extent and manner in which these ancient laws should be modified in the light of present knowledge and custom constitute another frontier issue of civil liberties.

The Impact of the Military

Those who fought the American Revolution, wrote the Constitution, and formulated the Bill of Rights, certainly recognized the dangers of dominance by the military over civilians. The Second Amendment's reference to a "well regulated militia" (citizen army) and the Third's stricture on quartering troops as well as procedural provisions of the Constitution, demonstrate the intent to subordinate the military power to civilian control. The inherent necessity of providing for the common defense is, however, recognized.

Threats to abridgement of individual freedoms become frontier issues today because they assume such different forms under such different circumstances than those which prevailed on the earlier frontier. Part of the problem lies in the situation where American GI's are stationed—and fighting— in various parts of the world without formal declaration of war or, in some instances, without presidential proclamation of a state of emergency.

In war time the precedence of military justice for military personnel—the court-martial proceedings which short-circuit many of the procedures of civilian courts—are accepted as essential to the prosecution of the war. In brief, court-martial proceedings are designed to bring swift and summary justice —with penalties ranging from imprisonment in a stockade to dishonorable discharge to lengthy prison terms or even the firing squad.

The constitutional rights of a member of the armed services in peace time—or at least technical peace time—are less sharply delineated.

Obviously, the draft itself impinges on the freedom of the person drafted. Peacetime selective service appears to have become accepted as a permanent feature of the American way of life since World War II, however contrary to the history and tradition of the nation.

How many of his rights does a draftee—or a volunteer—give up when he joins the military? The right to free expression of ideas, including criticism of national policy? The right to jury trial, to be represented by a qualified attorney, to appeal to civilian courts when charged with a crime or misdemeanor—or even to a military court of appeals? Must a person be a conscientious objector to all war under all conditions to be exempted from a particular military action he believes wrong and unjustified? Can military personnel who have enlisted for a certain period be held in service beyond that time in the absence of a formal state of war?

These are some of the questions which have been raised affecting the civil liberties of military personnel.

Chief Justice Warren once wrote in an opinion:

"Our citizens in uniform may not be stripped of their basic rights simply because they doffed their civilian clothes."

Today a soldier may wear civilian clothes part of the time when not on duty. Such a one participated in an anti-Viet Nam war demonstration, was court-martialed and given a two-year prison sentence and dishonorable discharge. That sentence was reduced by a reviewing higher officer and the soldier was later freed on bail on appeal to civilian court. The freedom of speech and association issue involved here is an undecided, but an important one.

A provision of the Uniform Code of Military Justice grants an absolute right of appeal to flag and general officers but affords lower ranks only a discretionary right of appeal. In reply to the contention this was arbitrary denial of equal protection under the law, the U. S. Court of Military Appeals held "the right of appeal was not essential to due process of law."

Three armed forces specialists whose particular skills were needed in Viet Nam charged that having their tours of duty extended beyond the period for which they enlisted constituted involuntary servitude. Their enlistment provided unlimited extension of service in case of war.

Former President and General Eisenhower's farewell warning against the power of the "military-industrial complex," with possible alliance of the scientific-education community, dominating civilian government goes, of course, beyond specific questions of rights of individuals in the military.

He was restating one of the oldest and most intractable of the dilemmas of freedom—reconciling indispensable liberties with the equally indispensable claims of common defense. The framers of the Constitution sought to solve the dilemma by allocating the powers of war-making among the separate branches of government to minimize the possibility of their misuse.

This becomes a frontier issue of the growing edge of freedom not because it is novel but because the scope of common defense—the technology, size, and economic impact of the military-industrial complex designed to meet it—has become so vast that intelligent decision-making has almost slipped beyond the grasp of the civilian arms of government.

Congress holds the purse-strings, constitutionally, on defense expenditures, but it must rely largely on the expertise of the Pentagon as to where and how much is to be spent. Likewise determination of the necessary and effective steps which must be taken to meet a real, clear, and present danger requires the President and Congress to rely on advice of professionals whose biases are not primarily civilian-oriented.

Most of the issues may require decisions on the policy-making level—political action, more bluntly. Problems of equitable and non-discriminatory application of the decisions reached, however, certainly involve basic rights. Operation of the draft is a sufficient illustration of this point.

Urbanization—Poverty and Affluence

It may appear somewhat absurd to link the poor and the affluent as facing similar threats to their individual rights under the impact of urbanization. Yet in at least two aspects of this general phenomenon (which could be characterized by a wide variety of terms all denoting mass sociological trends) the welfare client and the middle management employee face similar forces. These are mobility and bureaucracy—factors which, of course, affect all individuals but which present particular frontier issues for these particular groups.

Mobility is one characteristic of urbanized America. Immobility characterizes certain segments of the poor who never get more than a few blocks from home to take advantage of public facilities and services they hardly know exist. Nonetheless a greater problem—and certainly a frontier issue of civil liberty—is the residence requirement for public welfare eligibility. Migration from the rural areas—and from Puerto Rico—to the cities has been, and continues to be, an irreversible trend. These migrants are the least capable of finding and holding jobs and are most likely to require public assistance. Do residence laws making them ineligible for public welfare violate their constitutional right to cross state boundaries without penalty? Does the fact that a large proportion of welfare aid comes from federal funds make a difference in the answer to that question?

At the affluent end of the scale, the problem of mobility is not so much moving from place to place—although numerous corporations have a policy of transferring middle management employees periodically. Rather the right to job mobility is involved. Occasionally corporations have gone to court and prevented an employee with specialized technical know-how from accepting a position with another firm because he might reveal trade secrets. What are the rights of such an employee?

Does limiting his job mobility subject him to involuntary servitude? How does he assert his rights, if any? Union employees have used collective bargaining procedures to spell out their rights, but thus far no similar method of dealing with conflicts between the higher-up professional or managerial employee and the corporation has emerged.

Bureaucracy for the poverty group implies that those who receive welfare aid are subject to rules, regulations, and interpretations difficult to comprehend and almost impossible to appeal. Bureaucracy for the affluent "organization man" lies in equally obscure but certainly certain "rules of the game" within the organization of which he is a part. Here are special applications of the general problem of due process in governmental administrative agencies and in private organizations.

Are persons seeking or receiving various forms of welfare assistance required to divest themselves of their basic rights and personal dignity as they often must relinquish their meager material assets before receiving assistance? Abundant evidence can be cited which indicates many lawmakers and welfare officials would answer affirmatively.

Is an "after-midnight raid" by welfare investigators into homes receiving Aid to Dependent Children less a Fourth Amendment violation than an illegal search and seizure by police? Yet such probes have been justified as necessary to uncover fraudulent claims by ADC mothers—since the presence of a man in the household generally disqualifies them for ADC payments.

Should tenants of public housing be subjected to more inspection of their premises than tenants of private landlords? Should screening procedures for public housing applicants consider moral judgments of their "worthiness" as well as their economic need?

How can those seeking public welfare—or seeking to justify continued welfare—meet the more subtle methods used to discourage them? Delays in processing applications, regulations which are quoted but never shown in writing, lack of fair hearing procedures, unexplained agency actions, and denial of the right to appeal—such infringements of due process are charged against public welfare bureaucracy. Generally this bureaucracy is locally centered, although federal standards are playing an increasing role.

No moral or means tests are required of recipients of unemployment insurance or social security. Should welfare— or particular types of welfare benefits such as ADC and Aid to Needy Disabled—be also an "entitlement" rather than being doled out as sparingly as possible to the unfortunate who ought to be deserving, grateful, and meek supplicants? Various studies indicate that many persons who would be eligible for welfare benefits do not receive them for one reason or another. These people may exist on incomes well below welfare minimums.

"Ombudsmen"

An experiment that shows promise is a program to provide free legal service to the impoverished who are least able to know and assert their rights in dealing not only with official bureaucracy, but also with private sectors of the economy which exploit them.

Scandinavian countries have a public official known as the "ombudsman" who sees that an individual receives fair dealing when adversely affected by a governmental agency's failure to adhere to due process safeguards. Perhaps almost any American could use an "ombudsman" at some time or other in dealing with modern bureaucracy, but the poor need him especially.

Rights of the Affluent

For the affluent of greater or lesser degree the threat of private bureaucracy to their rights as individuals lies largely in the influence of the organization on their conduct and expression outside their role in that hierarchy.

Corporate employees in the middle and upper strata are usually not unaware of their rights to express their views on politics or participate in "causes." Yet they are much aware that unorthodox expression and activity is frowned upon by the organization and may limit their chances of promotion—

or even lead to their dismissal. Most of them choose to conform rather than jeopardize their status.

J. M. Shea, Jr., a senior vice-president of a Dallas-based oil firm, wrote a magazine article after President Kennedy's assassination, deploring his and other Dallas businessmen's silence while Dallas "became the victim of fanatic minorities." A furor ensued. A boycott of the firm's stations was attempted. Shea was not discharged but his company demanded that he agree never to "comment publicly without formally clearing each word in advance and in writing."

Shea resigned rather than agree to censorship which reached beyond company business into personal belief—his right and responsibility as a citizen. Yet other business executives argued that an officer cannot separate himself from his company, that the company had the right to protect itself from embarrassment, that the Constitution does not protect one's job.

One executive went so far as to say that part of his compensation—and that of his subordinates—went to cover the personal rights he—and they—give up. Therefore he—and they—ought to refrain from anything which could conceivably damage the company image.

In an era when increasing numbers of professional and managerial personnel work for large organizations, how is the frontier issue of socially-responsible personal freedom versus corporate-image judgment to be resolved?

Urbanization presents a mixed bag of restrictions on individual freedom—zoning regulations, noise, and pollution controls, traffic rules, etc., etc.—while providing greater individual permissiveness—anonymity, mobility, changing moral standards, etc., etc. Certainly the affluent society, which affects the lives of all Americans (except the one-fifth below the poverty level?) is both cause and effect of urbanization. Few, if any, would really want to reverse the trend, in spite of what they may say. Yet the problems of liberty and justice for all are vastly complicated by the social and technical revolution through which we are passing.

Over the Horizon

Over the horizon lies the frontier of the computerized or cybernated age whose impact on individuals as persons can yet be scarcely imagined. We can be sure, however, that we will be confronted with undreamed of problems of human freedom.

Whether through the genius of the Founding Fathers who formulated the Constitution and the Bill of Rights, or through the genius of the courts in interpreting constitutional guarantees, or that of lawmakers in applying those guarantees in new situations—or through a combination of these factors—the American Bill of Rights has served well for 175 years. Eternal vigilance, however, is still the price of liberty.

The Bill of Rights

Passed by Congress, September 25, 1789;
ratified by the States, December 15, 1791.

FIRST AMENDMENT

Congress shall make no law respecting an establishment of religion, or prohibiting the free exercise thereof; or abridging the freedom of speech, or of the press; or the right of the people peaceably to assemble and to petition the Government for a redress of grievances.

SECOND AMENDMENT

A well regulated Militia, being necessary to the security of a free State, the right of the people to keep and bear Arms, shall not be infringed.

THIRD AMENDMENT

No Soldier shall, in time of peace be quartered in any house, without the consent of the Owner, nor in time of war, but in a manner to be prescribed by law.

FOURTH AMENDMENT

The right of the people to be secure in their persons, houses, papers, and effects, against unreasonable searches and seizures, shall not be violated, and no Warrants shall issue, but upon probable cause, supported by Oath or affirmation, and particularly describing the place to be searched, and the persons or things to be seized.

FIFTH AMENDMENT

No person shall be held to answer for a capital, or otherwise infamous crime, unless on a presentment or indictment of a Grand Jury, except in cases arising in the land or naval forces, or in the Militia, when in actual service in time of War or public danger; nor shall any person be subject for the same offense to be twice put in jeopardy of life or limb; nor shall be compelled in any criminal case to be a witness against himself, nor be deprived of life, liberty, or property, without due process of "law" nor shall private property be taken for public use, without just compensation.

SIXTH AMENDMENT

In all criminal prosecutions, the accused shall enjoy the right to a speedy and public trial, by an impartial jury of the State and district wherein the crime shall have been committed, which district shall have been previously ascertained by law, and to be informed of the nature and cause of the accusation; to be confronted with the witnesses against him; to have compulsory process for obtaining witnesses in his favor, and to have the Assistance of counsel for his defence.

SEVENTH AMENDMENT

In suits at common law, where the value in controversy shall exceed twenty dollars, the right of trial by jury shall be preserved, and no fact tried by jury shall be otherwise reexamined in any Court of the United States, than according to the rules of the common law.

EIGHTH AMENDMENT

Excessive bail shall not be required, nor excessive fines imposed, nor cruel and unusual punishment inflicted.

NINTH AMENDMENT

The enumeration in the Constitution, of certain rights, shall not be construed to deny or disparage others retained by the people.

TENTH AMENDMENT

The powers not delegated to the United States by the Constitution, nor prohibited by it to the States, are reserved to the States respectively, or to the people.

Later Amendments
Affecting Civil Liberties

THIRTEENTH AMENDMENT

Neither slavery nor involuntary servitude, except as a punishment for crime whereof the party shall have been duly convicted, shall exist within the United States, or any place subject to their jurisdiction.

FOURTEENTH AMENDMENT

All persons born or naturalized in the United States, and subject to the jurisdiction thereof, are citizens of the United States and of the State wherein they reside. No State shall make or enforce any law which shall abridge the privileges or immunities of citizens of the United States; nor shall any State deprive any person of life, liberty or property, without due process of law; nor deny to any person within its jurisdiction the equal protection of the laws.

FIFTEENTH AMENDMENT

The right of citizens of the United States to vote shall not be denied or abridged by the United States or by any State on account of race, color, or previous condition of servitude.

NINETEENTH AMENDMENT

The right of citizens of the United States to vote shall not be denied or abridged by the United States or by any State on account of sex.

Citations

CHAPTER 13

CHAPTER 14

CHAPTER 15

CHAPTER 16

CHAPTER 17

CHAPTER 18

CHAPTER 19

CHAPTER 21

290

For Further Reading

This bibliography is suggestive rather than exhaustive. Except for a few "classics" in their field, only recent books are listed. Books covering several subjects are listed under the heading "general" Those in specialized areas are listed according to chapters covering the major topic, although a particular volume may also deal with matters discussed in other parts of this book. A few pamphlet titles are included. Many magazine and newspaper articles used as sources for this volume are not listed here.

GENERAL

American Civil Liberties Union, *Annual. Reports* (issued each year as pamphlets bearing different titles) NYC, ACLU

Brant, Irving *The Bill of Rights, Its Origin and Meaning* (N.Y.: Bobbs-Merril, 1965) 567pp.

Chafee, Zechariah *The Blessings of Liberty*, (Phila. J. B. Lippincott Co., 1956) 350pp.

Douglas, M. O., *An Almanac of Liberty* (N.Y.: Doubleday, 1954) 402pp.

————. *A Living Bill of Rights* (N. Y.: Doubleday, 1961) 72pp.

Emerson, Thomas I. and David Haber, *Political & Civil Rights in the United States* (Buffalo: Dennis & Co., 1958) 2v., 1536pp.

Frankel, Osmond K., *The Supreme Court and Civil Liberties* (N. Y., Oceana Publications, 1963, Supp. 1966) 189 & 53pp.

Jackson, Robert H., *The Supreme Court and the American system of Government*, (Cambridge, Harvard University Press, 1955) 92pp.

Kennedy, John F., *Profiles in Courage* (N. Y., Harper & Row, 1956) 266pp.

Konvitz, Milton R., *Expanding Liberties; Freedoms Gains in Post-War America* (N. Y., Viking 1966) 429pp.

Mayer, Milton, ed.,*The Tradition of Freedom, Selections from Writers* (N. Y., Oceana Publications, 1957) 766pp.

Norton, Thos. J., *The Constitution of the United States* (N. Y., Nesterman, 1943) 319pp.

Pfeffer, Leo *The Liberties of An American, The Supreme Court Speaks* (Boston, Beacon Press 1963-2nd ed.) 328pp.

UNESCO (ed.) *Human Rights* (N. Y., Univ. of Columbia Press, 1949) 287pp.

Way, H. Frank *Liberty in the Balance* (N. Y., McGraw-Hill, 1964) 136pp.

Whipple, Leon, *The Story of Civil Liberty in the United States* (N. Y.. Vanugard, 1927) 153pp.

CHAPTER 2

Farmer, James, *Freedom When* (New York, Random House, 1966) 198pp.

Flexner, Eleanor, *Century of Struggle; The Women's Rights Movement in the U. S.* (Cambridge, Belknap Press, 1959) 284pp.

Frazier, E. Franklin, *The Negro in the United States* (N. Y., Macmillan, 1957) 767pp.

Javits, Jacob K. *Discrimination,* USA (Harcoutt, Brace & World 1960) 310pp.

Morgan, Charles, *Time to Speak* (N. Y., Harper & Row, 1964) 177pp.

Roche, John P., *The Quest for the Dream* (N. Y., Macmillan, 1963) 308pp.

Lomax, Louis, *The Negro Revolt* (N. Y., Harper & Row, 1962) 271pp.

U. S. Commission on Civil Rights, 1961 *Report:* (Wash., U. S. Printing Office,)

Book 2, Education, 254pp.

Book 3, Employment, 246pp.

Book 4, Housing, 206pp.

Book 5, Justice, Indian Rights, 305pp.

————. *1963* and subsequent *Reports*

————. *Freedom to the Free, Century of Emancipation* (Wash., U. S. Printing Office, 1963) 246pp.

CHAPTER 3

U. S. Commission on Civil Rights, *1961 Report: Book 1, Voting* (Wash., U. S. Printing Office) 380pp.

CHAPTERS 4, 5, & 6

Chafee, Zechariah, *Free Speech in the United States,* (Cambridge, Harvard Univ. Press, 1941) 600pp

Douglas, Wm. O., *Freedom of the Mind,* (N. Y. Doubleday, 1964) 44pp.

Meiklejohn, Alexander, *Political Freedom* (N. Y., Harper & Row, 1960) 166pp.

Hudon, Edward G. *Freedom of Speech in America* (Wash., Public Affairs Press, 1963) 224pp.

CHAPTERS 7 & 8

Barth, Alan, *The Loyalty of Free Men* (N. Y., Viking, 1951) 260pp.

Chafee, Zechariah, *The Blessings of Liberty* (Phil., Lippincott, 1956)

Jennison, Peter, *Freedom to Read* (N. Y., Public Affairs Committee, 1963) 20pp.

National Council of Teachers of English, *The Students' Right to Read* (Champaign, Ill. NCTE, 1962) 21pp.

CHAPTERS 9 & 10

Amer. Jewish Committee, *Church, State and the Public Schools* (N. Y., Institute on Human Relations, 1963) 30pp.

Cogley, John (ed.), *Religion and the Schools* (N. Y., Fund. for the Republic, 1959) 96pp.

Bates, M. Searle, *Religious Liberty; An Inquiry* (N. Y., Harper, 1945) 604pp.

Blau, Joseph L. (ed.), *Cornerstones of Religious Freedom in America* (Boston, Beacon Press, 1949) 250pp.

Miller, William Lee et. al, *Religion in a Free Society* (N. Y., Fund for the Republic, 1958) 108pp.

Pfeffer, Leo, *Church, State & Freedom,* rev. ed. (Boston, Beacon Press, 1966) 768pp.

Stokes, Ansen Phelps, and Pfeffer, Leo, *Church and State in the United States,* rev. ed. (N. Y., Harper & Row, 1964) 660pp.

CHAPTERS 11 & 12

Barth, Alan, *Government by Investigation* (N. Y., Viking Press, 1955) 231pp.

Donner, Frank J., *The Unamericans* (N. Y., Ballantine, 1961) 313pp.

Rice, Chas. E., *Freedom of Association* (N. Y., New York University Press, 1962) 202pp.

Smith, Bradford, *A Dangerous Freedom* (Phil., J. B. Lippincott, 1952) 308pp.

Taylor, Telford, *Grand Inquest* (N. Y., Simon Schuster, 1955) (also paperback) 376pp.

CHAPTER 14

Brenton, Myron, *The Privacy Invaders* (N. Y., Howard-McCann, 1964) 240pp.

Ernst, Morris L. & Schwartz, Alan U., *Privacy, the Right to Be Left Alone* (N. Y., Macmillan, 1962) 238pp.

Orwell, George, *Nineteen-Eighty Four* (N. Y., Harcourt-Brace, 1949)
Packard, Vance, *The Naked Society,* (N. Y., McKay, 1964) 369pp.

CHAPTERS 16, 17, & 18

Barth, Alan, *The Price of Liberty* (N. Y., The Viking Press, 1961) 339pp.

Lewis, Anthony, *Gideon's Trumpet* (N. Y., Random House, 1964) 262pp.

————. The Supreme Court And How It Works (N. Y., Random House 1966)

(See also books by Barth, Donner, and Taylor listed for Chapters 11 and 12)

Lofton, John, *Justice and the Press* (Boston, Beacon Press, 1966).

CHAPTER 19

American Civil Liberties Union, *A Labor Union Bill of Rights* (N. Y., ACLU, 1963) 38pp.

Gilbert, Lewis D., *Dividends and Democracy* (Larchmont, N. Y., American Research Council, 1956) 242pp.

Harrington, Michael (ed.), *Labor in a Free Society* (University of California Press, 1958) 186pp.

CHAPTER 20

Dumbauld, Edward, *The Bill of Rights and What is Means Today* (Norman, Okla. University of Oklahoma Press, 1957) 242pp.

Rutland, Robert Allen, *The Birth of the Bill of Rights* (Chapel Hill, N. C., University of North Carolina Press, 1955) 243pp.

Index

295

Date Due

FEB. 11, JUN 7 '70			
NOV 5 '70			
NOV 7 '75			
JAN 31 '84			
SEP 23 '91			

Demco 38-297